D0871762

Community Journalism
A WAY OF LIFE

B R U C E   M .

Community

THE IOWA STATE

KENNEDY
Journalism
A Way of Life

UNIVERSITY PRESS / AMES

★ **BRUCE M. KENNEDY** began his newspapering career as a printer's devil while still in high school. Majoring in journalism at the University of Nebraska, he was editor of *The Daily Nebraskan*. At his graduation in 1951 he was named outstanding male graduate by Sigma Delta Chi. After returning in 1953 from army overseas service, he worked on weeklies in Neligh, Nebraska, and Lander, Wyoming, before becoming editor of the *Greybull* (Wyoming) *Standard and Tribune*. He was owner-publisher of the *Standard and Tribune* from 1959 to 1974. He is now president of Sage Publishing Co., Inc.; Publisher of the *Cody* (Wyoming) *Enterprise;* partner in the *Wyoming State Journal,* Lander; and partner in publishing the *Gillette* (Wyoming) *News-Record* and the *Green River* (Wyoming) *Star.* During his twenty-four years in the community journalism field, he has been winner of eleven national newspaper association awards in the areas of photography, column writing, news reporting, and general excellence.

ⓒ 1974 The Iowa State University Press
Ames, Iowa 50010. All rights reserved

Composed and printed by
The Iowa State University Press

First edition, 1974
Second printing, 1977

Library of Congress Cataloging in Publication Data

Kennedy, Bruce M   1929–
    Community journalism.
    1. Community newspapers. 2. Journalism. I. Title.
PN4784.C73K4   070   73–15551
ISBN 0-8138-0505-8

TO BETTY

Who has shared many Wednesdays with me

CONTENTS

Community Journalism

A WAY OF LIFE

The Weekly Newspaper

WHAT we want, and what we shall have, is the royal American privilege of living and dying in a country town, running a country newspaper, saying what we please when we please, how we please and to whom we please.

WILLIAM ALLEN WHITE, *Emporia Gazette,* DECEMBER 6, 1911

★

I SHOOK HANDS with a weekly editor the other day, a stranger from another state, and we looked at each other pretty frankly as if we were trying to find out what traits we held in common, what kind of men we were to involve ourselves in weekly newspapering. Of course nothing showed. The fraternity has no badge of identification. The ink was washed off, the hypo stains covered up. The deep mark of the last Wednesday was out of sight and, until another week, out of mind. We were just a couple of guys in our best suits, briefly being something else after the paper was out. But our friendlier feelings and warmer handshakes showed the kinship between us. We belonged to a profession which offers one of the last places a man can be truly independent, where his individual excellence is required in a variety of fields; and this knowledge had fed our lives.

All newspapering, big papers or small, weeklies or dailies, satisfies many followers. But because you're closer to all aspects of newspapering when you publish or edit a weekly newspaper and because the ink barrel is only a few feet away, the satisfaction in small-town newspapering is especially strong.

We're all things at once in weekly publishing—printers, yet competent ad salesmen, sensitive photographers, knowledgeable reporters, successful businessmen. Respectable trades, any of them. Yet we must also be on occasion society editor, mechanic, subscription taker, chief of the complaint desk, as well as the guy who sweeps out the front office. The trade calls it "country trained." A compliment. It means you can take over duties of any one of a dozen people. It signifies you're not afraid of work or of deadlines or plunging your hands into that ink barrel. It means you know newspapering.

For all of printing's technical advances and the world of science around us, weekly newspapering is still a frontier. We're isolated in our communities, fighting problems unique to us, hacking away at a maze of difficulties mechanical as well as intellectual, at attitudes indifferent as well as opinionated. It can quickly make you independent in action as well as thought.

Years ago a man could stake out 160 acres and clear his homestead. You can do the same pioneering nowadays in a town of several thousand souls who seldom see a local editorial in their daily, and see only politicians' pictures on the front page. You break ground in a different way. You can become one of those independent weekly editors with character enough to take editorial stands against your neighbors on public issues; who can still appreciate a finely printed graduation program in this age of mediocrity and stereotype; who can capture on Tri-X film the poetry of a spring day in this rush of one spring to the next.

It's a life of gratifying moments.

I was searching for pictures at a school picnic once, and the local park was filled with carefree and happy kids (they'd sung all during the walk from the schoolhouse). They were still singing, guzzling pop, and chasing each other around the trees. I think they all wanted their pictures taken. There wasn't a youngster who didn't say, "Take it of me, take it of me." They trailed me around, Pied Piper fashion, pestering and pleading. I finally gave in to one third-grade group of girls, shooting a special one of just them after I was finished with the rest of the planned pictures. As I folded up my camera and started for the car, they hollered "thank you" and "thanks a lot" and "goodbye" in a dozen different voices. Then behind me I heard a little voice pipe: "Three cheers for Mr. Kennedy." And they all joined in, the little tykes, all cheering and hooraying because it was spring and school was almost out and they'd just had their pictures taken. I left the park with those hip-hip-hoorays following me out, and I'll remember that bright May afternoon a long time.

Well, three cheers for the profession of weekly newspapering, too. There are many bright May afternoons in it, many hours of cheering. I'm supposed to be too restrained to give my own hip-hip-hooray when I hear someone enjoys my efforts at being a weekly editor, but I feel like it anyway. Watching people read my newspaper on Thursday morning is weekly affirmation of why I stay a weekly editor. Even though I know what's in an issue and I've tried all week to put something in to interest them, I'm always amazed at their eagerness to read it. They read it on the post office steps or in their cars. They'll walk down the street, heads buried in the front page.

They'll read it as soon as the mail comes or prop it up on the coffee counter. Or you'll be carrying in an armload of papers to the newsstands and someone is already waiting on that Thursday morning for you to bring their paper. One week when I was filling up a newsstand rack, a guy walked over, picked a paper out and said, "I can't wait until I get ours at home tonight." I could have given him the whole armload!

To know it happens in other post offices, in other towns and places, is even more gratifying. There's a postman in Connecticut who always read our *Greybull Standard* before he delivered it to a former resident because he "liked the pictures." A roomful of sophisticated Dartmouth College boys once became so interested in the papers we sent to a local boy there, he had to wait his turn to read his hometown news each week. There are navy buddies, uncles, fathers-in-law, office crews—all strangers to our town—who have become loyal followers of the paper. I don't know how you measure this satisfaction, but when a woman you've never seen before writes, "I think the world should have more editorials like yours," it's pay in part for those late Tuesday nights.

An editor writes for others to read, takes pictures so others may see. You know the paper should be read. You keep telling yourself they *should* read it; there's something in there for them. Yet when they do, when you actually see them reading it, it's cheering all right— but with a lump in your throat.

You don't make a newspaper like you do a tractor or a piece of cloth. You don't bolt it together with threaded metal or sheet iron. People go into a newspaper—people and life as it is from week to week. One of our community's older farm women came in one week with a story about her "perpetual milker," a cow that had given milk every day for nearly five years and had just stopped that week. She was sure it was a record of some sort. She was very proud of what she felt was a unique achievement in our community. She'd even figured out how many total gallons of milk the cow had given. The woman had it all ready for the paper.

After she'd gone I did write it up. When it came time for the headline, someone in the office suggested it sounded "udderly fantastic" and everyone clamored for that as the headline. But I knew the woman personally; I'd played with her kids when I was young. I knew how she felt about that cow, that "member of the family" who'd done so well with a milk pail. She'd milked it herself nearly every one of those 365 days each year, five years running, morning and night. It wouldn't have been a pun to her, not a clever piece of headline written for the laugh instead of the miracle. It would have hurt her, I knew, this poking fun at something she held dear, and I was a friend living in a small town with her, and I had no heart for it. I wrote some innocuous little headline, and "udderly fantastic," which might have seen print in a bigger more impersonal paper, never saw it in mine.

I was close to that woman as I'm close to many members of my town. I share their life as well as report it. I am not "the" editor always, but "our" editor just as it is "our" paper. This belonging gives small town newspapering a flavor of its own. It reminds you each week the place to live life is in a small town; the place to see it and feel it is on a small-town paper.

The life is not all rose-colored. I won't paint the bright side only. Another tough, soul racking side exists in weekly newspapering. All of us in it know it. A boss of mine was stopped on the street by a minister in our town and the minister asked him, "Did you know I was once a printer's devil? Worked at it almost a year before I decided to become a preacher?"

"Reverend," the newspaperman replied, "you had divine guidance."

Weekly newspapering has no peer for competitiveness. It competes with everything—for the advertising revenue, for job printing, for office supplies. It competes for the news, trying to beat the daily in the next town or the weekly across the street. It vies for subscriptions.

As editor, I compete with men's minds. I try to influence their thoughts, to mold opinions, to start crusades. I want people to follow me. I try to sway, to generate support. I plant ideas and desires in the hope they'll take root in the community's thinking.

Because I represent my town to the rest of the world, I become one of its spokesmen, too, fighting for trade area business, for community prestige, for high school athletic recognition.

And I extend the borders of competition to all places, because I compete professionally with other newsmen from one coast to another who are also publishing weekly newspapers, trying to make them the "best weekly newspaper published."

Finally, I compete with myself as I learn the profession by doing it week by week. I seek journalistic competence so that the words and typography and presswork are better this week than they were the last—a better lead, a picture that shows life more vividly, an editorial of higher calibre, more polished writing.

You don't always win. This is the hardest part. The money goes other places, the news is printed elsewhere. You lose an election. You make an enemy. Someone is forever winning, and not necessarily you. Someone is always stronger and better at one time or another. If you care about the winning, the days and nights when you lose are tough ones indeed.

Then there are the pressures and deadlines of every week, the long hours when inspiration falters or production is stalled. The paper can't miss its Thursday. There are deadlines from one hour to the next, from afternoon to afternoon, and how far the paper gets along depends on you. The long hours extend into the nights of council meetings, the late hours after the office door is blessedly closed. There are basketball games to cover and night pictures to process. It takes just plain hard work to publish twelve to twenty-four pages of newsprint.

You hear of the columnist wakened by the morning sun only to find her blank clipboard alongside her in bed in the same place she'd left it when she dozed off, uninspired. And you know exactly how it was.

People won't understand newspapering. "How come you put my story inside?" "Can you take a picture of our club's officers?" You finally educate one bunch of citizens, they move away, and school for newcomers starts all over.

You make enemies, too. It's inescapable. In the earnest struggle to influence men's minds, obtain their business, and publish their news, you must alienate some. A friend of mine told me of a person who was talking to him about my paper and me. "I don't like him," the guy had said, "but he does say what he thinks." It startled me, since you seldom hear about someone who admits openly he doesn't like you. I weakened then, and for a moment I wished it could be the other way—that I was liked instead of being an editorial writer. But it couldn't be, and in the end the editorials of the past and all those of the future won out. I was still an editor who wrote editorials; being liked was something else.

That's the way of newspapering, too. In the end it wins, despite the long hours and the battles lost. Even though the enemies and pressure of those endless Wednesday press days must be met, news-papering triumphs. You remember all the times you cut paper for Sunday school teachers, the scrap you gave away to the kids. You can see the varied-size piles of finished job work stacked on the counter, all colors and kinds, neat and sharply printed. You can remember the smells of the back shop, the red of the darkroom light.

Each week what you write on that piece of plain copy paper seems to sound more dignified, more worldly when it appears in black type. Sometimes you end up asking yourself: "Did I really write that?"

It's rewarding to be part of nearly everything involving your community, the printable as well as the unprintable. It's flattering to have your opinion asked for, your counsel sought, whether you're really as wise as all that or not. You build many monuments in news-paper business. Your newspaper and energy leave a wake of new buildings, successful projects, guidance, and direction. Helping others, boosting the community, the area, or "the cause" will become, like the Thursday paper days, endless.

Small-town newspapering is belonging. But I revel in the independence, too. Though I remain a part of the community, I am independent within it. It's my paper, they're my thoughts. I can do as I please, write as I choose. My Thursday product is mine.

It's the good living of the weekly field, the financial security, because it's a profitable business if run right. You can make good money while leading a challenging life.

The *Standard,* years before my time, was printed in an old wooden building on another street. The building has been repainted a dozen times and has housed several other businesses. But up on the old false front under all those coats of paint are still the words, "Greybull Standard," and underneath in smaller block type, "Printing." You can see the letters only when the early morning sun slants in just right, but I always look for them anyway.

There is a similar sign on my building, put up in my time, neon and far newer, but it announces the same message to my community: A newspaper is printed here.

I hope it stays there a long time.

CHAPTER TWO

I See by the Paper

THIS is the newspaperman's dilemma: If he mixes with people who make news, he must respect their confidence; if he does not mix, he cannot be a good newspaperman.

ARTHUR CHRISTIANSEN, *Headlines All My Life*

As AN EDITOR, two phrases especially warm my heart. One of them is, "Here's the money for that bill I owe you." The other one is to hear someone start a sentence with, "I see by the paper. . . ."

It's unfair to compare the two, for one warms my pocketbook as well as my heart. But for downright pleasure and pride, nothing can beat that Will Rogers phrase: "I see by the paper. . . ." It means I've done my job of gathering the news and passing it along successfully to my neighbors. No more important job exists than this reporting. For news is what sells the paper, dime by dime, week after week. You can sluff the pictures, you can jazz up the layout, you can write fence-straddling editorials once in awhile or not at all; but friend, your newspaper is a dead one if the man of the house puts it down and tells the wife, "Well, there's nothing in that thing."

The news should go in, by the pageful.

★ SMALL-TOWN NEWS

Small-town news and big-town news are identical fare of wrecks and deaths, floods and lawsuits, celebrities and common folk, socializing and congregating. The size of the world is all that differs. The weekly covers a world 3 to 30 miles wide instead of one 25,000 miles around. While thousands of newsmen and editors hover over the typewriters in the larger world, perhaps only one publication is concerned with what's happening in each smaller world. That's your paper or mine and that's where we get our strength.

Daily news is a stream of stories of the doings of strangers. Weekly news is of friends and neighbors. Yet gathering news is the same. The five Ws sound alike every day or every Thursday, in circulation of 2,000 or 200,000. The flood can swell the creek on the other side of town or the Mississippi. Families lose their homes, cattle are swept away, the river changes channel, the highway department works through the night. The New Orleans reporter asks the same questions, writes the same kind of story as his weekly counterpart.

The wire services dutifully report the ordinary happenings of extraordinary people—what they wore, how they looked, what they did, where they vacationed. Reporting these daily goings on of celebrities is regular fare to the daily newsman. His weekly compatriot, in turn, is writing ordinary happenings of the ordinary people—their siege in the hospital, their kids home from school, the fish they caught Sunday. So a weekly reporter has regular fare, too, though his deadline is once a week instead of once a day.

News is whatever happens to your town. Your typewriter will handle many police and justice court stories (and these will be among the best read stories you will have). The courthouse coverage is another separate field since it's your statehouse–U.S. Capitol–United Nations all in one brick building. School news is so rampant three-fourths of the year you'll wonder how to do without it that first week in June. And there's news of the business district, the disasters of nature, the stories of people, their calamities, their interests, the perpetual life of a town.

News of Public Officials. Public officials are a perpetual source of news. They are also a source of frustration. Invariably they think they know more about news reporting than you do; inevitably they are impressed with their own importance, particularly if newly elected; and they divide all news into two categories: that which they want publicity on and that which they don't. The "don't" category is usually the best news.

This is true in daily reporting as well, but our problem is compounded because everybody knows everybody's nature in a small community and because you often must deal with the official in other capacities than just his elected office. The fire chief may also be the head of the Lion's Club, many times the mayor is a businessman and an advertiser, or the president of the Chamber of Commerce may be on the school board.

This community closeness doesn't change the news, but it may make it harder to get. There is a tendency in community journalism to become so involved in what is going on in town that you forget you're a reporter. Reporting the news is your first concern. Establish in your own mind, and in the minds of your fellow townspeople, that your job is to report the news, not to help make it. You can express your opinion on the editorial page, but the news story, regardless of what you think, what your neighbor thinks, or what the mayor thinks, must go into the paper as unslanted as you can make it.

Let's take a few examples:

THE MAYOR *of your town is fighting for paving the streets. You are helping him on this project. You are tired of the dust and believe it will be a great improvement for the town; so do the majority of your readers. A small group is against it, particularly one man who says the plans aren't right. He makes quite an issue of it. The mayor feels undue publicity created by this sorehead will help defeat the bond issue. You discuss it with the mayor many times, and he asks your support. Should you soft pedal the objection of this man as the mayor wants you to do, or play it straight?*

Don't take sides in such an argument through the news story. Your job in the news is to present what is happening, not what you'd like to happen. The mayor will not understand this; neither will the majority of your readers (who are also many of your friends). They want you on their side, the "side of the right." They'll resent what they think is "your desertion," but fair play in the news is the only way.

This does not mean to overplay the sorehead or the minority point of view. Don't let a sorehead take advantage of his rights under an honest press to promote himself or his cause. Being in a minority does not entitle anyone to extra rights, only equal rights.

Sometimes the majority is notoriously blind, and the minority can bring a new light to an issue. In Nebraska in the 1950s an entire reappraisal of the tax valuation structure was started because one single taxpayer complained about it enough. The Nebraska governor, publicly giving credit to this one man, said, "Remember this one man and what he started, and realize that the democratic process of government rests with each individual citizen."

You may regret it if you dismiss the minority. Sometimes what it has to say is better news than that of the majority.

THE COUNTY COMMISSIONERS *are trying to build a road which will affect your area. So far no one in the competing town north of you is aware of the project. It has been hushed up; and while your town's chamber of commerce has been working hard with the commissioners, they have kept the project under cover. You discover it by accident in its initial stages and when questioning officials about it, none of them deny it; but they insist publicity on it will cause such a stink in the competing town the project will have to be dropped. They want it under construction before any announcement because by then it will be too late to protest. Your town is depending on this project. How do you handle this one?*

These situations happen all the time in small communities. People want to choose the time for publicity; they don't always understand your obligation to print the news as it happens. Sometimes you can tactfully make them see this, but if you can't there's only one course—to print it!

Something is wrong with a project that must be kept secret from the taxpaying citizens to insure its passage. I believe—and this is what I have learned to tell such officials—that if a project is defeated because of publicity in our newspaper, then we have done a service to our readers. Such a proposal, hushed up and undercover, should have been defeated.

If citizens feel strongly enough to defeat such a project, then the officials should have spent more time in selling it and explaining it than in trying to cover it up. Publicity never defeats a proposal. The proposal defeats itself. Your duty as a newspaper is to tell your readers what government is doing with tax dollars.

A SCHOOL SUPERINTENDENT *gives you a tip that something happened at an executive session of the school board, but he can't tell you what it is unless you agree not to print it. He promises you can release the story for next week's paper but not now. Would you accept his off-the-record remark and wait until next week?*

"I'll tell you something if you won't print it" is one of the most tiresome remarks in all of journalism. We should counter this plague with, "Don't tell a newspaper editor anything you don't want in the newspaper."

Off-the-record ties your hands. If you promise you won't print it, you cannot print the same story from another source. Would the school board president have given you the story if you had called him? He might have. But a promise not to print to one person is in effect the same promise to everyone. Off-the-record requests are often the way many public officials cover up their lack of confidence and fear for their position.

About that promise to "give it to you next week." It is better to have a story that something happened in executive session that they *won't* release than to have no story until next week. Invariably, when you agree to hold a story the news gets out anyway, or a stringer for a nearby daily picks it up, or it ceases to be news because something bigger happens. There is nothing like news when it is news.

It is a matter of whether you prefer to be on the inside reporting nothing or on the outside reporting as much as you can. Being "in" is a temptation hard to put down. "Off the record," "background gathering," or "I'll tell you something if you don't print it" will put you on the inside. But unless you can print it, there's no news in it.

YOU ARE COVERING *an open meeting of the town council. It is a routine meeting, until the mayor brings up a problem with a policeman. The council starts to discuss his qualifications. The mayor stops the discussion, turns towards where you are sitting and asks, "Can we have this part of the meeting off the record?" What do you say?*

One of the most tiresome requests a reporter hears is, "Can we have this off the record." If you haven't had your share of off-the-record fights with a public body, remember in an open meeting there cannot be any "off the record." Elected officials never seem to understand that anything they say in public meeting can be quoted. They tend to forget they are public servants, answering to the people. They feel they have the right to discuss what they please without any interference from those not on the board, but they are wrong in this.

If they want to avoid the press, a public body can always meet at a private home or at a special unannounced meeting. I've even found the school board huddling in a cafe. They can also outlast you in a meeting, saving a controversial subject (that's not on the official agenda and you know nothing about) until after the meeting is over. I've seen town councils vote secretly on a controversial issue when it is an open violation of the people's right to know and often against statute or ordinance.

In all of these cases the group officially announces the decision or takes a vote in a regular meeting. But the background, the arguing, the discussion, the real story, is lost forever.

It takes much patience and sometimes a long time to earn the respect of your fellow citizens and overcome this off-the-record business. You will never completely escape it. New officials, new board members are elected year after year and each time a new breaking in is required. If you continue to print the news as fairly and accurately as possible, they will ask it of you less and less. If council members are accustomed to being quoted, they don't mind half so much.

My newspaper is at open meetings to see if any news is there. If there is and we judge it to be newsworthy, it will be published. If not, it won't. We don't print news that would unnecessarily embarrass someone. We don't print libelous statements. We don't print every cuss word used in a meeting. Common sense and good taste keep some news out of the paper. But that responsibility of determining which news goes in and which news stays out is the responsibility of the newspaper itself. For an excellent discussion of libel law see the Chapter Appendix, page 23, by Richard W. Cardwell, recognized authority in communications law.

A GROUP OF TEENAGERS *holds a beer bust out in the country. They get rowdy and the farmer calls the sheriff. Only a fraction of the forty kids are caught at the time, but eventually all the others are found out. They are charged with illegal possession of alcohol in a justice of the peace court, an open record. All the offenders are in high school. It is the first offense for all but three kids. Do you print the names?*

Our paper would, and has for many, many years. We take each name as it appears on the docket, granting no favors to leave a name out, putting no special emphasis on any name. There have been advertisers' children, school principals' kids, kids of good friends and not-so-good friends. But they've all been in the paper.

Newspapers have been criticized—mine, too—for publishing names. The criticism usually is not just because we print names, but whether we should print them on specific occasions: first offenses or for "small" crimes. Yet it is not the responsibility of the newspaper to choose which are "good" or "bad" crimes. If one name is news, so is another, and the only fair way is to print every offender appearing on the police court book, line after line.

Some papers print names after the second offense. But I cannot keep books on who is in court for the second or third time. Actually, putting a stigma on a youth because he or she has committed two offenses is probably worse than for just committing one. It certainly draws undue attention to a youngster who may have committed two minor offenses.

Police and justice court proceedings are news. You can decide to ignore them or to publish them. If you choose the latter, the fairest way is to print the record exactly as it appears. The newspaper cannot judge which kid should receive the "punishment" of publication and which shouldn't. This is the job of the arresting officer or the county attorney. If they think a youth shouldn't be brought into court, they won't bring him. If the judge didn't think the child should be punished, he would have dismissed the case.

The one time we ever kept a name out of the court news was when a young parolee from the state penitentiary was picked up for not displaying proper license plates. His mother tearfully confessed the parole (they had kept it a secret) and what it might mean if they sent him back. That such an insignificant charge might return the boy to prison seemed grossly unfair to me. I gave in and left his name out. Yet it might not have been so trivial. The boy later went back East and killed a policeman during a robbery. He is now serving a life sentence. Publication of his name wouldn't have straightened him out. The parole officer had other sources for such knowledge than my newspaper. Yet my conscience has bothered me ever since, because I was party to a cover-up that continued a life of crime.

The kids understand what you are doing; the parents sometimes don't. Kids often have a greater sense of justice than they are given credit for. But kids and parents will understand and respect what you are doing if you print every single name. After a few years of such a policy, requests to withhold names are fewer.

YOU CALL *the school board president about plans for a new building which the school board is discussing. He gives you the information for a story but he says he'd like to read the story after you have written it. What's your reaction?*

One rule that eliminates many problems is: Don't let people read a story before it's published. They'll see it soon enough Thursday morning. Be jealous of what you have for the present week's paper. Don't let some public official act as censor. It weakens your position as a good reporter. It gives unwarranted power, authority, and responsibility to an unqualified person.

Rural News. The trend may be away from the rural life—fewer farms and fewer farmers—but the rural community and the small town go through life together sharing many stories. Town residents, quite a few of them farm people once themselves, are genuinely concerned about what happens on the farm. They react to an early frost, the insect pests, finicky markets, too much moisture or not enough. Townspeople hunt in the country, share a pew with the farmer on Sunday, they sell him groceries and marry his children. The farmer himself is just as loyal. Though he may live outside the city limits and pays no municipal taxes, he still considers it "his town." He sends his kids to its schools, he uses its services—the swimming pool, the baseball program, the community hall. He belongs to its organizations, contributes to its functions. The small town and the farmer—it's a kinship of long standing.

With a little encouragement, the obvious rural news—4-H clubs, your correspondents' news, county agent and home demonstration agent columns, Soil Conservation Service information—will take care of itself.

Dig deeper to the stories about a flooding creek channel that washes away an oat field, a single strip of hail on the lower bench, the cattle moving up to higher ranges, a successful feedlot operation, roundups and farm sales, new tenants arriving, old owners leaving, market information, freak animal births, neighbors helping out, rural fires, accidents, high yield, and weather news, always the weather.

Weather. We are all pulled, sometimes unconsciously, by the weather's whims. A windy day is jarring, disrupting, discordant to our dispositions. We suffer in the heat, or cold. We rejoice in the rain that breaks the drought, and in the first real spring day, and who can be sad in bright sunshine? Each day brings its own weather story, and a different story can be written almost every day of the year.

Of all the news we write about, weather is probably the most important to each reader. None of us—even the shut-in or the stay-at-home—can be oblivious to it.

Weather spawns an amazing number of other stories. There are muddy roads, icy streets, slick pavements, dangerously gusty winds, melting chinooks, typhoons, and tornadoes. Ducks fly south; deer come down out of the hills on the heels of changing weather. Tree limbs break off; dust swirls down the streets before a capricious wind. Antifreeze is needed and snow tires must be put on. Basements flood, creeks rise, the ice goes out of the river. Weather brings snow for skiers, ice for skaters, fluffy clouds for photographers, bright days for swimmers, and sun for the town's annual celebration. Crops burn up, mildew, freeze. They can be hailed out, blown down, flooded, delayed because of weather. It's part of every day—and part of every week's news you will write.

Historical News. A small town, fascinated by its own history and proud of its place in the world, will read in great gulps whatever local historical news you can uncover.

The eternal success of reprinting "yesterday's headlines" from old files of thirty, forty, fifty years ago indicates the continual high readership of those "good old days."

Recruit a literary old-timer to reminisce in print, or let him describe in more detail the happenings of other years. Search attics and trunks for old pictures to reprint. Publish an annual historical edition (a revenue producer as well as a historical contribution). Remind your readers of the history of a building being razed, of an old-timer's experience, of the coldest winter.

History doesn't have to be ancient to be interesting. Antiquity can start just ten years ago in a small town.

Obituaries. A death in the community is a death in the family. Strangers are few; nearly everyone is a celebrity of sorts, and a death, no matter whose it is, touches a small town. A man may have few close mourners, but he seldom dies wholly forgotten. He is recognized or remembered in varying degrees by many.

An obituary does more than report death. When I listen to people talk about a small-town neighbor who just died, I am struck by how thoroughly they read his obituary. They talk about how old he was and the cause of his death. They like to read where he came from, how much schooling he had, how long he lived here. They remember where he worked at different times in his life. They're interested in his survivors, in recognizing brothers and sisters who have moved away. They find out where his sons and daughters are now and who else he was related to (because keeping a genealogy table of everyone is a small-town habit). They want to know in which church the services were held. Finally, even the pallbearers represent a man's closest friends.

An obituary is important news with high readership, and each one deserves careful, respectful writing.

All the News That's Fit. Whenever I wonder if some item would be in good taste or whether this or that should be published, I think of my son in the third grade learning to read more difficult stories than Run Sally Run. He would take our paper each week and lay it all out on the living room rug to slowly read. So did many of the rest of the third graders in town, and the fourth graders, the fifth and on up in this little town's family of readers. The decision of what is "fit" news to print and what isn't becomes decidedly easier when I remember that little boy on his hands and knees reading every word I've allowed to be printed.

★ ADD THE DETAILS

You've room for the details. You have only one day a week (or two if you're semi-weekly) to beat the daily on timeliness. But you have six other days every week to explore new leads, call more people, take more pictures, write in greater depth. Search for those overlooked details, get more quotes, find eyewitnesses. Try to think of each person likely to be connected with it. Who might have seen it? Who lives nearby or in the same block? Who is a neighbor? Whom does it affect? These are the same questions the metropolitan reporter asks. But you know names and people. And they know you.

Weeklies can add a personal touch. There's license to "visit" more. You have time and space to be a small-town citizen talking with another about your community.

Small-town people are very fond of this visiting. As you go through the years in a community you realize more and more how comfortable talking with one another is. The group of men on the street, the ladies across that much-maligned backyard fence, the conversation floating over a pair of coffee cups. If you join them, you'll hear them talking about the weather, the ball game the night before, crops, politics, Mae West in her day and Raquel Welch in hers, business or farming depending on the profession, their neighbor's good luck or bad, and always old days and old times. Piddling items and big ones, important news and trivia, the world's first journalism was passing this along, sharing it with a neighbor who in turn shares it with someone else. The small town has just kept the visiting habit.

You can still observe journalistic good taste while you visit. You don't need to gush or slop into slang, cliches, bad grammar, triteness. If you mention in a burglary story that the safe was big and old and heavy and that the manager said "five men and Bill Unterzuber's winch truck" moved it into the building originally, the part that made the sentence comfortable (and more meaningful) to your small-town reader was moving man Bill Unterzuber. Not to mention his name would have deprived the story of a visiting touch.

Perhaps a new department store manager and his family move to town and rent an apartment at 514 Fifth Avenue North. Why not, "They are renting one of George Scott's apartments at 514 Fifth Avenue North." Or if they buy a house: "They bought the Lester Perkins house at 240 Pulliam Avenue." This information tells the small-town reader two facts, where the new manager is living and that the Les Perkins's finally got their house sold.

The same man may have three kids. Don't just say, "Mr. and Mrs. John Sawyer and three children." Make it, "Cheryl, 15; Don, 13; and Barbara, 7," and you introduce them to the community and seat them in the various rooms at school.

Harvest of the sugar beet crop is a general story, but an interesting small-town sidelight is that, "Walter Smith brought the first load into the beet dump." So is a fresh coat of paint, applied anywhere, or a town whistle that sticks, a bull that's bought, an arm that breaks on the playground, a farm that changes hands. It's all news, no matter how small.

Don't spare the details in writing your story. Use descriptive words—the "inch cable" that snapped is a more impressive break than just a "cable." A "Jersey bull" mauling someone describes what kind of a bull; a "red" Buick, a "claw" hammer, a "southeast" wind, "the old Braden store safe" are all added details. The big fish caught on a "Royal Coachman" fly tells all fishermen what they should have used. "Five miles east" may describe the site, but "across from the Ed Shafer farm" pinpoints it better.

People talk in specifics; don't write your stories in generalities.

★ GETTING ALONG WITH YOUR PUBLIC

People will become very cross with you. And you with them. It's inescapable in business, big town or little. Small-town feuding is complicated further because if you're a Hatfield you're constantly running into a McCoy—in the post office, during Rotary Club, at the basketball game. You won't wait for chances to put the old nose in the air if that's what you've both decided to do.

I don't know the McCoys in your town. But I've observed those who live in mine and I conclude that our small feuding blood is thin —easily fired, but as quickly cooled. People can't live together without creating friction. All families fight. All friends fall out. But hatchets in small towns, I think you'll find, are forever being buried. You bury your share. Your editorial office will see many hurt feelings, imagined slights, outright fights, passionate differences of opinion. But take this piece of advice from an editor who's seen his share of bickering: Never take the irritated Hatfields too seriously. Don't stew about people not liking you or being mad at you. Saints don't dabble in printer's ink. They leave it up to small-town editors who have imperfections and human failings, who make mistakes, who get mad themselves. But editors learn, if they stay in the business long enough, that hard feelings will be forgotten, fights ended. The public will nearly always come back to knock on the door.

Newspapering is one business that deals with almost everyone in town at one time or another. A football player's picture may please the heck out of Mom and Dad, but some other Mom and Dad will be sure you're playing favorites. A woman was upset with us because she felt her daughter's wedding story hadn't been long enough. She never told us this. Someone else did months after the story appeared! I always remember this incident, because that's when I realized I would never please everyone. If people were going to be mad at my newspaper for things I knew nothing of, my task of trying to please all the rest was impossible. Right now, in my town, someone is probably fuming over something I'll never know about. But he'll get over it and will be back in the office again someday with a local about his son being home. Or it'll be a want ad or a hello he'll have to return to me someday. Our little feud—even if it was one-sided— will be about over.

One of the more asinine threats—and I'm guilty of making it myself—is, "I won't trade with him anymore." It's natural defense. But retaliation can be ridiculous when you apply it to your newspaper. So you're mad at Sam Smith. What would you do? Leave his name out of the paper? And all his kids, and the wife? Put a big thumb print over his daughter in the glee club picture? When you newspaper as it should be done, you don't have a list of names you publish and a list you don't. A guy may cancel his subscription to your newspaper, but his name should appear just as regularly in its columns as if he were still a reader.

Your retaliation with an advertiser may take this twist: "Bub, you'll never get an ad in my paper even if you want to." But as a fellow businessman on my main street, older and wiser than I, reminded me once: "Whenever a person's mad at me and I at him, the thing that hurts him the most is having to spend money with me. That $5 bill he leaves in my store is the best retaliation I have. I let him spend it."

You may not have the opportunity to sell to this irate advertiser. He may stay away awhile on his own accord. Be patient. Treat him (in fact treat all those McCoys) as if the world was normal again. Just keep calling. Continue to strive for a good newspaper. Forget the feud yourself. And he'll be back.

Mistakes. When you make a mistake call the injured party first. Don't wait for them to call. You won't be able to prevent mistakes from happening, but you can prevent them from creating hard feelings. Your immediate apology cuts the sailing wind.

Admit mistakes and print corrections but don't make yourself into a buffoon. Don't make a big fuss correcting them. Don't say, "We made *another* blooper last week." Or "We got something *else* wrong," leaving the impression the customer should keep a running total of all the paper's mistakes. If you say you can't get anything right, eventually so will everyone else.

Some mistakes should be corrected and some should be marked off as impossibly human.

★ YOUR OWN STYLEBOOK

Your newspaper's own "stylebook" (how much to indent heads, what to capitalize, how to write dates, street numbers, abbreviations, etc.) establishes the right and the wrong. Your style doesn't need to be consistent with any other newspaper's. But it should be consistent within itself. Style takes away the indecision. If a street address can be written 324 North Avenue, 324 No. Ave., 324 No. Avenue, or 324 North Ave., your stylebook makes the decision as to which of these combinations is right for your newspaper. If you're not sure what your style should be, use a wire service or large daily stylebook to set up yours.

★ MORE TIPS AND TRICKS

Fight against sloppiness, wordiness, and inaccuracies, all slyly creeping up on you. You won't have the checks and balances of a big daily. The city editor, desk man, managing editor, rewrite man, and editorial boss may be you alone. You must be twice as careful week after week as you are day after day. If it's too vague, junk it. Don't "suppose" anything. Don't jump to conclusions. Check everything first. Find answers for every question you can think of. Call repeatedly for accuracy. A mistake printed one Thursday can't be corrected until an entire week later.

More mistakes in dates are made when days and dates are combined than when either is used separately. If you put the date of the month with the day of the week, as Saturday, Jan. 18, be positive Saturday *is* Jan. 18! It might be Friday.

Disgruntled politicians are willing sources of news tips, either in office or just out. Much of the time they are nursing a gripe or they want to get even. They'll reveal city or county government secrets you normally never would uncover. You don't need to agree to any deals or trades with them; obviously you shouldn't. Just listen.

Two generations of newspapermen have grown up without ever having used boilerplate or ready-print. That's passé. Our modern boilerplate is the stream of canned releases on all subjects that flood our desks. Shy away from those that do not directly affect your town or readers. (A reclamation project in Arizona does not mean much to Minnesotans, but Social Security benefits affect readers in both places.) The reader who is looking for local news recognizes canned releases as filler. They clutter our papers without performing enough service. They are seldom news, they can be pure propaganda, and they are sent to media all around us so they're not ours exclusively. If you do use the better ones, edit them strongly; invariably canned releases are overwritten. Never run a release verbatim if you can help it—at least rewrite the lead or give it a local tie.

The jungle telegraph amazes people who go on safaris. That invisible communication system of the bush is not so startling. Once you live in a small town you become accustomed to the "drums" beating at all hours, about all subjects. You begin to feel that the natives have nothing on us. The small-town bush telegraph can be garbled and embellished outrageously, but even the most flagrant rumor could have some basis. So follow every lead you hear. Small-town people, naturally curious, are bothered by strangeness—a car they don't recognize, uncommon activity in the neighborhood, the unfamiliar in the familiar setting. Though some drumming may be impossibly untrue, some may lead you to a story.

Some people are natural reporters, natural "drummers" if you will. They get that way by asking questions and by some sharp observing. In every town this staff of unpaid reporters will gladly serve without recompense if you will cultivate their support.

Proof should be read with copy, not by itself. Such double-checked reading reduces omission mistakes, typographical errors, wrong names and dates. It's better to double-check it with a second proofreader, but time and lack of manpower usually prevent this. Take time to read job work twice—once with copy and later to make certain you didn't overlook something typographical in your con-centration of making proof conform to copy.

Unless your memory is phenomenal, don't trust yourself to re-member all the details of your busy week. It's safe to keep track of it with a pencil. I've learned that if I don't write down my story notes, they slip away from me. If I don't mark my desk calendar for a picture appointment, it can be forgotten. If I don't remind myself of stories I must pick up, they are left out. Write it down—or it gets away from you.

If you can, write that story as soon as you get it. Particularly the small ones, particularly the sports. Some stories must jell or require more information. Others will be more complete and better written if written fresh. Developing the habit saves the step of writing extra notes and then spindling them. Saves wear and tear on the spindle, too.

Using the phrase "last week" to excess is a common weekly fail-ing. Unless it happened all week long, "Tuesday" is better than "last week."

It is difficult to be the brazen, hard-nosed reporter in a townful of people you know, but it is possible to be persistent. Just don't be patronizing. Don't ask for permission to publish some story. Don't give a wavering news source a chance to say "no." Let them assume if you're talking to them you're doing so because you want to print it.

Sometimes what people don't tell you is as much news as what they do. If a sheriff refuses to give you a story, print that he refused. If he says, "no comment," print that, too.

Don't be afraid to quote often. Telling the story in a person's own words is priceless reporting anytime. Also, in your small town, readers will recognize who's talking even though the words are not attributed.

Add background whenever you can. Bring people up-to-date. Explain rules, laws, ordinances. Tell what led to the situation the way it is. As you report more and more years, you'll find you're one of the few who will remember enough of the interesting, informative background. It may be up to you to furnish the continuity of a town's news as well as the interpretation.

And always remember that spry senior citizen who said every Thursday morning when she came for her paper: "I know all the news. I just buy the paper to see who gets caught."

CHAPTER APPENDIX

★ LIBEL THOUGHT PROCESS BY RICHARD W. CARDWELL, *General Counsel, Hoosier State Press Association, Indianapolis, Indiana*

A NEWSPAPERMAN without an understanding of the rules of libel is rather like a youth with a loaded gun and no knowledge of how it works. The odds are, sooner or later, someone is likely to be seriously injured.

Within space limitations (and with the understanding that nonconstitutional law may vary in different jurisdictions), I will set out the thought

process I use in determining whether particular material should be published.
The basic outline is extremely simple. It is:

1. Is the material defamatory of an identifiable individual, or a small,
ascertainable group?
    a. If it is *not* defamatory, print it.
    b. If it *is* defamatory, then—
2. Is the material privileged?
    a. If it *is* privileged, print it.
    b. If it is *not* privileged, then—
3. Is the material provably true?
    a. If it *is* provably true, print it.
    b. If it is *not* provably true, don't print it.

The conclusion is that one publishes defamatory, unprivileged, and not-provably-true material at his peril.

You will note I place *truth* at the bottom of the thought-process outline. The reason is simple. If one's reliance is on truth, that means it is in court, on the defensive, with the burden of proof to do so. That position is obviously a most undesirable one.

It is initially important to note that since the historic *New York Times v. Sullivan* decision in 1964 and decisions which have subsequently expanded the ruling in terms of coverage of individuals within it, the procedural rules of libel are dependent on *who* the prospective plaintiff is or *how* he has come to public attention.

The so-called *New York Times* rule, which today is a generally prevailing standard of law applied to most libel cases, is carved out of a *constitutional privilege* and will be discussed in the thought-process outline in that category.

DEFAMATION

What material is defamatory?

Published material which tends to expose one to public hatred, contempt, or ridicule or which induces an ill opinion of him in the minds of a substantial element of the community, is defamatory.

That may seem too vague a definition since it is a threshold question. But the fact is that no definite answer can be given. Without reference to established precedent in a particular jurisdiction, the most we can say is that a court will most likely decide whether material is actionable in accordance with the general and fixed opinion of the particular locality as to the damaging effect of the charge contained in the material. To an extent, defamation is like obscenity—one knows it when he sees it. When one's natural reaction after reading material is to think less highly of the individual referred to, then it is at least enough of a "gut" feeling to place one on guard that the danger of defamation exists.

There are several categories in which defamation dangers are high. They are holdovers from ancient rules of slander and include accusing one of suffering from a loathsome or contagious disease, or of unchastity or indecency, or of commission of a crime, or of incapacity or unfitness to conduct one's business or profession. But these are merely guides and not all-inclusive.

Illustrative words, such as "Nazi-like" or "Gestapo," or "reminds one of Hitler, Mussolini or Stalin," or other such references to heinous individuals or practices of the past should not be used to describe current situations. While it is not always clear that such references produce liability, they are the type of "fighting words" which produce litigation.

I only mention here material which may be called libelous per se, i.e., of itself. It is also possible for material to be libelous per quod, i.e., where the defamatory quality is ascertainable only from knowledge of extrinsic facts not apparent on the face of the material. The reason is that while it is desirable for a journalist to know enough about what is going on that he can discern hidden meanings in material, he quite often is not able to do so. So, the primary lookout must be to guard against that which is obviously dangerous.

As an aftermath of the *New York Times* decision, some types of material have been found nondefamatory in a constitutional sense when applied to one who falls within the rule. In the words of the United States Supreme Court if allegedly defamatory words are no more than "rhetorical hyperbole" or "vigorous epithets" and could be understood by readers as such, there is no defamation. Illustrations of this rule would be characterizing a legal, but obstinate, negotiating stance as "blackmail," or publishing a cartoon depicting attendants waiting for a politician with a strait jacket as a means of ridiculing his political aspirations. In other words, readers would not understand the material in the sense of making a specific charge of violation of a criminal offense or of mental incompetency, but would, rather, understand it as "rhetorical hyperbole."

Identification

It is well established that defamatory words are not actionable unless they refer to some ascertained or ascertainable person. Therefore, a reference in material may be so general and disguised that no reader would understand who was referred to. Yet, if an individual can show that readers understood the reference to apply to him, even if he is unnamed, he may have a cause of action.

A difficult question arises as to whether it is possible to defame individuals within a class or large group. The rule is that if defamatory words are used broadly with respect to a large class or group and there is nothing which points or can be made to apply to a particular member, no member has a right of action for libel or slander.

No cases have held that words spoken generally of a class or group in excess of more than about a dozen individuals can sustain a cause of action. For example, one might charge "jurors" collectively with ignorance or prejudice and not be liable. However, to charge a particular jury with ignorance or prejudice might result in a cause of action on behalf of any, or all, of them.

PRIVILEGE

If defamatory material is published there must be a relevant legal excuse for it. That brings us to the next area of inquiry—privilege.

Technically, it is not the published material which is privileged; it is the *occasion* on which it is published. Privilege is granted on the theory that the interests of the individual are sometimes outweighed by the public interest in the proceeding or with respect to the statement which is made.

Therefore, if the privileged occasion is present, it justifies the publication of the defamatory material and its publisher cannot be held liable unless actual malice can be proven. This holds even though the defamatory material may also be false.

A warning which runs through the entire area of privilege insofar as reporters of information are concerned, and an element which must be appended to every inquiry, is that *actual malice* always defeats the privilege.

It is also important to understand that "actual malice" has different meanings as applied to the constitutional privilege under the *New York Times* rule and as applied to regular statutory or common law rules of privilege. Under the constitutional rule, actual malice means publishing with knowledge of falsity or with reckless disregard of whether it is false or not. Under the regular rules, actual malice means publishing out of ill will, hatred, or spite with an intent to defame.

Constitutional Privilege

The constitutional privilege announced through the rule of the *New York Times* case was based on an occasion found to be present. That occasion was a "profound national commitment to the principle that debate on public issues should be uninhibited, robust and wide-open."

The effect of the rule announced there was to substantially shift burdens of proof in libel cases involving those falling into the categories of individuals to whom it applied. The shift was away from the alleged defamer, who previously was required, after defamatory material was proven by the plaintiff to refer to him, to defend on the basis of privilege or truth or to mitigate damages as best he could. The constitutional rule shifted the burden to the individual covered under it to show the falsity of the defamatory material and also to show that the material was published with actual malice, i.e., with knowledge of falsity or reckless disregard on the part of the publisher whether it was false or not.

Obviously, those covered by the *New York Times* rule have a substantially more difficult burden of proof to win their case than those not covered under it.

Therefore, the initial question in determining which rules of libel apply and where the burdens of proof lie is who the potential plaintiff is.

Potential plaintiffs who must meet the burdens of the *New York Times* rule include:

a. *Candidates* for public office; if the comment refers to their fitness for the offices they seek;

b. *Public officials* who are among the hierarchy of government employees who have, or appear to the public to have, substantial responsibility for or control over the conduct of governmental affairs; if the comment refers to their official conduct;

c. *Public figures,* i.e., one who commands a substantial amount of independent public interest at the time of the publication either (1) by reason of his position alone, or (2) by his purposeful activity amounting to a thrusting of his personality into the vortex of an important public controversy; if the comment refers to the position which places him in the public eye or to his activity in relation to the important public controversy;

d. *Those involved*, willingly or not, in a *matter of public or general concern*, even though they might be otherwise "private" individuals; if the comment refers to their conduct in such a matter of public or general concern or their connection with it.

The extension of classes of individuals to whom the rule applies came in a series of legal decisions. Therefore, the *New York Times* rule may apply to one potential plaintiff because he falls within one or more of the classes named. For example, a public figure might also be involved in a matter of public or general concern.

With respect to the last category, the question naturally arises as to what is a matter of public or general concern so that an individual's involvement in it brings the *New York Times* rule into play?

The U.S. Supreme Court declined to answer that question except in broad outline, leaving it to lower courts to make the determination on a case-to-case basis. The broad outline is that it may include "any issue about which information is needed or appropriate to enable the members of society to cope with the exigencies of their period." It has been held to include, for example, events which result in official action by public servants, such as a police campaign to enforce obscenity laws; comment about health and environmental hazards; religious "racketeering"; credit bureau practices; awarding of public contracts; hearing about drugging of race horses; a satirical article about a witness to a gangland slaying; the opening of a new play linked to an actual incident; an alleged "fix" of a college football game, and a church federation's receipt of a bequest under a will.

If a potential plaintiff is thought to fall within the *New York Times* rule, then in order to recover for a false and defamatory statement about him he must prove that it was made with knowledge of its falsity or reckless disregard for whether it was false or not. So, the question arises as to what facts might be shown to meet that burden of proof.

Since it usually is difficult to show that someone actually knew a statement was false before publishing it, most plaintiffs have tried to show a "reckless disregard" for truth or falsity. It is now established that "reckless disregard" means that it must be shown the publisher actually had serious doubts as to the truth of his publication.

Serious doubt is not measured by whether a reasonably prudent man would have published or would have investigated before publishing. Nor is it equivalent to a negligent misstatement. Often, if a source is relied upon in making the publication, the source's past reliability will become an issue.

The U.S. Supreme Court has hinted that serious doubt may be found when: (1) a story is fabricated as a product of one's imagination, or (2) is based wholly on an unverified anonymous telephone call, or (3) there are obvious reasons to doubt the veracity of an informant or the accuracy of his reports, or (4) if the allegations are so inherently improbable that only a reckless man would have put them in circulation.

The *New York Times* rule has also been found to apply in instances which involve not only straight factual reporting, but also with respect to statements of mixed fact and opinion. In such instances, the rule is applied to mean there can be no liability for statements of opinion if the facts upon which they are based are not made with knowledge of their falsity or serious doubts as to their truth.

In summary, the relevant questions one must ask with respect to the constitutional privilege of the *New York Times* rule are:

1. Does the individual who is the subject of the material fall within one of the categories of individuals who must meet the *New York Times* rule burdens of proof?

2. Does the material refer to his official conduct, to the position he holds or to his involvement in a matter of public or general concern?

3. Can the individual prove that the defamatory material was false and was published with knowledge of its falsity or with reckless disregard of whether it was false or not, i.e., with serious doubt of its truth?

Regular Privileges

Despite the fact that the *New York Times* rule sometimes has the effect of protecting against liability for lapses of good journalistic practice, it is still important to recognize other nonconstitutional sources of privilege. The reasons are two-fold: (1) if one guesses wrong about inclusion of one under the *New York Times* rule and a court holds he is not included, regular rules of libel will apply to his case with substantial burdens remaining on the publisher, and (2) routine utilization of privileged material helps build a strong record of defense even in *New York Times* rule cases.

The press is privileged to report judicial, legislative and other public and official proceedings and the contents of public records. The relevant questions are:

1. Is the proceeding or record, in fact, of a public nature?

2. Is the report a fair and accurate summary of what transpired at the proceeding or what is contained in the record?

Some courts have held that since such proceedings and records are easily accessible and the opportunity for accuracy thus enhanced, they will not apply the *New York Times* rule of privilege to defamatory misstatements of such proceedings or records.

A further broad field of privilege is publication of that which consists of comment and opinion, as distinguished from fact, with reference to matters of public interest. Included within it are two broad groups: (1) those involving matters that are inherently of interest to the public, such as the administration of government and of public justice, the management of public institutions and their conduct, and (2) those involving matters that are of interest to the public because individuals have voluntarily submitted themselves, their acts, or their accomplishments to the public's scrutiny.

For the "fair comment and criticism" privilege to attach, it must be shown that:

1. The matter is, in fact, one of public interest;

2. The factual situation upon which comment is made is true (or substantially true in many jurisdictions);

3. The comment may not extend to allegations regarding the private life of the individual whose work or qualifications are being criticized;

4. The comment is fair and honest as an expression of opinion, regardless of whether it is regarded as sound or correct by others.

Beyond these accepted privileged occasions, the law recognizes two others of limited utility:

1. Consent to the publication by the individual concerned, and

2. Right of reply to attacks from others, limited to material reasonably pertinent to a response which does not go beyond the scope of the original attack.

TRUTH

If defamatory material is published, and there is no privilege available (either constitutional or regular) because conditions set out above are not met, then a publisher will be obliged to prove its truth.

Truth in most jurisdictions is an absolute defense to libel (in some, however, even truth is not available if malice is present). However, proof of truth must relate to, and be as broad as, the specific charge. It is not sufficient to prove a different kind of misconduct if the charge is general. Also, a mistaken belief in truth, such as reliance on rumor or outside sources, is insufficient.

You will note I speak of *provable* truth. That presupposes the existence of evidence which may be competently introduced in a court of law to prove the charge. That means the existence and availability of pertinent documents and papers, the ability to rely on the prior statements or assertions of witnesses and other legal arsenal which may be necessary to sustain a burden of proof at trial.

Partial Defenses

There are several *partial* defenses available to attempt to reduce recoverable damages, but these go primarily to show absence of actual malice and are not available to defeat the action totally. These include: publication of a full and fair retraction; proof of partial truth; proof of honest belief in truth; mistaken identity; innocent republication; provocation, and bad character of plaintiff.

DAMAGES

If one publishes defamatory and unprivileged material, and if he cannot sustain the burden of proof of truth, then he becomes liable for damages.

Recoverable damages include *special* (a dollars-and-cents loss by plaintiff shown to be proximately caused by the publication), *general* (including compensation for loss of reputation as well as dollars-and-cents loss) and *punitive* (a punishment award against publisher, when actual malice is present).

As noted, this is a quick and limited summary of applicable thought processes in libel. It should be used as a springboard for a more thorough inquiry within your own jurisdiction.

CHAPTER THREE

More News Inside

I'M the voice of today, the herald of tomorrow . . . I coin for you the enchanting tale, the philosopher's moralizing and the poet's visions . . . I am the leaden army that conquers the world—I am Type.

FREDERIC WILLIAM GOUDY in "The Type Speaks"

★

IT'S THURSDAY morning and the paper's out and the phone is ringing for the first time. Someone must be furious! You can tell. The ring is loud and irritated; the phone fairly jumps off the hook.

"Is this the editor? I wish to register a complaint, a long overdue complaint in my opinion. Why don't you print my club's news?"

"We try to, but sometimes it's crowded out or has to be cut a little."

"Cut a little! How much is 'a little' to you if there's only one paragraph left? One solitary paragraph. It looks positively naked there on the page."

"I'm sorry," you say, "it isn't intentional, sometimes we just don't have . . ."

"You have enough room for that boring sports page. Column after column of dull figures and statistics and written in a jargon no one can understand. It's written by imbeciles for imbeciles about imbeciles who think more of a pumped up basketball than they do the finer things in life."

"Like your club news?"

"Of course. We do important work. It is enlightening. It is cultural and heaven knows this town can use a little culture. But you wouldn't understand that. You're too busy cheering at the amphitheatre."

"Ma'am . . . ?"

"Never mind. Fill the paper up with your precious sports if you want. But just don't bother sending it to me anymore."

And she hangs up in a huff. Scratch one name off the subscription list. And then the phone rings again, loud and irritated, like someone else is fuming.

"Who's the pantywaist down there who can't be bothered to write up the games?"

And you start in again: "Well, apparently that's us, but . . ."

"How come you don't put in more than just the score. No explanation, no high point men, no nothing. And there's a lot going on at the grade school we never hear about. How come?"

"I'm sorry, but sometimes . . ."

"Once in awhile you've got readers who like to see the bowling scores in, you know, and stuff like that. But you just put in that silly club news. That's all that's in that sheet of yours, news about women's coffees. Whydoncha say something about the games coming up? Instead we get bridge clubs. And birthday parties! You fill your paper up with it. Go ahead, stuff it full of that junk if you want but just don't bother sending it to me anymore." And he hangs up.

So scratch another name.

A newspaper, anyone?

Cooks discovered ages ago what printers should remember each week—the more dishes on the table, the more courses served, the fancier the meal. It's the same way with inside pages of weekly newspapers. Provide as many kinds of news and features as you can. I don't want to serve just sports, as my telephone sports "pal" would want me to do—nor only social items to please that society lady.

★ SOCIETY PAGES

We have formal society news, informal society news, and locals. These three kinds of inside news, although they are quite different, are usually gathered in the same breath by a society editor. Whether or not you put this news all in one department in your paper is up to you or sometimes, to the mechanical abilities of your plant. Ideally, most of this news should be run on a page or two set aside as a women's, or home and family, page. Here it displays to better advantage; you can change headline type to something lighter; add features on sewing, recipes, or household tips; group all wedding and engagement pictures.

Sometimes I'm forced into a combination of concentrating part and scattering the rest, but if I have to shotgun it through the paper I'm cautious of where I put it. No baby showers on sports pages or weddings alongside farm columns about livestock. And I've been through that bit about births too close to the engagement announcements.

Society Editors. The small-town society writer is really a greater in-stitution than the rest of the world realizes. Weekly editors all over the United States rely on a local woman (often the publisher's wife) to gather socials and locals each week.

The perfect society writer keeps the town's genealogy in her head and commits to memory the relatives of every subscriber. She is keeper of the social register and understands who fits where but is not im-pressed by it. She will show up at 8 A.M. Monday with three galleys of copy, all typewritten, double-spaced and on one side of the page. She will stay with you and keep right on working through the babies. And she reads the sports page herself!

Formal Society. Social gatherings you dress up for—fancy teas, parties, the weddings and inevitable showers, bridge clubs, endless coffees, all the places where the little finger raises so delicately from the tea-cup—those assemblies of true "high society" do exist in a small town.

My little town is perfectly capable of generating its own social strata. The country club can foster the same feelings of social differ-ences among the souls in a community of 5,000 as in one of 500,000. While we don't need to dwell on the frailties of human nature which cause this class consciousness, our lot in the weekly press is to report it.

Weekly society news is justly criticized many times for being long-winded and superfluous. Often, a trained journalist doesn't write it. A woman at home or the girl in the office may write these society pieces. The weekly publisher must share the criticism because he is the one who publishes columns of society teas and bridge parties because someone else gathered and wrote it for him.

The temptation to use reams of social news copy is very real to the weekly editor. Here are a couple fistfuls of copy on my desk Monday morning and the operator is hollering for something to set. It's no wonder so much of this society news finds its way to the machine and into the paper.

Wedding stories are another problem. I can almost leave up a wedding story in standing type, changing only the names of the prin-cipals and maybe the color of the bridesmaids' dresses. The rest of the story will contain the same trite phrases, dwelling much too long on the material of the bride's gown or how the cake looked. Are the tablecloths and wedding music really necessary? Each wedding story is a revelation, a written record of a memorable day to each bride and her family, and we editors are caught in tradition's web. Is there among us a man brave enough to decide which girl in his community will be the first to have a three paragraph wedding story?

Yet always keep the blue pencil poised for what one editor I know calls "lather." His society editor was forever "lathering it up" as far as he was concerned. It isn't a bad word.

Names are important news—but not the same names every week. I try not to overplay one prominent family or one clique. Society "doings" occur in all levels of my town. Not just "that 400." There are the affluent and the influential, those who are almost affluent and influential, and those who probably never will be either. But each group has its clubs and its birthday parties and its social gatherings and it all makes social news.

Informal Society. Meetings you don't have to dress up for—the town's organizations, fraternal groups and their activities, church groups, the service clubs—these are generally written by a society editor. This is often more public service reporting than social writing. A finance drive, a church meeting, notices of forthcoming events, plans for some town-wide activity—it's all news of the many organizations that flourish in a small town.

Church news, usually much different than this organizational news, follows a similar pattern. In every town you'll find cooperative ministers who have items about their churches' forthcoming evangelistic services and related activities.

Locals. Nothing packs the news wallop of those five to ten line notes of information—all kinds of information—about my readers. Of all the news inside, locals have the most general readership. Their appeal comes from the make-up of the small town where people are genuinely interested in each other. Locals are friendly gossip, the "visiting" kind of news of Chapter 2, street corner conversations, and friendly backyard chatter wrapped up in six lines of type.

"My son was home over the weekend," is the biggest event in the Jones family all week. It is part of the small-town phenomena that many other townspeople share this interest in knowing young Jones was home. Locals don't affect just one family. They affect friends, relatives, classmates, neighbors.

Strictly speaking, locals are "society." In her telephone sashays around town, the social editor picks up the bulk of them and in practice "socials and locals" are lumped together. Locals, however, cover the news of what's happening to individuals, not to cliques or organizations or the country club social groups. The local's appeal lies in its concentration on people, all people. In a small town, news doesn't have to be big news to be read.

In locals I've discovered that:

• It's good newspapering to train all the staff to pick up locals when they hear them. It's a pretty dull town that won't produce five locals on one trip down Main Street and a pretty dull paper that lets that kind of news slide by.

• Readers themselves help gather locals. I begin to understand how wide their readership is when I receive locals already written or given over the phone and I don't have to change a line. People have read locals for so many years the style comes automatically. Our paper receives dozens of locals weekly that require only minor polishing, including some from a little old lady every so often who invariably says she and her husband "motored" someplace. You can tell how long she's been calling the paper with her news. "Motored" was a newspaper word back when horses were going out! But it proves, I think, locals have been around a long time and how much they are read.

• A local need not always be about people. Those one paragraph items about a new coat of paint or a little job done by the town crew fit comfortably in a column of locals.

• I print locals at the expense of other inside news. They reach a wider audience.

• Locals are published respectability, sometimes the only chance a person has to be recognized in a community. They mean a great deal to people who aren't members of the Main Street crowd or who don't "belong" to a social group.

• I try not to overlook locals. My readers may obliquely refer to a potential item. I need to follow it up. Or they may want to have some personal happening in the paper but they're reluctant to say so. A man will remark, "My sister was here over the weekend and she was telling me . . . ," or, "When I was in Des Moines last week I saw . . ." It takes me only a minute to ask him, pencil in hand, who his sister is or what he did in Des Moines. And I have the local he was trying to give me. (I make sure he sees me writing it down, so he knows he got his message to me.)

• I make locals simple. I eliminate, for instance, the reference to my town. It doesn't have to be repeated after each name. If no town is mentioned, the reader understands it's his own town. I don't put too much into one local; they become complicated enough. And I don't list every sight a family saw in Yellowstone Park.

• Locals are universally adored by make-up people. Mechanically they can be a godsend. A galley of locals will wrap around several short columns of stacked ads. With a proper standing head, they can be pasted into odd-sized places, exactly to the line if necessary. A newsworthy local, given a small headline, makes a far better filler for five to ten line holes than the canned ones about China tea or muskrat babies. Locals will fit anywhere. Give a make-up man a galley of them to use in a run and he'll bless you.

★ COUNTRY CORRESPONDENTS

Traditionally, country correspondents have carried many pages for weekly newspapers, an old-fashioned habit with much merit. We've mentioned how your town becomes "our" town for the farmers living around it. The country correspondents gather these farm families into their respective rural communities, giving the people of Snavely Lane and Willowdale and Orchard Bench their only published news. Part of each paper becomes theirs exclusively, a column of space every Thursday for visiting in print. It's no wonder the country correspondent (who's writing the same kind of locals about her community that I do for mine) finds such a receptive audience.

All kinds of country correspondents take pen in hand. A weekly newspaper does not always have the luck to find only good ones. It becomes a question of using a mediocre correspondent or none at all. Not every community can come up with talent. It won't be the pay that attracts, certainly! But if you keep searching and encouraging you'll find someone who'll do it. Eventually she (or sometimes he) may even become the ideal correspondent—a better than average writer with a personal touch, maybe even a columnist's touch; one who has a feeling for people and their everyday happenings; who will recognize and emphasize legitimate news as well as the rest of her socials and locals.

What to Pay. Weekly editors can't afford to lay out too much money for gathering this country news, yet we must pay enough to induce a person to write it. If I pay 15 cents an inch, I must do the book-keeping and I encourage that old "lather." If I pay a flat rate of $5 for each week's efforts, I will probably overpay the columnist who doesn't do much and underpay the diligent ones. You have to adjust the pay scale to fit your community and your situation.

★ SPORTS NEWS

The appeal of sports recognizes no population limit. The small town, too, can become frantic about favorite teams, athletic stars, play-offs, the 300 game, the hole-in-one, the tie-breaking touchdown. Only one Yankee Stadium exists, but there are thousands of small-town ball-fields, sandlots, and backyards. Some athletic competition is generating interest—and thus news—someplace in my town during all four seasons. It can be bowling, hunting, archery, town basketball, Golden Gloves, Little League, American Legion baseball, swimming, fishing, skiing, or all those varied and frenzied sports programs of the school months.

In a small town, school sports engulf the community. You can't involve a small town's kids without involving nearly everyone else. It's not "the" team but "our" team, representing us to the rest of the world. With September's first arching kickoff, school sports sweep up mamas and papas, old grads, the undergraduate rooters, old-timers and grade school worshippers. And the sports field is no longer just for the boys, either. Girls' sports are rightfully and excitingly in the spotlight now, too.

You'll find sports stories everywhere. I spend a half hour once a week with the various coaches. As a frustrated athlete I like the locker room talk in the first place and I've found it's a good source for background, inside tips, and camaraderie. I talk with the kids and encourage them to tell their own story of the game. I'm curious of their opinions of opponents. A player saying, "Livingston was the toughest linebacker we faced," is authentic praise.

I use names galore. Opponents' names, too.

All-opponent teams, picked by the players, are usually surprises. The kids see it differently on the field than I do on the sidelines.

I cite the small achievements of individuals—an intercepted pass by a lineman, a good fast break, a double play combination—opponents as well as "my boys." In a sentence or two my sports readers will share the excitement.

As a fan myself I have a weakness for reminiscing. Sports fans would almost as soon talk or read about past glories as the new ones. I write of old stars, of teams of other years. I don't say, "the kid hits like Mickey Mantle." Instead, he "hits like Tom Wilkinson used to do a couple of years ago."

Statistics are fun, too. Those cold facts can balance the fever of the game itself. A football summary tells its own story. A rebound record can describe a game better than the score. A complete play-by-play record of a football game not only gives yardage statistics and yards gained per carry by individuals, but is often the only record of the game. End of season summaries make welcome stories—the most points scored, the longest pass completed, the most hits, the fastest 440.

These are ideas for school sports. They will work, too, for your town's other sports. Sports coverage is universal, regardless of age group.

Give it Some Space. The larger daily, though it recognizes the value of sports to build its own circulation in my town, normally will be too involved elsewhere to do more than skim my area. I may be nearly a week late in reporting them, but I can still find stories the daily would not.

I work hard for the different angle. Does the loss complicate the standings? How many undefeated wrestlers are left after last week? Who is the leading ground gainer so far? Which quarter was the disastrous one? What was the key play? Dig for details—the girl who hits the best free throw percentage, the shot made just before the half, the tackle who gave away twenty pounds, a good block, the long punt. The hometown viewpoint again is a big asset. No other paper cares as much about my town's teams as I do.

Writing Sports. Sports language is universal and although purists shudder at sports jargon, a sports reader knows exactly what is being said to him. Don't slip into poor writing, though, because of the liberties. Sports writing, for all its slang and local color, can have dignity, too. Sports deserve as high caliber writing as any other news.

We should vary the use of sports verbs, and avoid the same old ones. A sportswriter often lands on a verb or a phrase and stays forever. A basketball team might be "walloped" 85 to 55, but swamped, smothered, buried, plastered all can describe the disaster, too. No word remains untried in sports (and the worst cliches come from the most banal ones). Take words in common usage elsewhere and find a place for them in sports. It was a "plodding" quarter, for instance.

I like school sports written from the kid's angle. I don't believe editors should be first assistant to the coach or leader of the downtown quarterbacks. I don't like wailing in print over post-mortems. It is not my philosophy to criticize high school athletes or to single out individual mistakes. It's the kids' game. They're not professionals; they're supposed to be playing for the fun of it. They don't need a bunch of adults chipping away at them, especially in the newspaper. I try to report the game the way it was and leave the handwringing to someone else.

Covering sports is a big job, no matter what size your town. You don't need a junior college and several high schools to create enough copy. You will stretch your hours to cover what's already there. Report the junior varsity programs more extensively; add the neighboring town's sports, country schools, intramurals, junior high. Dig deeper into wrestling, swimming, and minor sports. It takes only two competing kids to make a contest—and a story.

On a weekly we can encourage an unpaid staff among the local sports fans. Bowlers will furnish you with weekly results; archers can keep track of tournaments. I've had high school boys not out for sports keep statistics, run down information, even take pictures. Many daily newspaper photographers started their careers in high school sports.

Sports Column. A lively sports column (like all columns) appeals to a wide readership. The sports fan wants to know your opinions about a game. Even though he has seen it himself, he wants to see if you saw it as he did. He wants published confirmation of his ability to understand sports. He wants to know if he missed anything. The fan in the stands who plugs in his transistor radio earphone to hear what is going on out on the field in front of him isn't joking.

The average fan does not follow the game closely enough to understand its finer points. He is aware that a basketball going through the hoop counts for two points; he'll welcome your telling him how it got there.

Be specific in all your writing, but especially in your column. Generalities cover a practice session, but specifics explain it. "The team is working on a fast break" says it, true enough. But my reader instantly knows more if I say, "The speed of Jim Brown and Jerry Jones is making a fast break click for Coach Hank Smith in this week's practice sessions." Specific evaluations and explanations are far more interesting and more accurate. Don't be timid about expressing your opinion. But don't be unduly critical.

Personal writing gives a special touch to sports. It really is "our" team. Be objective about a strange team, but not your own. Small-town fans want to hear someone else remind them how well their team did.

The Appeal of Sports. National sports are concerned with the cream of the crop, the authentic stars, the pros. But sports is really the average youngster throughout America, the boy who kicks a football high into the backyard air or the boy who tries to get a basketball through the hoop above the garage door. I've watched these boys and their basketball hoops many times. They typify for me what sports means to a youth—his dreams of excelling, his "play" game at home, the fun of throwing a ball up toward a makeshift old hoop, and the practice, practice. Boys and hoops. You can see them in farmyards as you drive along—in front of garage doors, on vacant lots, in backyards. The hoop is usually slightly askew from a hurried father's quick nailing; the net has long since rotted and been battered away. Invariably there's an odd-sized, scrap lumber backboard, unpainted so the nails eventually show through and run rusty-colored trails down across the cracks.

But as any boy knows who has shot away the hours, a basketball will go through it if aimed just right. The shot he makes against this old hoop may someday be the same as the game-winning, last-second heart stopper he dreams about.

This dream of making the team, of winning the game single-handedly, can be a story someday on some small-town newspaper's sports page. We should be around to write it.

★

I Don't Always Agree with What You Say, But . . .

. . . I worked over the phraseology of that editorial (To An Anxious Friend). I cut out every adjective and used a verb instead which greatly strengthens one's style.

WILLIAM ALLEN WHITE, *Autobiography*, 1946

★

AN EDITORIAL is sitting up half the night trying to put your thoughts down so they make logical, coherent sense.

An editorial is having to write something against a friend or in favor of an enemy.

It's saying goodbye to someone you respected. It's reprimanding a mayor who didn't do a job. It's writing confidently about the future; it's reliving comfortably the days in the past.

An editorial is Thursday morning with the phone ringing and you know it's someone to give you the devil about what you wrote.

An editorial is sharing some thought or phrase or an idea you liked. It's tongue in cheek and sword in hand; it's laughing and crying and unashamed flag waving.

It's winning a battle; it's taking on the cause of the minority.

It's being alone and misunderstood; it's prophetic on the one hand and completely behind the times on the other; right one week and wrong the next.

It's not wanting to write because you're tired and don't think you have anything to say.

Black type of an editorial is all of these, yet each one is as different as the editor who wrote it. Which is the way it should be. For the editorial page *is* the editor, where he wears his heart on his sleeve, where he speaks his mind, where he shares his ideals and ideas.

★ EDITORIALS

I believe an editorial must be governed by the rules of good taste and common decency so that it can be read by all people, of all ages, of all walks of life.

It should be independent of every other page of a newspaper so that the opinion expressed on the editorial page has no bearing on the advertisement of any other page, the news story of the front page, the name of any person in the social columns.

An editorial should not try to mirror what the majority is thinking. Nor the minority either. It is one editor's beliefs publicly expressed.

An editorial should choose sides whenever it can, but if you cannot choose sides, be careful of your attempts to please both pro and con. Such pleasing is next to impossible. Write what you feel and if you are not sure of your own convictions, it's better not to write it at all.

On this kind of editorial page there is no place for rabble rousing. Leave invective out. Forget personal battles. Forget the editorial that seeks to criticize for criticism's sake. Present what you feel as logically and respectfully as you can. Do not insult your reader by attempting to appeal to his emotions or his personal prejudices to gain your point.

Don't ask that everyone agree with you. Agreement of the majority doesn't strengthen an editorial or make it good or effective. It is your opinion or your idea and maybe yours alone.

Don't be afraid to open your heart. You will delight the cynics and give them hours of snide remarks. However, you will find most of your readers aren't cynics and disbelievers but young people and understanding grandmothers and sentimental men and appreciative contemporaries—and they all have hearts, too.

Do not be afraid to praise, but mete praise discriminately. Many things are good, few are excellent. To praise everything that is merely good is to weaken the praise of that which is excellent.

Keep in mind that editorials should be as long as it takes you to make your point, but Horace Greeley wrote once: "Make your editorials only as long as your pencil."

Don't be alarmed if an editorial of one year or one month seems inconsistent with that of another year or another month. An editorial opinion, like the news, is the opinion of this time, of now and now only. Events, change of attitude, new facts can transform old editorials into closet specimens. It was an opinion of that time. Be proud of it. Don't revise it. Trying to strike a consistent mark can often drift into bigotry and blind stubbornness.

Be unpredictable enough so the reader can't pick up the paper each week and know exactly what you're going to say.

Write for no class or group. Write as you see it and if you like it, the chances are great someone else will like it, too.

Don't forget to laugh at yourself, your ideas, your pet peeves. And laugh at the other fellow's, too. A sense of humor can save this world.

Don't think you must print every editorial. Many of the best editorials never get into print. The power of disclosure is many times editorial enough. A phone call to the right place, a word of advice, has alleviated many situations, and your Pulitzer prize-winning editorial never got past the typewriter.

Share all ideas you run across. They don't have to make a point or strengthen a philosophy. Just share them. The ideas will do the rest.

Be resigned that editorial writing is lonely work and your editorials will offend your friends as well as your enemies. But don't stop writing them.

Editorial writers often get discouraged, and on a small-town paper this discouragement is the toughest part of all. Because if you're human and if you like people, if you're dedicated to your principles, editorial writing is a tough job. There are many uneasy moments. It seldom can be done quickly. It takes precious time to research, to consider angles involved, to check facts, to reconcile your own feelings. Some editorials write themselves; some of the firebrand kind roll out of your typewriter. A great majority of them take intense, comprehensive thought. Indeed, sometimes you must agonize over your own opinion about a subject before a typewriter key ever strikes paper.

Editorials are easily put off. Subject matter seems desperately hard to find sometimes. Some days, withstanding the guff and gaff about one of your editorials seems too much.

You cannot remain aloof or detached in small-town editorial writing. You must answer more personally for what you have to say. A reader who doesn't like an editorial stand in the big paper blames that paper; in the small town he blames the editor. The writer of the big daily writes with an anonymous pen miles away; the reader knows the small-town editorial writer personally. This closeness can dull the sword.

It is easier to forget an editorial page. It is easier to eliminate the long hours of preparation and the longer hours of bickering and explaining after publication. It is easier to put in a couple of galleys of correspondent's type, or better yet, ads that pay! It is easier to believe, "I don't have time" or, "I don't have anything to say."

But if you want to reach your community, if you want to dig into life, then lay out an editorial page someplace in your newspaper and start writing across the top, "Here is our opinion."

Local or National Editorials? A persistent movement in journalism has advised the small-town editor to write only "local" editorials. We weekly editors aren't supposed to comment on national or international issues, just the local ones. This is poppycock.

Editorials deal with ideas, and there are no city limits to ideas. Of all the mediums of thought, a newspaper should be the last to restrict these ideas. Our reader isn't so limited. He thinks about his nation and the world and the state all at once.

Then, let's be practical. There aren't that many local issues in many small communities. Towns go through great upheavals and things then taper off. Improvements are made and the tax burden strained, but only so many hospitals can be built, so many schools erected, swimming pools dug and streets paved. One quick way to lose your reader is to keep pounding him week after week with some pet project of yours. When editorial writers rely on local issues entirely it can become pretty sparse fare. You can always find something to write about locally if you feel you must. But why write a forced, second-rate editorial about garbage cans on Main Street when the country is torn apart over civil rights?

Should You Publicly Support Candidates? Since I believe it is a responsibility of an American voter to choose a political party or a political candidate, I believe it is an editor's responsibility, too. Yet I do not advocate blind party loyalty in an editorial column. Nor the same party this year as last. As a member of one party, I have not been reluctant to criticize editorially the members of that party.

Whether you support political candidates is, of course, a matter of preference. I don't like to think the courage of personal journalism is dying, but after the *Publisher's Auxiliary* ran an article about the subject a rash of letters took the position that editors should not support candidates. What is an editorial if it can't take sides? In my paper one election year, some people argued that I should not tell them who to vote for, but to urge everyone to go to the polls. My belief then and now is best expressed by the following editorial I wrote in answer to the criticism:

An Editorial Or A Poster?

Let's straighten out one apparent misconception.

You can write all the letters to the editor you want, cuss us out, disagree with us, give your side of any question. But don't tell us how to run our editorial page. Don't tell us that we can't give you OUR opinion of a problem, of a theory, of a political candidate. Don't tell us what to write and what not to write.

We reserve this page in each issue of the *Greybull Standard* to express this one editor's opinion. Sometimes it has been the opinion of the majority; sometimes of the minority. It doesn't have to agree with anyone as far as we are concerned.

But each week there's some subject we'd like to comment on. Just as you do in your homes, to your neighbors, out on the street. Obviously this is freedom of speech and of the press. Do with yours what you like. We'll continue to print ours. And if we don't want to listen to yours, we don't have to. If you don't want to read ours, neither do you have to.

If you want an editor's published opinion of what he thinks about a political candidate, read his editorials. If you want to read information about getting out and voting, read those posters in the U.S. Post Office.

"I" or "We". For years I used the traditional editorial "we" and never signed editorials. But as I write more, I find I make a point stronger if "I" write it. When I wish to express a conviction that belongs to me alone, the "I" is the only pronoun I can honestly use. Signing my name or initials at the end of each editorial has the same, more personal, impact.

Leave 'em Laughing. Editorial thoughts at times may run only a paragraph long. If you string them together in one-paragraph-after-another form, arrange them so the final paragraph is a snappy one. The show biz principle of leave 'em laughing needn't be confined to the stage. Your exit from the editorial page with a good laugh or a chuckle sends the reader away in good humor. The good impression lasts. It gives the potpourri a climax, a punch instead of tailing off. Column writing utilizes the same principle. Don't give away your best before the evening's over.

They're Separate. The front page is for the report of what others are doing. The editorial page is for the report of what *you think* they should be doing. And that's why the two are separate.

★ READER RESPONSE

People aren't usually shy about disagreeing with your editorials. They aren't always as vocal about telling you they like what you've written. The standing joke on our paper is that an editorial is a good one if we register two comments. If three or four people say something, you've really scored. If more than five say complimentary things, clip it out and send it off to the Pulitzer committee. You've really got a gem!

Your editorial writing will never want for readers. This Thursday procession of interested readers comes from all parts of town to see what you have to say. For a long time you will be sure only a few read the editorials. But stop and remember some day all the comments from different people and you will be amazed to find they come from many directions. If a farmer from the south end mentions something you wrote one week and a housewife does the next, you can be sure your printed word is reaching a broad audience in between.

You should understand this editorial reader of yours. He wants to retain his individuality and his independence. He doesn't want to be kept. That is why people say, "I never voted a straight ticket in my life." And that's why someone invariably tells you, "I don't always agree with what you say, but I read your editorials."

Actually the reader would just as soon be convinced. He welcomes being informed. He's hungrily interested in facts and information. He's anxious to see "what the other guy has to say." People start a new conversation with, "What did you think of such and such?" Readers pick up a newspaper editorial or a column and wonder, "What will he have to say about this?" The reader wants to know your opinion so he can better make up his own mind. That is why fence straddling can lose its audience. The reader, with his double standard, believes it is okay for him to straddle the fence, but not the editorial writer. From you he demands an opinion.

When you feel yourself writing for a certain person or to a certain group, put on your hat and go out for a walk. When you come back, vow again to write for yourself. Not for one person or one group. Don't wonder, "Will so-and-so approve?" It doesn't matter if he does. The question is: Do you?

If you left it to the reader to choose your editorial policy, it would be fiery indeed. Your reader is a bloodthirsty creature. He delights in an editorial that flays someone. He's eager to read the give-'em-hell editorial. He wants someone blasted. He wants you to browbeat rather than logically argue. He is mildly disappointed when you persuade with anything smaller than a 2-by-4 club. It's like a boxing match. Though the spectator has no intention of getting in the ring himself, he's hoping someone else is bloodied up!

Your obligation is not to the fist-shakers. Editorial logic and cool persuasion may be slower and less popular, but more honest.

Letters to the Editor. Your editorial page can be bolstered with some lively letters to the editor. However, you can't do much about them if they don't come in. Or if the letter writers are nothing but crackpots. Good letters to the editor vary with the community. Some communities join in wholeheartedly to express their opinions. Others are extremely reluctant. It seems to be cultivated in one sector and not in another.

Generally, though, the reader dislikes saying what he thinks in print. His opinions are loud enough on the street corner; but when he has to sign his name to a published letter, his courage fades. Your job is to encourage him to make these opinions appear in type.

I try, for instance, to be extremely fair with all who write letters to my paper, especially those expressing opposite views. I refrain from commenting editorially about a letter appearing the same week. This is real sacrifice sometimes. The temptation to blast back immediately is a great one. But that's having the last word, and it's unfair to the letter writer. He would never catch up with my rebuttals. I have the time and facilities to pick his letter apart the same day it appears, on the same page, and he never enjoys this advantage. Not only does the letter writer recognize the unfairness of this—so do all the future letter writers. Many of them will hesitate to risk the same treatment. So if I feel I must answer the letter writer, I wait an issue before I do.

The same policy of fairness should be true of editor's notes on letters. Point out corrections in facts or straighten out misconceptions if you can, but leave the sarcastic remarks to someone else.

The normal person who sits down to give his opinion is not doing it to match wits and pens with you. He concedes that advantage to you. All he wants is to be allowed to say what he thinks. If he feels strongly enough to put it in black and white with his name signed to it, give him that opportunity. Don't try to show off your own ability with a sharp pen.

If his letter is ungrammatical, correct it for him. You're not trying to ridicule his education or to weaken his point by letting him appear illiterate. Your object is to give him a way to express an opinion in your paper.

If a potential letter writer knows what he wants to say but feels he can't write it, invite him to sit down and tell you what he wants to say. And you write it for him. It's still his opinion. All you've done is to put it down on paper. More people would write letters if they felt capable of expressing themselves with a pen.

Kids may write you letters once in awhile. Give these youthful letter writers extra consideration. We are trying to teach our youth fair play, freedom of expression. We encourage them to be independent and individualistic in their thinking. The lessons are wasted if the editor stifles a high school student's try at a letter to the editor. Though his letter may be naive, misdirected, maybe even bigoted, I give him the chance to participate, to speak his piece. I may cut off some overzealous adult who should know better, but I try to be considerate of a youngster's attempt.

Print all the sincere letters you receive, but don't feel obligated to print those which are more interested in personally attacking the editor than in making a point. Or those from the letter writer who keeps sending letter after letter. Don't turn your paper over to the fanatic. He'll take advantage of your patience and understanding. Give him his fair say, then cut him off. He usually gets the message. (National statistics show more letters come from fanatics and rabble-rousers than from all the rest of the writers together. You'll find your statistics are comparable.)

I don't print carbon copy letters to the editor (i.e., those sent to all newspapers at the same time). If a particular group wishes to pay for advertising to make a pitch, I'm perfectly willing to sell them the space. I don't provide my letters to the editor column as their propaganda means. If someone wishes to make a point with my readers, and only my readers, I'll publish his letter. If he wishes to take issue with something I have said, he is offered that privilege in my paper, but it is exclusive privilege.

Watch for libelous remarks in letters to the editor. You're responsible, not the letter writer, no matter how many times he signs his name.

Don't hesitate to cut the letter's length if you can do it without ruining the intent. You usually can since letter writers are notoriously wordy.

One of the biggest inducements for encouraging letter writers is offering to withhold their names. Many papers successfully do this; I've always felt it was wrong. Even if I know the name, no one else does; this makes my newspaper part of the innuendo. For the same reasons, I'm against editors writing anonymous letters of their own as a readership gimmick or to start more letters.

How Do You Handle an Irate Reader? In any editorial writing—more particularly in small-town editorials—you must be prepared to answer personally to every person who's been on the sharp end of your pen. Dealing face-to-face with those you write about is one of the reasons local editorials don't always get written. It's easier to editorialize against some senator in Washington than the school board president down the street. Not many of your editorial victims will be mad enough to storm in with upraised fist, but those who do will make some memorable moments. Before you reach for the tranquilizer bottle, remember that generations of editors before you have had to stand back of their printed word; except for those rare, tough-skinned, belligerent ones, few ever enjoyed it.

There is only one smart way to handle the man who is infuriated with what you wrote. That is to accept his right to criticize you as he feels you criticized him. The most calming words, the biggest soother of ruffled feelings, is the phrase, "you may be right." The editor doesn't say he's wrong. He's only saying the other guy may have his point, too.

William Allen White is said to have listened for several minutes to an incensed politician who felt White's editorial was damaging. Finally when the politician finished his tirade, White is quoted as saying, "Well, now that's settled. What else is there to talk about. . . ."

"You may be right," or "Well, that's settled," are much better approaches than arguing with the irate reader. Don't try to interpret your editorial for him. He read it. He knows what it said. Stand by it, but don't try to explain it, or apologize for it.

I can think of several sleepless nights and bad Thursdays that could have been avoided if I had taken this advice earlier. At one time I fought through the points in the editorial all over again. But if I couldn't make the reader see my point in the editorial, I had little chance of convincing him in a verbal argument.

Accept the other guy's point of view, but don't apologize for yours. Keep your good humor, and your temper. And if all this doesn't work, *then* reach for the tranquilizers.

★ COLUMN WRITING

Whether you write an editorial page column yourself or use others, you'll find that a good one makes many friends. No one can cultivate your own column-writing ability, but you can be pointed in the right direction. Of all copy you'll write in your newspaper, none will be more individually creative than the columns you sign. Yet while good columnists write from no generalized rule book, they write with similar pens.

I've noticed the successful columnists share several talents. They have a way with the ordinary so it becomes important in print. They can find the worthwhile among the commonplace; they can twist the everyday into the holiday. Their sense of humor is quick and ready but they usually laugh more at themselves than at others. They don't hesitate to express private thoughts; they share their families generously. Their choice of words is distinctively theirs. The typically good columnist is very much alive, very much aware of the world; and because he can be so in print, the world becomes very much aware of him.

The more personal the column, the bigger its success. The reader likes the conversation of a good column. He enjoys the listening. When the columnist shares a thought with him, it becomes a personal affair between the two of them. While this may happen in editorial writing, it is easier to pull off in a column.

There is a certain lilt to column writing. You'll find you can express thoughts and opinions easier in a column than in the colder, more formal editorial. You have license to be freer, more relaxed. Your heart is closer to your paper. You may feel the obligation of the editorial, but you seek a corner someplace for your private thoughts; so you may end up writing a personal column because you want to, not because a hole needs filling in the paper.

Take extra pains with your creativity in the column; work at developing your writing ability. Timing is more important in column writing than anywhere else, especially if yours is a humorous effort. As the comedian knows, laughs come from the way he tells a joke, not necessarily what the joke is. Learn the pause—that momentary halting of the reader's eye in a line of type—which leads him into the punch line. The climax should not be told too soon, don't give away a surprise ending, or use too few words instead of too many; employ astonishing comparisons, incongruous descriptions, above all, the right word. The fat lady who "waddles" into the store creates her own humorous atmosphere that isn't there if she "strolled" in. Seek descriptive verbs or adjectives which will contribute to the humor. Just one word can make a column item.

Sharpen your ear for native dialogue. Your community will have a dozen clever people whose everyday conversation is better than anything you can write. They usually won't mind if you quote it or borrow it.

As many kinds of columns exist as there are column writers. An editorial is usually bound by some tradition, in form anyway. With a column the roof's off. Many people can write with a columnist's pen—the editor himself, the editor's wife, a sports fan, the gardener, the housewife, the old-timer, the high school student. Your paper will seldom lack for column subjects. Leave room for a "Life in This Part of the United States," that popular gathering of short squibs from the town's happenings or your own Bill Vaughan style "paragraphing." You need a place for the pieces of a week's life. Such a column requires no theme, no relation between items. It has the advantage of appealing to all types of people with all kinds of humor. The material is constantly available—some weeks your readers will write it themselves.

Humor in Columns. There are some melancholy exceptions, but more people in the world want to laugh than cry. So the mother lode of column writing always has been humor. Nowhere does it succeed better than in the small town where the less formal atmosphere creates a continual abundance of joke swapping and humorous repartee. Small-town people laugh easily together because they know each other. They live in a family where the miser, the crazy dresser, the drunk, the oddball, the whiner, the Senator Claghorns all are real. So are the perpetual family jokes, the constant cliches of conversation, the repetitive phrase. The small town doesn't need any props. The props are there already. And so are the laughs. Share them in a column.

Anyone who has worked at writing a column will appreciate Red Smith's comment on the art. "Column writing is easy," Smith was quoted in *Time* magazine once. "I just sit here at my typewriter and let the blood ooze out of my forehead."

★ A PAGE OF DISTINCTION

The editorial page, being different from the other pages of the newspaper, should look distinctive. Experiment with various measures or type sizes: ten point instead of eight; 18 ems instead of your one-column measure. Give the page typographical distinction. It has its own flavor; it needs its own dress—liberal white space, two columns of type in a three column space, large size heads on each letter to the editor, alternating boldface paragraphs, indentions, special logotypes on by-lined columns, pictures, cartoons, boxes on special informative features.

A picture can occasionally make a point better than, or in addition to, the editorial. A picture of poor streets, a tree in the park chopped down indiscriminately, vandalism of historical relics, a public eyesore, a narrow bridge, an unmarked crossing gets its message across swiftly. However, you can't run a picture of an editorial subject too often without losing the emphasis. A picture is often inadequate if the point is elaborate or abstract, nor can a picture offer the liberties of the cartoon.

The editorial page should be in the same place each week. It helps your own operation (deadlines, make-up), and the reader feels more at home on the same page week after week.

Cartoonists, if you can find them, are priceless. If you try to confine your editorial page to local issues, however, it may indeed be difficult to find a local artist with that knack for puncturing and biting and stabbing with the brush tip.

How about ads? Ideally the page should be open, without advertising. But if your newspaper is a small one and you're being pushed into an extra two pages by keeping the editorial page open, look twice at your no-ad policy. Filling a full page of editorial matter is a herculean task some weeks especially if news, pictures, and advertising all fall on the same shoulders. A rule about no ads isn't realistic if you have to devote too much time to filling the page or if you wind up in more pages than you want, but do keep ads to a minimum and your page will look better. Make the rule fit your operation.

It Is My Page. I am very jealous of my editorial page. I protect my right to express my opinion on it, to say what I feel, to mount crusades, to wage wars. I enjoy this privilege of saying what I think, of answering to no one, asking only my own conscience if something should be written or not.

I mistrust those "balanced" editorial pages which present at the same time both the editorial opinion and what an opponent feels. I provide a letter to the editor column for anyone who wishes to answer an editorial of mine. News columns are for both pro and con; the talents and facilities of staff and newspaper are dedicated to both sides in the rest of the paper.

The editorial page is my soapbox and I do not wish to be pushed up on it, or off it, by anyone. I don't want to be restricted or obligated to any group or political faction; I want no shackles, no indebtedness. This is why I cannot reconcile editors holding public office and at the same time actively running a newspaper editorial page. You have an obligation to the board or office you hold; you can't ethically use your newspaper to take either side of a controversial issue involving that group. You cannot write an editorial as an independent newspaperman and not be read as a member of the board. While it is every citizen's duty to serve publicly, a newspaperman's greatest service lies in the good he can do with his newspaper.

★ NEWSPAPERING AT ITS BEST

Type is at its best on the editorial page—in an editorial that enlightens, in a column that entertains, a short paragraph that brings a laugh, a bit of satire that strikes quickly home, or a marshalling of facts and figures that swings the tide. Black type, column after column of it, is more instructing, entertaining, cajoling, and enlightening here than anywhere else.

Filling such a page is the most demanding job on the small-town newspaper. It makes you face up to your obligation as an editor as no other part of the paper does. Naturally, such a page won't allow you to follow all the "rules" all of the time. You will feel you've neglected your obligations sometimes; that you've missed a service you should have done. You will have small-town pressures and reservations and you will duck an issue sometimes to avoid a fight among friends and neighbors. You won't always be the crusader you'd hoped you would be. Don't despair. If you try hard, if you publish the best page that's in you as honestly and fairly as you can, the bad moments will be forgotten among the memorable ones.

You can make a reputation as a reporter with a good, lively front page. You can take exceptional pictures and be known as a good photographer. But it is on the editorial page where you make your reputation as a *newspaperman*.

CHAPTER FIVE

I Like Your Pictures

THE people in the audience looked at the pictures, and the people in the pictures looked back at them. They recognized each other.

EDWARD STEICHEN, *speaking about his exhibit,*
"The Family of Man"

★

AN EDITOR'S CAMERA isn't as powerful as an editor's pen, but some marvelous "copy" can be written with a roll of film.

I can tell you about a Little Leaguer who hits a game-winning home run, but I'd rather show you his face. Flood waters are trash-laden, roily, and filthy and that's the way they look in a photograph. You can almost reach out and touch the cuddly fluffiness of a pictured March lamb. And a pretty girl's smile—well, that has inspired poets for years!

Taking pictures, as you can see from any number of good books on the subject, is not hard to learn. But there is no substitute for learning it. Photography is not so much the right camera as it is the right lighting; not so much the film as it is the painstaking hours, the inspirations of a dozen restless nights. There's no secret film and developer combination, no magic camera art, no lens so perfectly suited that it will automatically guarantee good pictures. The photography is that guy or gal behind the camera, not the camera itself or anything that's in it.

Photography hasn't changed much over the years. Film is astronomically faster than it was in the old days, but you can take excellent pictures with good, slow Plus-X film. Sunlight is still constant light. The right shadows still make a picture. An overhanging tree branch will always furnish frame and balance. The basic rules haven't changed, though we use ASA-rated films instead of glass negatives.

There are constant reminders of this. One of the West's most talented photographers was Chas. J. Belden of Pitchfork, Wyoming. The pictures he took in the 1920s still adorn hotel walls or show up

in the annals of the West. He was a sensitive painter with silver ni-
trate who could catch a cowboy reading a letter from home or snow
falling on a mountain cabin so you'd long remember it. He had a
special way of capturing animals on film—a cow licking its calf, a long
line of trailing sheep, horses streaming out of a dusty corral. By today's standards his equipment was cumbersome and outdated, but he
had the talent to make memorable photographs.

Once when I was searching for old pictures of my town, a man
brought in some negatives he had taken a half-century before. He
had only been a fourteen-year-old boy when he rigged up a homemade darkroom, found an old box Kodak and shot pictures with great
abandon. They were superb photographs. When I put those old negatives under my "modern" enlarger they came out clear and sharp with
subjects relaxed and natural. Knowing they were taken fifty years ago
by a youth with what we'd classify today as a youngster's camera only
enhanced their appeal. Here, again, was a photographer.

What made both of these old-timers different from the modern
photographer? Only the years between then and now. The principles of photography practiced by the old professional and the eager
lad were essentially the same. Their heartwarming graphic results
remain examples of good pictures through a photographer's abilities,
not from his superfast film or finely-ground lens.

Of course, we modern photographers have many advantages over
the old-timer. The long minutes of fiddling with a ground glass under a dark cloth or lugging a big, heavy tripod are gone. I'm grateful
for that (and for high speed film on Friday nights during football
season). But we can never improve on the old photographers' ability
to shoot excellent pictures—that talent must be learned.

We who take pictures for the weekly newspapers of today may
share some of the old-time photographers' circumstances. Our general
run of pictures in the weekly is not the highly-specialized work of
magazines or the more progressive dailies. The average American
weekly has one staff member taking most of the pictures. He takes
all kinds of pictures, and his assignments are sandwiched between his
other duties. He can't afford a different camera, ideally suited to each
type of picture; often he can scarcely afford the time. He is only a
part-time photographer, just as he is only a part-time ad man or reporter. But taking pictures is within his grasp. Any number of
cameras, films, and developers will produce exceptional pictures—*if*
he knows what he's doing.

★ **SYSTEM FOR GOOD PHOTOS**

You'll find taking pictures becomes automatic. Your technique develops after the battering and hammering of experience and fail-

ure. All techniques are individual, like a style of writing is; but all techniques incorporate similar rules.

My system incorporates ten rules, none of which are secrets or anything new. Taken separately they're all common rules, but combined they guarantee the best odds for making good pictures. Combining as many of the rules as possible in making one picture is the secret of adopting a system. A low angle makes a good picture, but poor light can spoil it. A properly lighted picture can be dulled in the darkroom. A good shot is robbed of impact by running it too small on the front page. You may not be able to incorporate all of your rules in the same picture (the picture itself may not call for a low angle or bright light), but try for as many as you can.

My system, or technique, includes ten rules I have found work best for me most consistently. (These ten points are in no special order of importance.) They are:

1. Search for the best, brightest light.
2. Make certain light comes from an angle to the subject.
3. Strive for the good contrast that makes a good picture—black blacks and white whites.
4. Shoot from a low angle to dramatize your composition.
5. Get close enough to your subject and focus properly to get a good, sharp image.
6. Help the people in your pictures look natural.
7. Print the pictures large enough.
8. Shoot enough pictures for a variety of choices.
9. Use tender care in the darkroom and work for quality.
10. Be a poet with the camera; tell a story with film.

You can see how these rules of the system work in this picture of a March lamb (Figure 5.1).

The picture was taken in bright sunlight on a very fluffy-cloud-and-blue-sky day.

The light fell at right angles across the lamb and gave dimension to it by casting tiny shadows in the woolly fleece and shadowing the areas on one side of the face and in front of the legs. The shadows highlighted the texture of the wool and gave form to the lamb's body. Even the shadows cast by the little rocks on the road added detail.

The blacks of the picture were good solid blacks and the whites very white.

The low angle dramatized the lamb's direct look right at the camera and made the lamb seem near enough to touch. Its head and back went up into the sky.

The picture was shot very close and the focus was correct.

The picture was the best one of eight taken.

And a poet would take many words expressing what this one picture says!

FIG. 5.1. This "March Lamb" illustrates the ten-point system.

1. Brightest Light. Bright light makes bright pictures—and bright reproduction. I may get by with a gray picture once in awhile, but most of my pictures will be better if they're shot with the brightest light conditions possible. A gray face in a glossy print is muddy in reproduction. Washed out whites, flat-looking scenes, and lackluster shots with the same gray cast throughout are all caused by lack of light.

A passable picture can be made on a gray day, but I prefer to wait for the sun if the picture doesn't have to be shot at a specific moment. It's a long wait sometimes; in those endless days of overcast sky often a futile wait. Yet the sun puts that brightness in the high-light areas, gives depth with shadows, provides black and white contrast to make outstanding halftones. Cloudy days are full of dreary adjectives. Sunlight sparkles. The wait is worthwhile.

Stinginess with light makes dull pictures. There is no reason for underexposure, for instance; or being satisfied with gray instead of bright white; or shooting in the shade instead of the sunlight, not waiting for clouds to pass, or not looking for shadows. Indoors, don't try to shoot available light under poor light conditions or use an undercharged flash gun. Don't pose a dark subject against a dark wall or both will blend in together. You need a good reflective background so the subject will stand out. Placing your subject a few feet away from the wall helps eliminate harsh shadows in back of the subject.

Sunlight falling on a face lights it up. A gray face lacks detail and the character that good lighting will put into it. Misjudging flash output or shooting available light under questionable conditions will wash out the face tones. Don't settle for any old light; use the best source you can.

Light, flash or sunlight, must be able to bounce back at you. This is the easiest way to consider exposure and to understand why a dark background or subject absorbs more light and needs more exposure than a group of white-shirted businessmen. A certain amount of light you "throw out" from the camera must come back to you. You expose for the amount of light that returns. Your flash goes out to a yellow wall and comes brightly back. Overcast sunlight looks fine on the faces of the group by the evergreen tree, but the deep green keeps most of that light from returning to your camera.

Finding proper exposure may become a beginning photographer's biggest hurdle. The beginner invariably overcompensates. He seems to feel, "If I have all those f/stops, why shouldn't I be using them?" He worries more about exposure and shutter speeds than picture composition and the subject before him.

Most outdoor pictures won't vary much on exposure. Sunlight is nearly constant. If you kept track of the meter settings you use on bright sunlit days with the sun over one shoulder, you'd find they'd be nearly always the same. If the bright sunlight gives deep shadows and bright whites at f/22 one day, it will the next. This is the "norm," and you compensate for those other pictures—extreme brightness like a snow scene or the dullness of late fall afternoons—from this constant setting. When you have more time and you're shooting critical scenics, your light meter will be invaluable; but under the pressure of shooting and obtaining pictures quickly and efficiently, remember the constant light source.

Flash photography has a similar story. Flashbulbs or a properly charged electronic flash give out the same light at every shot. What controls your exposure is how much light comes back to you. If at 15 feet in a normally lighted room a flash unit provides enough light at f/16, then it will the next time. If you're closer than 15 feet, stop down. If the room is darker or if you must be further away to include all of a big crowd, open it up.

Once the normal f/stop is established for a particular camera and film combination, memorize the variations and the extremes:

- Get a printable picture at dusk and remember the f/stop.
- Bounce light in a normal room.
- Try a picture of a person sitting at his desk and don't use a flash.
- Remember the exposure for a patient in a hospital (white nightshirt, white bed, white room).
- Take a snow scene on a bright day.
- Try back light on any subject.
- Shoot a time exposure at night (e.g., Christmas decorations).
- Photograph a person's face on an overcast day.
- Take a night football shot or one in the gym during a basketball game.

These variations in exposure—and you can add many more to your own list—become your built-in light meter. This experience prevents you from laboring over each exposure or shutter speed. Fretting over exposure steals important time from picture making. Remember a lousy picture with the best possible exposure setting is still a lousy picture.

The automatic light meter shooting of 35 mm photography will eliminate many exposure worries, but you must understand lighting regardless. A 35 mm light meter registers correctly on a gray face, but for a gray face! Since you want brightly lighted, not gray, pictures you must first watch your light, get it correct, and then read your meter-shutter combination. The meter is only showing you what the light is, not if it is the *correct* light.

Skimpy light is what faults many available-light shots. A pho-

tographer whose ability I respect says he shoots with "light available," not "available light." The emphasis is correct. When light is
"not available" your natural shooting will be muddy and underexposed. The gray tends to take over.

Sometimes in shooting available light I get so carried away with
the candid technique and ease of shooting, I forget the weekly newspaper's reproduction limitations. Grays and darker shadows of some
available-light photos hold up in magazines' high grade reproduction
facilities and their fine paper. But the average weekly paper can't always show off poor available-light pictures to the best advantage. It's
those percentages again.

Generally, you control artificial light from a flash unit, but available or natural light controls you. You can shoot available light with
any kind of camera, but larger format cameras with the slower lenses
need extra development sometimes to provide enough "pushed" light.
It is possible to use available-light shooting if you know your camera
and if you know light.

The trend towards 35 mm photography has given available-light
shooting a real boost since 35s have good depth of field and very good
lenses. But light source still controls the available-light shot. If the
light is there, the picture will be good. If the light isn't there, you
will create just an average or fair picture.

In available-light shooting, no one disputes the fact that the picture can be taken without artificial light. The real question is: Is the
picture well lighted enough to reproduce well?

2. **Light from an Angle.** I want light to fall from an angle on my
pictures. Sunlight coming from one side creates shadows, encourages
contrast, chases away flatness. If I move my flash off the camera on an
indoor shot of a person, I create shadows on the cheekbones and
around the nose that improve the face and keep it from being an un-
attractive, flat-looking mug shot. The shadows supply that interesting
black and white contrast so necessary to the average picture. And the
shadows come from angled light. (A plain white sheet of paper isn't
as interesting as a white and black checkerboard.) Candlelight going
up to light a choir boy's face, sunlight filtering through branches, and
light stepping shadow by shadow down concrete steps are all examples
of light reaching a picture from an angle.

A pine tree against the snow has character and mood when the
sun strikes it from an angle. It's only another tree in the forest in flat
light. A field of baled hay at one angle can be lifeless. When you walk
around to the side, it becomes a field of shadows.

I work for shadows that will enhance the even pattern of bricks
or the rough texture of stucco or wood, or make canyon walls stand

out. Shadows show symmetry of architecture and are a must in aerial photography. Cross-light on a lamb's fleecy coat makes it soft enough to touch; or it can mark a ski trail across white snow. The slightest bit of shadow helps show detail.

We weekly photographers have certain leeways in our schedules because of the lack of spot news pictures. We often have time to choose our light from an angle for feature pictures, ad cuts, or posed people. We can avoid the middle of the day shooting in the summer, for instance. Morning and afternoon sun is always better than noon. When I have the choice, I tell them I'll be there at 10 A.M. or 3 P.M. instead of 1 P.M.

3. Contrasty Pictures. Gray pictures and soft tones can reproduce well sometimes—a mood may be spoiled without them—but contrasty pictures create excellent newspaper halftones. In black and white newspaper photography the percentages favor as much contrast as you can get.

To maintain this contrast in pictures, I remember to shoot in bright light for the whites, shoot from an angle for shadow, develop film for good contrast, and use a contrasty paper.

In Rules 1 and 2 we've already discussed the bright light providing the whites and angle light for black shadows. The search for contrast, though, doesn't stop at the darkroom door. Inside under the red light you must be as conscious of what makes good contrast as out in bright sun.

Film development and f/stop exposures are equally important for contrast. Shooting at f/22 and underdeveloping as if it were f/16 will give loss of contrast. Your normal f/stop for sunlight pictures also has a "normal" development time. You can't vary one or the other without changing your final pictures.

Weak or old developer will affect the contrast of your picture. I mix new developer or replenish often. I also consistently use as high a contrast paper as I can, whether tray development or an automatic processor is used. I avoid the brown-tone or dull finish papers, too.

Manufacturing firms and graphic arts representatives will advise you to use flatter, grayer-tone photographs for your halftones, but they don't run weekly newspapers. If they did, they would begin to see that your percentages for sharp halftones in weeklies go up with sharp black and white photos.

If you're still tray developing prints, contrast can be affected if you jerk your prints out of the developer too soon. Probably overexposed in the enlarger in the first place, the print is not allowed to come to full development and ends up in the hypo before it should. The secret of developing prints by tray is to expose properly in the enlarger (perhaps underexpose slightly) and then allow the print to develop fully before taking it out. Contrast comes up as the print develops, and it must be allowed to come up fully before the print is pulled from the developer.

4. Shoot from a Low Angle. Shooting from a low angle has saved so many of my pictures that I've become a rabid low-angle convert.

Sky is an excellent background. Lowering the camera sends the subject's face into the neutral sky, away from buildings, trees, billboards, and on all the ground-cluttered world. A sky darkened with a filter, or maybe laced with a few pretty clouds, gives strength and body to a picture. It will set off a subject looking at the camera. See what happens when you pose a girl in front of a building and when you move her out, and up, into the sky.

Dark sky is easier to reproduce, contributing again to the black-white, white-black combination so necessary to newspaper photography.

When taking scenics, photographers use the foreground (a tree branch, a person, edge of the canyon) to give depth to the panorama behind. This same solid principle works for newspaper pictures. The foreground accentuates the rest of it. With a low angle, foreground shooting finds perfect expression.

An example of how low angle shooting can improve a picture shows up in these shots of a temporary earth dike bulldozed alongside a potential flooding river. In the haste to get the dike up, a seven-foot street sign was almost buried and became an obvious way to show the dike's depth. When the first picture was shot (Figure 5.2a) the sign is hard to see against the background. The normal level angle makes the dike look only a few feet high.

When the camera was moved to a lower angle and the street sign pushed into the sky, the dike's height became more dramatic (Figure 5.2b).

In Figures 5.2b and c the foreground at the left of the picture is important. In Figure 5.2b the dirt and the rising dike show what has happened. The street sign is visible and helps the perspective. In Figure 5.2c the buried sign dominates the foreground, it's easily readable and the sweep of the dike more pronounced. Lighting had to be at an angle so the clods and hastily piled-up dirt shows.

Foreground emphasis with a low angle helps fill up a picture, and I can use more area of the square or rectangle. Also, if I have an important part of the picture in the foreground, I don't need to stand across the street to get everything in.

Lower angle shooting helps the photograph appear more as your

FIG. 5.2.   Low angle shooting improves this shot.

(A)

(B)

(C)

eye sees the subject. When you approach a person, your eye level is at his eye level. But your eye compensates and you take in his full height, placing his legs and trunk in proper perspective. With a camera held at eye level, you see the person with the top half of his body in proportion, but not the bottom half. His legs appear shorter; you seem to be looking down on him. The camera held slightly lower compensates for this loss of perspective.

If you have a reflex camera, try it yourself sometime. Look at the subject with the camera held high, then watch in your ground glass as you lower the camera. One of the reasons the twin lens reflex camera (and the bulky reflex cameras of the old days) have been such good producers is because a certain amount of low angle shooting is built in. You don't hold this camera at eye level for most shooting and consequently since you hold it lower you're unconsciously shooting up.

Admittedly, low angle shooting is not for all pictures, but shooting at a low angle (or *lower* angle) can improve many pictures.

5. Close Enough and Sharp. Pictures should show details. The wrinkles, the strands of hair out of place, the design of the lace shawl. I can produce these in a newspaper engraving if I remember sharp focus, if I don't move the camera, and if I avoid excessive enlarging.

A picture out of focus is the one fault that can't be corrected before the print appears in the paper. You may be able to improve the contrast of an underexposed negative, but you can't refocus the picture. A fuzzy glossy print becomes a fuzzy engraving, so focus carefully. It takes only a few seconds in the field. If you don't know the depth of field capabilities of your camera, learn them right away.

If camera movement is ruining some of your pictures, shoot a fast shutter—1/200 or 1/250—to take care of the jiggling when the shutter is snapped (especially in quick shooting). The larger the camera the more chance for camera movement. Snap shooting, that quick movement to catch an expression, increases chances for fuzzy pictures.

The closer you are to your subject the easier it is to make a good print. Fill the frame. I stand as close as I can without distortion (depending on the subject and depth of field). Then my enlarging is cut down, focusing is better, contrast holds (a picture tends to gray out when you must enlarge excessively). The less you need to enlarge, the more you will avoid showing graininess, which naturally looks worse as the picture gets larger.

If I stand close to my subject, I'm already doing some of my darkroom cropping. Cropping, after all, is only part of the composition. It's better if the wasted parts of the picture are being cut out by the camera in the field rather than on the enlarger.

In 35 mm photography, using a good telephoto as a "normal" lens gives 2¼-by-2¼ advantages to the 35 mm format because it eliminates excessive enlarging and automatically crops by filling the frame more.

6. Help People Look Natural. Although there are fires and animals and fields of corn to photograph week after week, most of my pictures seem to be of people. My fellow citizens (and their children) somehow participate in an amazing number of activities worthy of a little film, so I find my camera pointing in their direction most of the time.

People must look natural and relaxed in pictures. I want to use my camera to "describe" people just as accurately as if I were using words and a pen. It's seeing people as they are. The big smile old John Brown gives me on the street should be the same big smile in the picture I take. I don't want his eyes half-closed or staring out into space. I don't want him looking startled, pained, tense, apprehensive. If I catch him with his mouth open or a blank look, I'm embarrassed and so is he and so are the rest of the people who read the paper. A small town is sensitive to feelings of others. It's like the class play or a fumbling attempt at public speaking. The audience squirms in a mixture of pity and embarrassment and not a few of them think, "That could be me."

Most people actually like having their picture taken. They're not so nervous about having it taken as they are of not posing well. They want to look good; you should help them.

People who stand in front of a camera are amateur models. Professionals turn on a smile when a camera swings their way. Less-practiced subjects will wait warily for something to happen. Make sure to *let them know* when the picture is going to be taken. Give them a chance to turn on their charm, better expressions result.

You can help people relax by saying anything, even if it isn't clever, to reassure them. Or joke them out of their stiffness. Assure them as far as you're concerned this is going to be very easy, they're doing very well already. If your subject looks tense and sober when you're ready to shoot, have him move his feet slightly or turn more sideways—any kind of movement to make him forget momentarily about the camera in front of him. Don't give confusing, verbal directions. Don't say right and left (which is left and right to your subject). If he becomes confused or can't seem to understand, he'll only become more nervous. Point your finger the way you want him to move. And don't fiddle unnecessarily with the camera before shooting. Be efficient yourself.

Don't try to be a comedian when you're trying to make them relax. Hearty laughs move subjects' heads; the harder people laugh, the more they throw back their heads and the more movement you're likely to get. If you are too quick on the trigger, everything in the picture will be in focus except the person's face.

Don't take extreme low angle pictures of people, especially women. Holding the camera too low creates wrong lines, puffiness, and most of all, double chins. It may not matter as much to a man, but a woman may not be flattered by low angle shooting.

Don't let people plant their feet in front of you and face you head on, mug shot style (Figure 5.3a). Although this subject makes an acceptable picture, notice how the lines are improved if you have her turn slightly to the left and look back at the camera over her shoulder (Figure 5.3b). This creates a more flattering pose. You're not in a studio, but this is what a portrait photographer does. A 45-degree turn on the chair creates about the proper angle. Then have the subject turn her head back and look directly at the camera. Make sure the subject turns her head so that you can just see the other side of her face. Do not make the mistake shown in Figure 5.3c. There the subject has not turned her head enough and is moving her eyes, not her face, toward the camera.

You can make consistently good shots using the principles of Figure 5.3b in many picture assignments where you want a single- or two-column picture of a person (news story, employees in an ad). Watch that the subject does not tip her head too far to either side and that she doesn't carry her chin too high. You should be able to make a quick portrait-type picture like this of a person almost anywhere with just one flash for a light source. (The flash is held off the

Fig. 5.3. Portrait-type pictures: (A) mug shot style, (B) at a good angle, and (C) body turned, but head not turned toward camera enough.

(A)

camera and high so that the shadows fall under the chin and interesting shadows are created on the face.)

Don't let people take off their glasses when they pose for a flash shot. They may be afraid of the reflection, but without their glasses they won't look natural. Holding a flash a little above the glasses level and to one side angles the reflection and keeps it from glaring in their glasses and back to the camera. Be careful not to hold the flash too high, because horn rims or thick frames will cause a shadow across the eyes.

Shadows also can be pesky nuisances when photographing people outdoors. Baseball caps or wide-brimmed western hats cast too much shadow for good pictures of faces. What is especially tough to correct in the darkroom is the half-shadowed face. Remedy this situation by asking your subjects to tip their hats back until their faces are all in the sunlight (or use a flash fill-in). Some photographers try for all shade falling across the face, but I prefer the bright faces for newspaper reproduction. (I'm such a bug on bright sunlight on faces, I've been accused of advocating, "When in doubt, squint.")

A high noon sun, especially in the summer, causes the same unwanted shadows on faces that hats do. If the picture calls for a subject to look down or if I'm using the sky for a background by shooting low angle, I don't shoot at noon. Sell ads during the noon hours if you want, but wait on the pictures if you can.

When you take indoor photos, pose a subject away from the wall several feet so the shadow doesn't ruin his outline. Holding the flash

(B)   (C)

up helps eliminate the shadow behind the subject, but always hold
it so the light falls evenly on the subject. Aiming the flash unit to
one side or the other overexposes that one side.

Available-light shooting with good 35 mm equipment eliminates
flash problems when taking pictures of people, but you must still
watch your artificial light source. If an overhead light puts harsh
highlights in wrong places, you must move your subject or change
your position. Light streaming in from an unshaded window behind
your subject will create uneven light—too much from the window, not
enough on the face. Work for even light on faces.

7. Print Pictures Large Enough. Skimping on the size of the halftone ruins many newspaper photographs. You see two-column pictures that should have been at least three, and many threes that could
have been bigger. A good picture needs room to grow. Bigger pictures
are dramatic, they show more details, they create a bigger splash, and
attract more attention. Even a mediocre picture can look good when
blown up big enough, so a good picture blossoms in big enough space.

I use the "extra column" principle. I try one extra column than
originally intended. If it looks good in a three-column, I try it in a
four.

You can't make faces big enough if you try to show a person's
shoulders, so crop pictures close to the head. Take out excessive foregrounds. Crop to the essentials and then enlarge. This takes a certain
courage. A picture hypnotizes you. You may think part of it is vital
but as soon as you crop it out, you never miss it. Cropping *makes* the
picture of the Happy Fiddler in Figure 5.4a and b. His great expression is what is important, not that he was playing with a partner before a microphone in the school gym.

Don't try for too much in a picture. The entire first grade class
in a four-column picture can't have the punch that three kids color-
ing pumpkins would have in a three-column. Don't feel you must re-

FIG. 5.4 The fiddler's gaiety is the best part
of this picture (A). The rest can be eliminated
(B).

(A)

cord all the class for posterity. Make a rule about the number of people in one picture. Five or six, for instance, as a maximum. No more. Too many people, like cooks, can spoil the result. As the noted artist Rembrandt said, "A crowd I make with five people."

8. Shoot Enough Pictures. I don't like to skimp on film. There's always a different angle, a pose from a different side. If I shoot too few pictures I decrease my possibilities for a good picture, I may have to spend precious time retaking a picture, I reduce the chances for a good expression or a good pose, and worst of all I may lose a picture forever. It makes an 80-cent investment in a roll of film seem pretty cheap.

Taking enough pictures of people is especially important. Your amateur models will present a different expression or turn of the head with each shot. Don't cheat your chances. The odds for a good pose increase with the number of pictures taken.

9. Tender Care in the Darkroom. It isn't enough to just *take* good pictures. You must also be able to *make* good ones, although darkroom work becomes tedious to many photographers.

(B)

In weekly newspapering darkroom work always seems to come at the wrong time—in the middle of ad calls or newsgathering or when I'm trying to tie up a Tuesday's loose ends. That's why the time under that red safelight should be efficient time.

I make my darkroom work as simple as possible—loading film while one batch is developing; fixing, washing, drying continuously; watching the clock to prevent overfixing and overwashing; using hypo clearing agent to speed washing time; drying films faster; heating or cooling developer with a heater-fan combination. I always keep chemicals fresh, mixing and replenishing often (especially film developer). It all makes for consistent results.

Work speedily but not sloppily. Don't lose quality in the darkroom. It's the last stop before the engraver; how the picture looks when it comes out of my darkroom usually is the way it will look in the newspaper. If a picture needs an extra five minutes work (dodging to correct uneven exposure, perhaps) then spend that five minutes. It's photographic sin to leave uneven exposure in the final print when dodging could have corrected it. Suntanned faces in a group need extra care, or the sky may need to be burned in longer on one side than another. All these precautions must be taken to produce quality pictures. No amount of make-ready, no engraving adjustment can compensate properly for a print that should have had more—or less—exposure. Take the time to make it right.

To save fiddling with sizes of paper, I use only the 8-by-10 size. An 8-by-10 sheet can be cut down to every possible size for pictures up to five columns by eight inches deep with *no waste*. Cut in half, an 8-by-10 is perfect for a two-column width shot or narrow depth threes and fours. Cut in half again, it's the right size for one-column head shots or small twos.

I use a full sheet of paper for a test strip, because my time is more valuable to me than one sheet of paper. Actual picture-size paper shows the areas that need dodging *and* what the proper exposure should be. A test strip two inches wide shows only the exposure.

Pick one developer and one method and stay with it awhile. Don't be experimenting every week. I'm not afraid of change, but I don't want to be changing all the time. Once you find a satisfactory film and developer combination, give it a long, fair trial.

Your efforts to achieve quality in the field and the darkroom should extend to make-ready and presswork, too. Take the same special pains on the press you've taken elsewhere. Don't gang engrave pictures of various contrasts or shoot several halftone negatives the same way.

Above all, get enough ink on the picture. Some pictures need more ink than others, and that's what the ink fountain is for—to regulate the flow of ink over the form. If you want your pictures to print as they should, adjust the ink.

10. Be a Poet with the Camera. Good feature photography is done with a poet's eye. There's rhyme and meter in a picture field of tasseled corn or on the faces of happy kids. There's poetry in an old man's wrinkles, a lilting verse in a young girl's smile or a pretty day. In all these directions your camera should be pointed.

You must be conscious of emotions your photography will evoke. Will this bring a laugh? Will this picture make people say, "Isn't that just like life," or, "How natural that is."

The old *Saturday Evening Post* covers, especially Norman Rockwell's great ones, touched thousands of people every week. In a sense that is what many community newspaper feature pictures try to do. A weekly newspaper photographer may find news pictures scarce, but he should never lack for material for these "cover" pictures. He should ask himself: If I could find one incident, one expression which will typify this occasion or evening, what would it be? A valentine held shyly behind a back? A forlorn dog? A grinning pumpkin? A flag flying at half-mast? Raindrops in a mud puddle? What is it that tells the story without words? Find it and photograph it.

Figures 5.5 through 5.11 show how my ten-point system has worked for me.

★ TOUCHING UP

Those grease pencils (a black one and a white one) that mark on glossy prints will salvage some crippled pictures. Combining the two pencils can produce any shade of gray. Scratches, dirty negative marks, unwanted background all can be penciled out quickly on the finished glossy. You should break the line or feather out a mark to make it blend in.

A jar of red opaque will eliminate entire parts of the picture before it is halftoned or screened.

If you're stuck for arrows and circles to emphasize something in a picture, you can clip them from an old type catalog and paste them right on the glossy.

★ EXTRA-LARGE PICTURES

Big pictures, those that run full page depth or width, are irresistible eyecatchers. The reader is overwhelmed by size and detail and dramatic impact. Any good picture is improved by enlarging, and when you're short of type, a big picture will do more for your total page layout than a slapped-together house ad or a filler about U.S. savings bonds.

I invested early in a large full-page halftone screen and created

FIG. 5.5. Catching the natural expression of people is like writing exactly what happened. The first day of school may be sad for some, but not this little boy. Getting him in front of the school with this look stopped readers. The low angle let the tablet and the face dominate. Light came across the subject at an angle. And the school in the background filled the rest of the frame.

Fig. 5.6. Even if you didn't know this painter who obligingly climbed up on this painted horse in the middle of the job, you could appreciate his paintbrush and hat high in the air. If you know him, it's even funnier. That's why small-town pictures can pack such a wallop. This picture was published with the caption, "Painter Goes Rodeo."

Fig. 5.7. A camera has to watch life with a poet's eye, too, to see things like this frosty morning in January.

FIG. 5.8. The system isn't always able to work. You can only drag a runaway pig back in one direction regardless of where the sun is! The poor backlighting can be overlooked if your picture can capture the story.

FIG. 5.9. Low angle was absolutely necessary to this picture. It gave Mrs. Leghorn some class and importance she should have appreciated. She is strutting down both the middle of the picture and the middle of Main Street. Any other angle and she'd have been just a stray chicken.

FIG. 5.10. Something dominant in the foreground greatly strengthens a picture. This shot of a flooding road would not have been so compelling if it had been taken of the entire road. Letting the reader see this closeup of the muddy water pouring over the shoulder of the road described the situation better than any words could have.

FIG. 5.11. A photographer must get as close as he can to his subject. This flock of cedar waxwings outside the window had to appear only an arm's length away to be anything but just some more birds in a tree.

some sensational results. I've made a panoramic view with two four-column pictures by putting these together across the top of the page. If you take care with the prints, making them the same contrast and tones, the pictures appear as one. If you can't make a perfect match up, leave a thin, six-point stripping space between pictures and the panoramic illusion is retained.

You can even do this with letterpress engravings by butting the two engravings. The trick is to minimize the joint and to cut the pictures apart on a natural break. Don't cut on a change of tones. Halftones or engravings should be developed (or made) together so the two look as nearly alike as possible.

If you're an offset paper, big pictures are no mechanical problem. They only take a large-sized screen. You don't have to enlarge your photograph any larger than 8-by-10 since your line camera will blow that size up to full page. Stripping is no problem. Remember to turn the ink up on that page.

★ AVOIDING GRAINY PHOTOS

Grain is the worst kind of sloppiness in photography and causes as much reduction in final quality as anything. Besides avoiding those common faults of irregular temperatures in development, fixing, washing, and too much "wet time" or time in solution, here are other ways to eliminate grainy photos:

• You may be enlarging your negative more than you should. So stand closer to your subject when taking the picture to eliminate excessive enlarging.
• Don't be careless with exposure so that negatives are overexposed. Modern film gives leeway for mistakes and compensation for inexperience but film can't cover up forever. Learn to expose properly and you'll lessen chances for grain.
• Don't rely on overdevelopment. You may be pushing your film as far as you can, maybe too far. One hazard of available light is overdeveloping to make up for underexposure or poor equipment. If you're consistently having to overdevelop your film to get better contrast, you should be shooting flash or looking for another film–developer combination.
• If development is wrong or you're using grainy film because you're sold on its speed, try a slower film. You don't need fast film for top pictures although it does improve your depth of field and it does make night football and other sports shots possible. But slower film can take marvelous pictures too, and you may not have to fight the grain.

★ QUALITY NOT QUANTITY

Time and money limit weekly newspaper pictures. A newspaper, to
be run economically and efficiently, can't use picture pages week after
week. Heavy ad weeks may crowd out some inside pictures. Other
weeks, picture ideas and situations aren't there. A few good pictures
throughout the paper will interest more readers than one full page of
mediocre ones, just as one good picture on the front page is worth
three or four so-so shots inside. Finding enough time is also a con-
tinuing problem. Strike a balance between enough pictures to sup-
plement news and feature coverage, but not too many to strain the
time and money budgets.

It takes a little longer to shoot a top-notch picture than to slop
through a bunch of average ones. A picture costs you time to think
it out, some more time to take it, part of a roll of film and the cash
to get you there. Then you must develop it and spend more for
chemicals and paper, and more of your time. Finally you wind up
paying engraving or halftone costs. As long as you're going to spend
this money for pictures, spend it on quality.

★ WHICH CAMERA

Photographers have argued film and cameras for fifty years and will do
so again for the next fifty. Every time a new camera hits the market,
new converts and new missionaries are made. Once it was the four-
by-fives, then, the twin lens reflexes, then the 35 mm's, then different
35s, then the best lens to use. If the "perfect" camera exists, it is probably the one you are comfortable and happiest with right now, the
one that suits you. No matter what camera you use, it will still need
your skill as a photographer. The real question has always been: Am
I taking this picture right? not, Am I using the right camera?

The 35 mm now dominates the field. Its development in the past
decade has generated an increased interest in newsphotography and
put cameras in more newspapermen's hands than ever before.

In other days, the 4-by-5 Speed Graphic was the workhorse. I
never thought I could ever get along without it. Its flash system is still
the best ever—a big negative properly lighted, one picture ready for
development, or a dozen—and if you have a solenoid with push-button
release on the flash gun, it's perfect for action shots. The rising front
on a Graphic makes it ideal for pictures of buildings without distortion or basketball shots from floor level. Its bigger negative causes
fewer grain problems, less care needed in the darkroom, less enlarge-
ment.

But when the twinlens reflex became more popular, I picked up a Rollei and then wondered how I could ever part with it! The twin lens reflex ground glass focusing was probably responsible for more good pictures than any other one piece of camera equipment. Composition became as nearly automatic as possible. You see exactly what you're getting and the natural low angle gives pictures of distinction. You also get a good-sized negative to work with.

But both of these have given way to the 35 mm whose range of lenses and mechanical improvements have made it the most productive news camera ever. Its great depth of field can let you shoot in tight places, its fast lenses make available-light shooting a pleasure, the cost of film decreases, speed and ease of shooting are a joy. All those interchangeable lenses actually give you more than one camera. And the ability to shoot rapidly and candidly with it has blessed photojournalism.

Whatever your camera system, keep it simple. Concentrate on the picture before you, not on the equipment.

★ IMPROVING HALFTONES

The darker the sky, the better the halftone usually. Clouds show up in contrast against a darker sky—so do people and most everything else. A simple yellow filter can do the trick. I just leave my K2 filter on my twin lens reflex. I've found I take more pictures with it on than off, but the K2 yellow does require good lighting conditions and blue sky to work. An overcast sky, since it is white, is darkened very little by a filter. Because the sky is brighter near the sun and therefore less blue, any picture angled toward the sun will have less filter effect. Light near the horizon is subject to the same principle. The filter effect increases as the camera is pointed toward the bluer sky. Finally, overexposure tends to ruin filter effects, while slight underexposure increases them. But without a filter you'll have more "snowy" days.

Generally, the less pure white in a background, the better the halftone. The white background fades into the newsprint and becomes no background at all. There are no sides or top to the picture. A shade of gray "makes" sky and squares off the picture.

Even patterns, like a brick wall, make good backgrounds. That alternating dark and light provides good contrast.

Don't let large blotches of gray creep into the foregrounds of your pictures. Gray is fine as a background—in a sky or the side of a building—but let the whites and blacks dominate the front. Don't substitute gray for black.

Don't rely on an engraving or halftone negative to correct your picture taking faults. While it's true that less shadow dot can improve the contrast of a gray picture, a few rules followed out in the field or in the darkroom would have been easier.

★ CUTLINES

The most neglected space in America's newspaper is the three or four lines of type underneath each picture. These cutlines usually say the obvious, oftentimes the very trite, most of the time the very dull. We could all improve our pictures by what we have to say below them.

Our town once had an anniversary celebration with the normal amount of horseplay. We even "hung" a fellow one afternoon and I got a picture of him just about ready to "swing." Someone in the office put an extremely clever cutline with the picture, and I'll never forget the reaction of one reader who saw the picture. He was in the barber shop when I was and, as any editor would do, I watched his eyes as he read the paper. He came to the "hanging picture" and looked at it for an appreciable length of time. Then I watched his eyes travel down to the cutline. As soon as he finished reading it, he glanced back up at the picture and broke into a big grin.

What a lesson for cutline writers! I had watched a clever bit of black type mean the difference between a so-so picture and one that really tickled the reader.

Words can enhance a picture and give more meaning to it.

Another good example is Frederic Remington's western sculpture of the four cowboys on horseback, galloping abreast of each other, guns out, firing in the air, whooping it up. What did Remington call it? "Coming Through the Rye." A classic example of a "cutline" that made the "picture."

Say something different in the cutline than what's in the story. Why repeat what's been said in the story?

★ SELLING PICTURES

There's extra money in pictures if you want to take the time to make it.

People will want to buy copies of pictures that appear in the paper. Or they'll ask you to take pictures of weddings, babies, or shots of their businesses. This sideline photography will cost you valuable time. If you can afford the time, fine; but don't let selling $1.25 8-by-10s interfere with selling $125.00 ads. Put selling pictures in perspective. If you're really going after this newspaper business, you'll begrudge the time spent in the darkroom or out on some social assignment for the picture business. If you like doing that kind of pictures or fooling around in the darkroom, by all means do it. It's good therapy and good relaxation. But there's very little extra profit in it if you count your time as anything.

If you have a commercial photographer in town, he may make some deal with you to furnish those reprints. You'll still make money without having to do the work. A commercial photographer, by the way, is a good source for pictures. He can furnish those wedding shots, anniversaries, school night functions you miss; he may waive his fee for the credit line.

★ AERIAL PHOTOS

When taking aerial photos, remember to take the picture so the shadows falling across at an angle will show the details. Without shadows all the terrain below you will look flat.

Use a filter, like a yellow K2, to compensate for haze. Be sure to open your f/stop accordingly.

Have the pilot throttle down to reduce chances of jiggling. Hold the camera firmly, away from the vibrating fuselage. Don't touch the window; shoot a fast shutter.

★ OTHER PHOTO HELPS

Be careful of red. It photographs black. Every beginning photographer has tried the red apples against the green tree only to have it all look the same in the picture. Red is perfect for color shooting, but in black and white, don't back a red tractor up against a dark building.

Business windows in the daytime aren't very successful pictures. There is too much reflection in the glass of cars going by, the other side of the street, even of you. Wait until evening and make a time exposure if you can, or get a polarizing filter.

Don't be afraid to use bounce light. It will give softer, more natural (yet even) light all over.

In big rooms or gymnasiums, light evaporates. If I can, I avoid taking crowd pictures in the middle of a big room. That flash must hit something (one basketball player, for instance) and bounce back.

Put enough information in cutlines. Identify everyone in the picture. It's a weak cutline that refers to "the picture above," "when this picture was taken," or "as the picture shows."

Line up the edge of your picture with horizontal or vertical lines. Don't have a telephone pole slanting off to one side of the picture border or let the horizon run diagonally (unless there really is a hill). Keep the lines straight.

Hide the sun (when you have to face it) behind a sign or a tree or a corner of a building.

If light reflects in eyeglasses in your final print, take a grease pencil and lightly pencil in a pupil. No one will ever know.

Unrestricted shooting can cause a tendency for careless shooting. It becomes "shooting" instead of "taking pictures." Systematically posing twelve good shots, trying for different light, another angle, is much different than indiscriminately squeezing the shutter twelve times. Don't let extra film become a crutch.

Try hard to make every photo say something. Don't line up six people facing the camera. This police lineup shot is the worst in journalism. No, the second worst. The shaking hands bit is worse! Use your imagination.

People continually want pictures taken that aren't good newspaper pictures, like a routine six-year-old's birthday party or a social gathering. I get requests for these all the time, but I keep saying "no"

tactfully. I can't take pictures of the doings of one organization unless I'm prepared to take them all; obviously I can't do that. New officers of one social club or a "pretty table of flowers" arranged by another happen over and over each year. You can't publish one without offending the other. The best way is just not to take them. The fewer of these nonsense pictures published, the less often you will be asked.

Organization scrapbooks are another pest to community newspaper photographers. "We want a picture of all the officers in the paper," says the lady, "because we have to have it for our scrapbook. It goes to national, you know." I say let's enlist a crusade to eliminate organization scrapbooks.

Some of world's best pictures are "shot" at a photographer's desk before he ever goes out. Planning a picture ahead of time or anticipating problems that might come up makes shooting in the field much easier, and usually much better.

Bless Those Ads

THERE is really no such thing as "Hard Sell" and "Soft Sell."
There is only "Smart Sell" and "Stupid Sell."

CHARLES H. BROWER, *Batten, Barton, Durstine and Osborn, Inc.*

★

THE STUDY of weekly journalism
is inescapably the study of small towns. This chapter on advertising
is the study of the town Main Street and its 8 A.M. to 5 P.M. inhabitants, the small-town merchants. If you're conscientious about your
job of selling advertising, you will probably know this street better
than anyone else in town. You'll lose a couple of years of your life
to it, leaving countless miles of shoe leather on its surface, because
your financial security depends on how well you understand the
street and how well you work it.

Dozens of small-town Main Streets have flashed by my car's windshield over the years; I know you have watched them flash by yours.
You too have probably wondered what the people feel, what they
do, how they think behind those hundreds of small-town buildings
and houses.

I once thought every town's problems were unique to that town.
I know now we fight the same battles, wrestle the same problems.
You can't take the grain elevators of Nebraska and put them on
California's seacoast or fit the desert flavor of the Southwest into the
outskirts of a Pennsylvania farming community, but you can switch
the people—and the businessmen—around. The man who runs the
hardware store in New York City runs it much like the Montana
hardware merchant (except for those Montana saddles).

The businessman is no different in one small town than another
because the customer is no different. All these businessmen face the
same problem—how to persuade more customers to buy more mer-

chandise! The universal Main Street preoccupation is to find someone to buy a dollar's worth of goods the merchant purchased wholesale for sixty cents. You're involved because the merchant enlists the
help of your paper. He wants you to tell the world what he has to
sell. Thus our newspaper advertising is born.

If the merchant needs our advertising help, it is also true we
need the merchant's advertising. For without it our community newspapers cannot exist. Nor can any large newspaper. The ads, bless
them, make publishing newspapers possible.

It is wrong, though, to assume advertising's attraction is all green-
backs. Advertising is also an art in itself. Anyone competent can sell
a handsaw, but good advertising is created and sold by the professional. The advertising salesman who tucks his notebook under his
arm and steps out to do battle on his Main Street must be a good
enough salesman to sell it, a near artist to lay it out, creative enough
to provide ingenuity, persuasive enough to convince, printer enough
to make it pay in the backshop, and crusader enough to promote and
explain an intangible product few merchants really understand.

If, after you've thought this over, you suddenly decide to stay in
the office, prop your feet on the desk and take what walks in the
front door, you can't be blamed. The prospect of facing Main Street
has chilled my heart more than a few Monday mornings. But let's
assume you've tipped your lance toward Main Street as hundreds of
other newspapermen have done, and you're determined to be back
Monday afternoon with enough advertising for a twelve-page paper
that week. What awaits you on that street?

★ IT PAYS TO ADVERTISE

Your first task is to convince the advertiser he must advertise to be a
successful merchant. No easy start! One of my personal discourage-
ments in selling advertising has been the failure to convince more
businessmen they can make more money if they advertise.

If he is an average merchant, he doesn't realize advertising can
be the cheapest, most productive salesman he has. He is overly fond
of institutional advertising and advertising that talks about what a
good merchant he is or how many years he has been in business, or
how he has "the largest stock in town." He thinks of advertising
only from one week to the next. He is sure it is a waste. He has
trouble distinguishing between a cookbook donation and a good,
solid selling ad in your newspaper. Above all, he is sure you have
your hand in his back pocket, trying to high pressure and coerce him
into buying advertising he neither really needs nor wants.

These doubting merchants don't know, as I do, how much personal profit they missed by not advertising regularly and correctly. I've watched advertising perform well in too many businesses, including my own, not to have become a fanatical believer in its power to earn a businessman money. Advertising is the single greatest selling tool there is, sometimes a miraculous way of producing more customers which in turn produces more profit. The merchant who reduces his advertising to cut expenses has only cut his own profit. He has cheated himself by skimping his advertising. The money that was his to make if he had adopted even the simplest advertising precepts and kept with them religiously was left to be made by somebody else.

However, you will enjoy business relationships with some merchants who do understand the part advertising plays in merchandising. Company-trained businessmen like chain store managers such as J. C. Penney men are grounded in advertising principles. Company programs and policies help them plan their campaigns. The bigger the town, the more good businessmen there are. Let's be candid and admit the smaller the town, the less progressive the merchant. The merchant is in the business to make money and if he is capable of making more money, he goes to a larger town to make it. Small towns are training places for talented merchants and football coaches who later move on to greener, more lucrative pastures.

The normal small-town merchant thinks he is doing you a favor by buying an ad. Actually, you're doing him the favor. Trying to convince a businessman he's being helped by you rather than donating to you is a perpetual fight.

Al Look, a long-time advertising salesman in Colorado, has written an excellent advertising book aiming it as much to the retailer as the ad salesman. This approach makes much more sense. The merchant is the one who should be educated to advertising. He needs help in understanding advertising; he needs the convincing.

Too many ad salesmen start their jaunt down Main Street without being sure themselves what advertising is all about. They end up (especially in competitive situations) selling against the competitor instead of educating the merchant on advertising itself. The mistake in this approach is failure to improve the advertising potential of your town. You're not building the next week's ad. You are not cultivating the merchant so he is "pre-sold" on advertising.

Before you sell, have a talkable philosophy of advertising. If you know your own theory of advertising, you're more convincing to the businessman; confidence encourages confidence. Take some advertising books home on weekends. Dig into national advertising, study success stories of national products; this type of advertising shows how advertising creates a demand for certain products. If your faith is lagging, restore it by running your own ad campaign in your own paper for subscriptions, job work, or typewriters; and see the results it brings in six months. Find a merchant in town who has had good luck with an ad program and quote him unmercifully.

When you've studied advertising, thought about it, pounded it into a workable, talkable philosophy, your pitch on advertising might go like this:

> "Think of advertising as a salesman. You can hire advertising to give a sales message every week to an amazing number of your customers. If you, as a merchant, could go into the majority of homes in your trade territory regularly and tell the people what you have, that's the best advertising in the world. But you can't. Advertising comes closer to doing this job than anything else. It's a selling tool, a piece of your merchandising that helps create a demand for your store, for your products, for your services. Advertising will increase your revenue because, if done properly, it will increase your sales. If you don't use advertising, you're missing your share of the legitimate market. People are 'passing by' the store—and doing it without leaving home. Encourage them 'inside.' Show them what's for sale. Give your sales pitch all the time. All this can be done through advertising. Unlike the light bill which doesn't help you produce anything, advertising expense can return its cost to you by creating more sales. And creating sales is *new* business, *new* revenue.
>
> "Advertising hustles this new business for you all over your trade territory. It can tell people, old customers and new, what kind of a store you have, what merchandise you sell. It sells for tomorrow as well as today. It builds customer confidence. It introduces you to new customers you've never seen. It helps retain the old customers.
>
> "Advertising can be a real salesman, the most economical, efficient one you can hire. Yet, just like a good clerk, it won't overcome understocked shelves, unclean stores, old-fashioned fixtures, dimly-lit counters, or selling indifference. Advertising is only as good as your store. It will help you sell your store and your merchandise, but it won't carry you. If you feel you have a good store and good merchandise, hire advertising and it will make you money."

As I sold more advertising I began to incorporate this pitch into my selling. Telling a merchant how to make more money always finds a ready audience anyway. I tried to impress him with

advertising's respectability. If he could accept advertising as a
sophisticated way to produce a profit for him instead of just another
grubbing expense like the light bill, he could begin to understand
its capabilities. If he understood advertising would generate many
times its expenses in returned profit, he could embrace it as a
welcome partner.

I kept telling him over and over:

> You should be advertising this merchandise. You
> should let advertising reach out to those hundreds of people
> who are not coming to town this weekend or who won't
> come in your store to see it. Tell them something your
> competitors aren't saying. Let them know you want their
> business. Tell them your store is modern and up-to-date
> and progressive and you are happy to give service. Don't
> wait for the customer to come in to see the merchandise
> or to look at it in the window as he passes by. Go right
> out and see him this Thursday morning and the next
> Thursday morning and the next and the next. Money
> invested in advertising returns in more customers. If you
> get more customers, you realize more money. That's what
> the game is all about.
> "If I were to say to you, give me $500; I'll keep it a
> year and give you back $1,500, you would accept that as a
> 'great business deal.' Advertising is capable of generating
> this kind of business for you. The dollar you spend in
> advertising is not to pay for lights already burning, but to
> find customers to come into your store to buy your
> merchandise. If you don't use advertising as you should,
> you lose this customer potential. Don't cheat yourself out
> of legitimate profit by not recognizing advertising's great
> power to make its user money."

Once when I was talking with one of my advertisers in front of
his furniture store, his competitor pulled up in a delivery truck across
the street and loaded a bunk bed. Our conversation lagged noticeably
as my businessman friend pretended he wasn't watching the other
side of the street. Finally, though, when he could stand it no longer,
he lamented, "Look at that guy over there. We sell a bunk bed with
better quality, better springs, a better mattress; and believe it or not,
it sells for $1.98 less. This week he's sold two that I know of and I
don't know how many more. And I haven't sold one."

"There's only one difference," I couldn't resist replying. "Your
friend across the street told his customers about his bunk beds by advertising them this week. You didn't. He put in a simple ad, only a
3-by-8 in our paper, didn't cut the price, attempted no spectacular

sale. All he did was tell people he had a bunk bed. He sold its good quality; he offered a solution if a home was crowded or if the youngsters had outgrown their smaller beds. He described the construction, mentioned the color, marked it at the regular price. He pushed them, thought about them, then he moved them to the front window. He was *trying* to sell bunk beds. And you weren't."

I wish I could report my friend advertised happily ever after, but he didn't wilt easily. I needed more days of selling. But those bunk beds across the street made the original point.

Another time, one of my merchant customers got a moonlight dealership with a typewriter repair house to sell typewriters. The first typewriter he got in was a brand new red portable, the exact brand and price I was selling at my newspaper office. Although he was a nonadvertiser, I called on him relentlessly (hoping I could wear him down, inch by inch). Each time I went in that store, I pretended I didn't notice that bright red portable blazing away on the counter; one day I worked up enough courage to ask how typewriter sales were doing.

"That's the same one I started with—haven't had anything but lookers."

Again I couldn't resist. "Can I tell you why? Because people don't know you have typewriters for sale. Back at our office during this same time, we've sold six portables just like that one sitting there. We advertised ours. That's the difference. People in the market for a typewriter came in to see us. They might just as well come in to see you."

Once more the merchant should have told people he had something to sell.

★ ADS MUST BE GOOD TO SELL

If the businessman lacks education about advertising, he will lack knowledge of what is a good ad. The principle of advertising is lost if the ad itself doesn't do its job. Your next major task is to throw out the garbage cluttering much retail advertising and help your merchant understand "sell" advertising.

If I were to single out one principle which helped my promoting of "sell" advertising, I would have to give credit to the simple thesis that an ad is no more than a clerk in the store.

An ad should appeal to the customer. It should try to interest the customer in buying a product or a service; it should provide description of the article to be sold, the price, an outstanding feature or function. It should be simple, uncluttered, pleasing in appearance.

These requirements fit a good clerk, too, don't they? Interested in the customer, willing to wait on his needs, to answer his questions, to give price, to point out features the customer is not able to see or understand, to convince him he can't be without this item. At the same time the clerk must be neat, pleasant, and eager to please.

An ad that announces, "We have the largest stock of hats in town," tells the customer nothing. What would happen if you had a clerk who met all customers at the front door and grandly announced: "We have the largest stock of hats in town!"

An ad based on one brown Stetson with the description, price, and its picture will sell more hats than 60-point type blaring; "The largest selection." Advertising one hat gives the correct impression of more hats in the store. The customer reading the ad has something tangible to look at, to speculate over.

Or what if the clerk refused to tell a customer the price of a dishpan. Some ads forget to mention price. If the clerk said, "I don't know much about this electric drill, but you can probably figure it out," you would probably walk out without the drill. But some ads carry only fragmentary descriptions. Or they can only describe an item with that weary catchall: "All types and styles." What styles? What types? A clerk who would talk in such generalities is a poor clerk. And it's a poor ad that only does these things.

If an ad doesn't sell, it is wasted effort. A clerk who does well at straightening shelves, but who can't sell, is wasted, too. I don't imply selling means high pressuring. The clerk who can suggest and smile, who knows his product and can interest the customer in it, is the clerk who can sell. An ad must sell, too.

If you will remember that an ad should sell as a merchant would want a good clerk to sell, your ads will be better. J. C. Penney is often quoted as saying, "I talked with the people in the newspapers just as I would in my store or if I met a neighbor on the street." That's what ads should do—talk to customers.

"Sell" advertising is simply that. Put the customer in the headline, inform him in the copy, let him look at the product, let him "feel" it in the illustration if you can, let him see the price, encourage him to want it, tell him where he can get it. "Talk" to him; sell to him.

Human nature being what it is, you will find that the poorer the ad, the easier it is to sell it to the merchant. This frustrating phenomenon stems from his lack of advertising education. Poor advertising has been with us a long time. We've been deluged with ads that aren't specific ("Stop in and look at Joe's tires"), ads that talk about the store too much and the customer not enough ("The largest stock of tires in town"), ads that use worn out words and phrases ("Now is the time to put on winter tires") and ads that fail to make a solid sales pitch ("See Joe's for tires").

With the exception of grocery advertisers (who learned the hard way they must advertise price, push their leaders, make their ads sell, sell, sell), most of the rest of the businesses have been exposed to more poor ads than good ones. Naturally they think of advertising in the style set by several generations of poor advertisers.

We must upgrade this standard of exceptionally poor advertising. We have to reeducate our advertisers to what good advertising is, to change their inclination for institutional advertising about themselves to "sell" advertising for their customers, to introduce them to the willing salesman they can hire in advertising.

This reeducating comes hard. You can lay out an ad that specifically pushes men's shoes and the merchant wants something "more general." He seems to prefer "shop for shoes" instead of "shop for loafers." He believes general advertising is a better bargain. He reasons, "If I can get all the information in a 2-by-5 ad, I'll save money."

It will take much tact and patience to convince him he is wrong. He won't want help; he'll want to advertise his way. Your conscience will hurt when you take his lousy ads instead of selling him good advertising. The pocketbook can take a jolt, too; you can win the argument this week but lose ads for weeks to come.

Facing such an uncooperative customer is discouraging. He won't want you to tell him his advertising education is lacking. He won't always appreciate your concern or theories.

Keep trying, because you never know when your words may fall on fertile ground. I've had my sales pitch played back to me several times by merchants who I was sure hadn't been listening. They may argue and exasperate you with their stubbornness while you give your pitch, but they are listening. Just keep selling. Practice what you're preaching to them. You're encouraging the merchant to push specific merchandise, to make people aware of his service, quality, price. Do the same with your own pitch. Make it persistent. Make it appeal to the merchant himself. He'll especially listen if you're talking about him. Tell him what *he* gets for his money, how many people *his* ad will reach. Put his store, his gross, his merchandise into your sales pitch.

What to Advertise. The same merchant who is bewildered by advertising will be the one who asks you: What do I advertise? Usually this is the fellow who can't see advertising as another salesman. He is hiring it for something else. He misunderstands the clerk theory again. Would he ask one of his clerks to sell nothing else but marked down wool sweaters when the rest of the store is frantic about swim wear?

I've seen this happen. A merchant will display seasonal mer-

TABLE 6.1. Percent of Year's Total Sales Done Each Month—Sales by Type of Store

	Jan	Feb	Mar	Apr	May	June	July	Aug	Sept	Oct	Nov	Dec
All Retail Stores	7.1	6.8	7.8	8.3	8.4	8.6	8.5	8.3	8.3	8.7	8.8	10.4
Car, Auto Dealers	6.4	7.0	8.6	8.8	8.7	9.4	8.6	8.0	8.6	9.4	8.9	7.7
Department Stores	5.9	5.6	6.9	7.9	7.8	8.1	7.6	8.0	8.2	8.5	10.0	15.5
Drugstores	8.1	7.8	8.1	8.0	8.2	8.1	8.1	8.2	7.9	8.1	8.0	11.4
Eating, Drinking Places	7.4	7.0	7.8	8.0	8.7	8.8	9.1	9.3	8.5	8.7	8.1	8.6
Family Clothing Stores	6.6	5.7	7.1	8.2	7.9	7.8	7.7	8.3	7.8	8.4	9.2	15.3
Furniture, Home Furnishings	7.2	6.9	8.1	7.8	7.9	8.4	8.4	8.5	8.2	8.9	9.2	10.5
Grocery Stores	8.2	7.5	8.0	8.4	8.5	8.3	9.0	8.1	8.1	8.5	8.1	9.3
Hardware Stores	5.6	5.7	6.5	8.1	9.0	9.7	9.4	8.5	8.4	8.9	8.9	11.3
Household Appliance, TV, Radio Stores	7.3	7.1	7.5	7.6	7.8	8.6	8.0	7.8	8.2	8.3	8.8	13.0
Jewelry Stores	6.0	5.0	6.0	6.0	8.0	9.0	6.0	7.0	7.0	8.0	9.0	23.0
Lumberyards, Building Materials	5.9	5.7	7.1	8.2	8.4	9.4	9.3	9.7	9.5	9.5	9.1	8.2
Men's, Boys' Wear Stores	7.3	5.8	6.6	8.1	8.2	8.6	7.3	7.4	7.5	8.0	9.3	15.9
Service Stations	7.7	7.1	7.9	8.0	8.4	8.6	9.0	9.0	8.5	8.6	8.6	8.7
Shoe Stores	7.2	6.2	7.8	9.6	8.2	7.9	7.5	8.4	8.9	8.3	8.6	11.4
Tire, Battery, Accessories Dealers	6.4	6.3	7.6	8.6	8.7	9.6	9.1	8.6	8.2	8.6	9.2	9.1
Variety Stores	6.0	6.2	7.2	8.2	8.2	7.9	7.7	7.9	7.7	7.9	8.9	16.2
Women's Apparel Stores	6.5	6.0	7.3	8.4	8.1	8.0	7.6	7.8	8.1	8.6	9.2	14.4

Source: Bureau of Advertising, "1973 Newspaper Advertising Planbook"

TABLE 6.2. Percent of Year's Total Sales Done Each Month—Sales by Product

	Jan	Feb	Mar	Apr	May	June	July	Aug	Sept	Oct	Nov	Dec
Air Conditioners	3.2	4.0	8.0	11.1	13.1	20.4	15.8	7.7	4.4	5.6	3.2	3.5
Auto Batteries	8.7	6.7	5.3	6.0	6.0	6.7	9.3	10.0	9.3	10.6	10.7	10.7
Books, Stationery	6.1	6.1	6.0	5.5	6.0	6.3	5.0	6.3	6.8	7.5	12.6	25.8
Cameras	7.5	6.5	6.0	6.5	7.5	9.5	9.0	7.5	7.5	7.5	7.5	17.5
Dishwashers	7.4	7.1	8.5	7.6	8.6	7.3	8.5	7.4	7.1	8.3	8.8	13.4
Dryers	8.7	8.1	8.2	6.8	6.9	6.7	7.6	7.9	9.0	10.4	9.9	9.8
Freezers	6.1	5.9	6.5	6.5	7.9	9.3	12.2	12.1	10.2	8.6	7.9	6.8
Home Furnishings (total)	6.8	6.8	7.5	7.2	8.0	7.8	7.6	7.9	8.4	9.2	10.3	12.5
Infants', Children's Wear	3.9	4.6	7.8	7.4	5.7	6.1	5.6	9.3	8.4	8.1	12.2	20.9
Life Insurance	6.0	6.6	7.4	8.0	7.1	7.9	7.5	16.2	7.2	7.2	7.6	11.3
Liquor	7.4	6.8	7.4	7.6	8.1	8.3	8.9	8.1	8.1	8.4	8.7	12.2
Luggage	7.4	5.7	5.5	5.7	8.7	10.9	7.9	7.9	6.1	5.7	8.1	20.4
Men's, Boys' Wear	5.3	4.9	6.2	6.7	7.2	8.9	5.9	6.5	7.1	8.2	11.1	22.0
Paint, Wallpaper	6.3	7.0	8.0	9.5	10.1	9.8	9.8	9.9	8.9	8.4	6.5	5.8
Piece Goods	7.6	8.1	10.6	8.8	8.2	6.7	6.3	7.9	9.2	9.8	9.1	7.7
Radios	7.5	5.7	6.2	5.1	5.1	6.6	5.4	7.4	10.3	9.7	8.8	22.2
Ranges	6.3	6.8	9.4	7.8	8.7	8.1	9.8	7.8	7.9	8.7	8.6	10.1
Refrigerators	5.9	6.0	7.8	7.8	8.3	9.8	10.6	9.6	9.4	8.8	7.8	8.2
Rugs, Carpets	12.1	11.2	11.1	9.9	9.7	8.2	8.9	9.9	11.2	12.8	11.4	6.6
Silverware, Jewelry	5.0	5.4	6.1	6.6	8.2	8.1	5.7	6.6	6.8	8.0	10.7	22.8
Sporting Goods	5.7	5.8	6.7	7.2	7.7	8.3	8.2	10.7	10.7	8.2	8.7	12.1
Television, Black and White	8.4	7.5	7.7	7.5	6.7	7.1	7.2	7.2	8.1	8.7	10.3	13.6
Television, Color	9.1	8.0	7.5	6.8	5.8	6.1	6.4	7.3	9.3	9.9	10.7	13.1
Tires	6.9	6.1	7.9	9.2	9.7	9.7	9.5	9.4	7.7	8.6	8.0	7.3
Vacuum Cleaners	6.8	8.8	8.2	8.3	6.7	7.9	7.2	8.7	10.4	10.4	8.9	7.8
Washers	8.1	7.8	8.8	7.7	7.8	8.3	8.6	8.6	8.5	9.3	8.3	8.2
Water Heaters	9.0	8.6	9.1	9.2	7.1	8.2	7.8	7.4	8.3	7.2	8.6	9.5
Women's, Misses' Apparel	5.9	5.7	8.4	8.4	8.2	7.0	6.1	7.6	8.7	9.2	9.7	15.1

Source: Bureau of Advertising, "1973 Newspaper Advertising Planbook"

chandise in his windows, ballyhoo it throughout the store and then try to use advertising to push some other slow, out-of-season merchandise. So his advertising "doesn't work." Advertising will be more successful at less cost to the advertiser if he uses it on current merchandise. This rule may seem too general since a store carries all kinds of merchandise, pushes slow items as well as hot ones, has sales, markdowns, and clearances; but basically, to make advertising work, adopt the "Christmas" philosophy—advertise when customers have the money to spend and advertise seasonal merchandise.

Every business has its best merchandise months. A chart on what sells best for various businesses each month (Tables 6.1 and 6.2) gives me some idea what my confused merchant should be pushing. It helps me make suggestions, I think more about the accounts I'm servicing, and I have some ammunition for the guy who wails, "What should I advertise this week?"

Ad Copy. The world's best advertising copy appears in mail-order catalogs. If you keep one of these catalogs around the office, you won't be stuck for ideas about what to say about curtains or a power saw or little girls' school clothes. There's more good description, more real sell, for all kinds of merchandise in these mail order catalogs than anywhere else.

Price should be used as often as possible in classified or display advertising. Price is a specific; the ad without price loses selling punch. Every item in a merchant's store is marked. He's not ashamed of the price on the shelf. All his ad is doing is shelf selling. Merchants often hesitate on putting the price in ads because they're afraid the customer will think it's too high; they're afraid to tell their competitors what their price is. A merchant may believe by not saying anything about price he won't lose customers. The customer has the opposite reaction. He assumes the price is high if it's not advertised. He wants to know what the price is; he's suspicious if it's absent.

★ MISTAKES COMMONLY MADE IN AD LAYOUTS

Incorrect Illustration in an Effort to be Clever. The ad in Figure 6.1a is selling one product (air conditioners) but illustrating another (shovels). The punch of the ad is lessened because the reader has to read the entire ad before he reaches the sales message. There is immediate mistaken identity for the casual reader—shovels or gardening or clean-up, not air conditioners.

There is more sell in Figure 6.1b. The caption sells immediately and it doesn't make the reader wade through a puzzle.

(A)   (B)

Fig. 6.1. Illustration is incorrect in (A), but is correct in (B).

Fig. 6.2. Reader can easily pass over the caption in (A), but is drawn into the caption in (B).

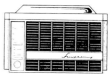
(A)   (B)

RADIOS

Take One
Wherever
You Go

GOOD BUYS

Don't Fail
To See
This Sale

McHale's APPLIANCE

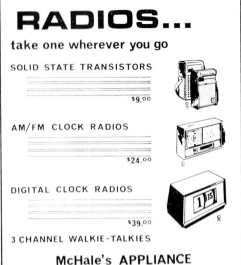

RADIOS...

take one wherever you go

SOLID STATE TRANSISTORS

$9.00

AM/FM CLOCK RADIOS

$24.00

DIGITAL CLOCK RADIOS

$39.00

3 CHANNEL WALKIE-TALKIES

McHale's APPLIANCE

(A)   (B)

FIG. 6.3. Too many gimmicks in (A), but additional buying incentive and clean lines "sell" in (B).

FIG. 6.4. Dull spacing reduces "sell" in (A), but better layout helps the same ad in (B).

AIR CONDITIONERS
Reduced for final time

There's just no more room on our floor for these late season air conditioners.
We'd like to move them out to be ready for our fall merchandise and we're willing to sacrifice price for space.
THESE ARE GOOD model air conditioners--not second rate, no lemons, no faulty parts. We've sold dozens just like these during the hot weather. Now we'd like to move these last remaining ones out of stock.

save at our expense! $150

McHale's APPLIANCE

AIR CONDITIONERS
Reduced for final time

There's just no more room on our floor for these late season air conditioners.

We'd like to move them out to be ready for our fall merchandise and we're willing to sacrifice price for space.

THESE ARE GOOD model air conditioners--not second rate, no lemons, no faulty parts. We've sold dozens just like these during the hot weather. Now we'd like to move these last remaining ones out of stock.

save at our expense! $150

McHale's APPLIANCE

(A)   (B)

(A)   (B)

FIG. 6.5.   Ad (A) is too full of "attention getters," but ad (B) puts
the message neatly across.

No "You" in the Caption. Most advertising captions can be strength-
ened by pitching the message directly to the reader. This adds sell.
It puts "You" into the headline and sells directly to you.

There is more sell in Figure 6.2b than in Figure 6.2a. The headline gives a reason for air conditioning. It draws immediate attention
and requests an answer.

Borders and Gimmicks that Detract. Gimmicks in layout do not improve the sell of an ad (Figure 6.3a). It may even detract enough to
make the ad fail. If attention is called to the ad layout—the mechanical instead of the sales message—the sell of the ad is lost.

The headline in Figure 6.3b gives more sell by listing several
models. Description and illustrations provide additional buying incentive. Walkie talkies are a related sales item.

Poor Line Spacing and Emphasis. Failure to emphasize the various
parts of the sales message results in a monotone pitch. Everything

looks and reads alike in Figure 6.4a. The same spacing between all lines discourages readership. Instead, type should be laid out in blocks with the paragraphs each having a separate pitch. Additional emphasis can be given in increasing the size of type in one of the most important paragraphs or using bold face and enlarging the "Save at Our Expense" line.

The ad in Figure 6.4b is better because there is no indifference in the sales message, it draws attention to the different reasons for air conditioning, and is easier to read.

Putting too Much in the Ad. There is too much information in the ad in Figure 6.5a. White space sells too. It gives breath and fresh air to the layout; it encourages the sales message. The simple layout in Figure 6.5b utilizes the white space and makes the ad easier to read and understand.

★ PLANNED ADVERTISING FOR THE MERCHANT

Experts advise the community newspaper publisher to "plan an advertiser's program for him." Taking over these merchants' accounts much like an advertising agency would do sounds easy but it's hard to do in practice.

Yet planned advertising can be applied in a limited way to every merchant. We know the merchant should spend his money at the right, not the wrong, times; and by planning his advertising he can have full pages at Christmastime, ads every single month, and still stay within his budget. He can achieve better results from advertising that is planned, promoted, thought out, and regulated.

Planned advertising is arriving at an amount Mr. Brown, a jeweler, wants to spend for advertising during one year, and dividing it up over 12 months, in proportion to the best months to advertise. A $600 advertising budget for Mr. Brown should not be broken down into $50 each month, but proportioned to those months when jewelry and watches are selling best.

Mr. Brown has three top months—June when the wedding season arrives, and November and December when Christmastime approaches. He has slack time in January, February, March, and April and again in July, so he shouldn't advertise in these slower months as he does in June, November, and December when his customers are buying more.

If we spread out his advertising by percentage, here are the amounts for each month: January, 5%; February, 4%; March, 5%; April, 5%; May, 7%; June, 10%; July, 5%; August, 6%; September,

6%; October, 9%; November, 10%; December, 28%. Each month Mr. Brown is consistently telling people he has fine jewelry and watches to sell in ads from small-sized 1-by-5s to 2-by-10s or in 3-by-8s in better months. In December he is able to use half pages and bigger because he's budgeted properly. The same budgeting can work for any merchant.

The theory of planned advertising is solid and worthwhile think-ing, but the average small-town merchant isn't really ready for some-one else to do his advertising for him. He's suspicious of the offer, he doesn't believe it will help him any more than his present week by week advertising, and he can't, or won't, see its advantages.

Other obstacles hinder the effort, too. Planned advertising is for the good merchants, not for the guy who can't keep up his stock, who refuses to put his advertised merchandise up front, who has poor clerks, or a run-down store. Advertising, planned or otherwise, won't overcome these faults.

But the merchant isn't always to blame for the failure of the theory. Equal difficulties result from the harried ad man who doesn't have enough time to give these accounts. Considerable study and work is required for the advertising of one business on a fifty-two-week basis. The merchant who hires the ad man to do his adver-tising will expect him to do it all, and that takes time. Ten mer-chants take ten times more time. If you have two competitors in the same business, a conflict of interests is difficult to avoid when you sell advertising to both.

We weekly newspapermen might have neither the kind of mer-chants it requires to implement such a program nor the kind of time necessary for it, but we still can encourage it on a week to week or month to month basis.

When to Advertise. The advertiser is often plagued with when-to-advertise doubts: The good times? Or bad? When people are spend-ing anyway? Or when they're not? Two weeks before Valentine's Day? Or just one week? He's going to ask you what you think. What will you tell him?

Tell him to advertise when people have the money and are buy-ing, in his "good" months more than his "bad." The world has given up predicting the customer's whim. Generally, the customer buys most when he has the money to buy. During this buying time is when advertising dollars bring back the most revenue. A merchant may need extra business in slack times instead of the harried Christ-mastime. But his advertising program in the dead of February falls on its face compared to one in busy December.

You should urge your merchants to lay out a graph like the

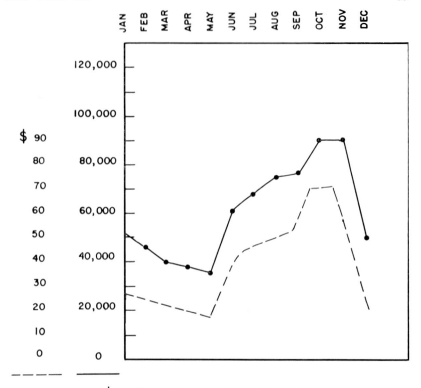

$ 450 TOTAL ADVERTISING SPENT

FIG. 6.6. Planned advertising which runs parallel to a merchant's retail sales.

one in Figure 6.6. It gives the ups and downs of a merchant's retail sales. The theory of planned advertising is to parallel advertising with the ups and downs of sales. The dotted line should be the proportion of advertising spent by the merchant. There is good reason why the two lines parallel each other. If the merchant's retail sales are good in March, then his advertising does him more good if it's heavy during March, at that time when his customers are buying.

Take a look at the second graph (Figure 6.7). This is what happens when the proportion of sales and advertising run counter to each other. Visualize the dotted line as money spent. You can almost see the waste.

Every business will have a different graph. The clothing retailer will have a tremendous season in December during Christmas, when farm machinery and feed dealers are in the doldrums. Incidentally, this is one of the reasons newspaper advertising is so profitable to

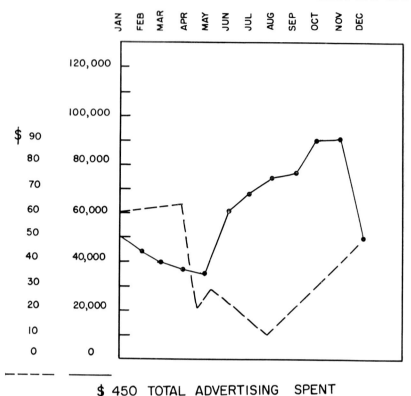

Fig. 6.7. Merchant's retail sales and advertising running counter to each other.

publishers. There is always someone who is having a good month and who can advertise it. Advertising is a constant source of revenue with fewer fluctuations than other businesses.

In his merchandising the merchant unconsciously knows when customers have money and want to buy. The hardware dealer sells at full price and diligently promotes lawn mowers during April and May. But in his preseason or postseason sales he cuts the price trying to attract the off-season customer by price cut alone. The mowers sold better in April and May at full price because the merchandise was right for the season. Out of season, they needed special promoting to sell. The merchant doesn't want to give away the merchandise when it's selling. You don't cut lawn mowers to half price during May and June. When the money's around—and Christmas continues to be the classic example—people will buy, buy, buy. That's when to advertise.

Here are some other ideas:

- Even within a month there's variation, especially in payday towns. Ads just before paydays are consistently better pullers. Saturday night shopping may be fading, but payday shopping never will. If a customer doesn't have the money to spend, a well-advertised product doesn't sell as it should. Merchants can practically give merchandise away during the poor months and not get any takers.
- Being far enough ahead with an ad is much better than a week late. Back to school buying starts in August.
- When a merchant doesn't think he can handle any more business, he should keep on advertising anyway. He is drawing more customers for less money, handling more gross sales on less gross expense.

Special Occasions. Christmas greeting ads from the merchant to the customers can be hard on your conscience as the ad salesman. How many barrels of cough drops did a Merry Christmas ad ever sell? Yet 90 percent of the merchants on your main street are affronted when you don't include them in the holiday greeting section. The only time three of my advertisers ever come into my office instead of my going to theirs is just before the Christmas issue. They don't want to be missed!

Special edition and special section ads are similar. Once, on the advice of a fellow publisher who had already been tortured with the agonies of his 50th commemorative paper, I made a list of every merchant on my main street, even the barbers and beauty operators. Then I estimated wildly what size ad I believed they "should have" in our fiftieth edition. In the subsequent ad calls I made for that big issue, only one advertiser took less space than what I'd believed he should have. It was the easiest sale of "advertising" I've ever done.

All of us have had to sell signature pages, the worst blight on advertising there is. We should abolish them. Years ago the Red Cross in a town where I worked was short of their goal by $150. "We'll go out and sell a page to help them get that money," my boss told me. "We" meaning "me," of course. And I did manage to struggle back with enough signatures to please him. When we counted, our ad had taken in $165. But the Red Cross was still $150 short even at the end of the next week. The Red Cross could have used the money spent for the ad to a better advantage than the merchant. It didn't do the merchant any good, and just took the money away from legitimate advertising.

Your conscience is strained when you ask yourself how much

real selling this type of advertising did for your merchant. The answer is usually "none." That's why I don't encourage such selling.

Even if you know how much more good "sell" advertising does for the merchant, you may sometimes *have* to look at other advertising. You may have to take some promotional and institutional advertising or not take any at all. My crusade for legitimate advertising for my merchants has had to be postponed during some FFA weeks and anniversary observances. I couldn't turn down advertising revenue—I owed it to my business to keep it as healthy as I could.

But it was only a postponement. I keep trying to promote good advertising week in and week out, to one merchant or a dozen, whenever anyone will listen. Good advertising is the foundation of my business and if I succeed in convincing merchants to use the kind of advertising that brings them the most results, I have sold for the future as well as this week.

★ WHICH PAGE IS BEST?

No one page is particularly better than others for advertising. Studies have shown a good ad will pull on any page, so it is not so much position as how good the ad is. A compelling ad will do its job regardless of page position.

I don't give an advertiser a certain page week after week. I've found that with position selling hard feelings are created among merchants, there are not enough so-called "choice spots" to go around (everyone will want the back page or the editorial page or some other one), and mechanically it can be very confusing and hindering. You can't always afford to hold up a run waiting for a position ad to come in or to be set.

★ COOPERATIVE ADVERTISING

Cooperative advertising can greatly bolster the merchant's ad program. Since the distributor will pay part of the retailer's advertising cost (to push a certain product) the small-town advertiser receives a boost in his advertising budget. It's money in your pocket, too, you know. All the merchant needs most of the time is encouragement from you. Some don't even know such advertising exists.

★ RERUNS, DISCOUNTS, AND CONTRACTS

Now we're into the gimmicks, into newspaper's own brand of merchandising. What we try to do is entice the merchant into taking more advertising by making his "deal" more attractive. I question sometimes whether it helps as much as we think it does.

A rerun rate allows a merchant to run the same ad more than once—after the first time at a special rate. The theory is to give the merchant the benefit of savings you gain by not having to reset the ad.

Discounts reward the merchant for using more inches by lowering the rate. Sometimes the discount is given for local lineage exceeding a specific amount; sometimes only to lineage over that certain amount.

A contract rate ties up a merchant for a year at an encouraging rate. It often applies for a shorter period of time as in a ten-week advertising program. This is what radio does so successfully, capturing a merchant for a run of advertising instead of week by week. Somehow contracts haven't caught on as easily with newspapering as with radio. The merchant seems to insist on week-by-week control of his newspaper ad, but will agree to let his radio ad keep on blaring.

I hate to show my suspicious nature, but I always wonder if the merchant doesn't take undue advantage of these rate services. Many advertisers think of advertising in one lump sum. They allot so much to that program. If they can save money in one place, they'll spend it on another.

My newspaper has never had good luck with discounts and contracts. Maybe my merchants aren't as progressive as other towns'; maybe my lack of enthusiasm killed the idea or dulled the execution. It has seemed to me through the years the merchant thought about his discount only at statement time, and then only to see if he got it. I feel I just gave away some of my legitimate earnings. The sharp merchant who keeps track of his monthly inches of advertising doesn't need a discount inducement. He'll buy good "sell" advertising ideas and be more impressed with your sales pitch on coverage and circulation than on how much money he's saving.

Rerun advertising can be a sales incentive. The merchant seems to be as much a bargain hunter as his customers. The idea of saving money if he runs an ad twice can be too much temptation to pass up. "Run it twice and it costs you less the second time," does work.

Small service advertisers such as plumbers and electricians will appreciate the rerun rate, e.g., twelve weeks of advertising—first week at regular rate, then next eleven at rerun.

Running an ad twice is an easy way to take care of next week's advertising, but if you're conscientiously giving your businessman a good advertising program, rerun advertising isn't the answer. The danger in selling by discount and rerun is the preoccupation with selling advertising by price instead of its service to the advertiser. Advertising, if used right, is worth every penny you must charge an advertiser. If he is buying advertising on price alone, he may be missing its value to him.

The contract will protect your advertising sales to a merchant. He will cut uncontracted expenses first, not yours. He feels committed to the contract in spirit as well as physically. It's a way to provide a discount while keeping the merchant wedded to your newspaper advertising. It works especially well with big chains, discount stores, and the larger advertisers.

If contracting and discounting help your sales, by all means use them, but if you're relying on these price inducements to sell advertising, study again what advertising is. Gimmicks aren't necessary to sell advertising if you approach the merchant as you should.

★ TRADE TERRITORY

To talk advertising and its pulling power with your merchant you must also talk trade territory.

The CB&Q Railroad, in its lonely journey across central Wyoming, used to make one short stop at a little place with a combination general store and post office, one other nondescript building that always looked empty, two houses, and an abandoned tarpaper shack. The place used to be "town" to a half-dozen nearby ranchers before oiled roads and faster cars. But the little burg still rated a trainstop and coaxed in a few of the ranchers, especially those who picked up their mail there.

Whenever I went through this original way station out in the Wyoming wind and sagebrush, it struck me that even this Main Street had its trade territory, though surely it was the smallest one in the United States. From this little "town" on up to the big city, you can find as many different sized trade territories as people and as many ways to work them.

One generality which can be emphasized to help the advertiser is: *A town's trade territory is strongest closer to home.*

A successful rodeo promoter once outlined his advertising formula for drawing continuously big crowds. "First," he wrote in a rodeo trade magazine, "we decided what our immediate trade territory was, the area most interested in us, the countryside that traded in our town and thought of it as theirs as much as ours. We saturated this area, flooded it with advertising, even billboards. We unashamedly went after our local people to attend this rodeo. We found it cost less to interest people already in the trade territory than to advertise fifty miles away for customers. Our town had always hoped to gain big crowds from these other towns and other trade territories. We lived in a dream world about getting thousands of people to drive down to attend our small celebration. This never happened. And when we woke up one day to the obvious fact that we were neglecting our own trade territory trying to influence an indifferent one, that was the day our problem started being solved."

I've always felt this was good advice for any merchant. Figure out what your trade territory is and saturate it. Fret little about the fringe areas or that lucrative-appearing big city seventy-five miles away. Invite your own people to buy from you by advertising for their business. Concentrate on the people at home.

Every small-town Main Street exerts its influence upon an area. The size of the town measures the amount of influence, but never very accurately. You can't call a farmer living forty miles from a city of 10,000 and twelve miles from a small 1,500-population town an exclusive customer of either Main Street. He'll trade both places. So will the resident of the small town. The city always beckons. Shopping in the big city has more competitive prices for the customer, an infinitely better selection, and is downright more fun. The city's circle of influence extends down to the small town and the larger the town or the city, the wider the circle. If you drew legitimate circles for every town and city in the United States, you could hardly see where one began and others left off.

All towns are guilty of exaggerating their trade territory. They extend their borders too far, expect too much from people living on the fringes. The small town believes it can cut into the bigger town's territory; the bigger town is positive it will soon swallow all the business in the little town. What makes this all impossible is the nature of the small town and its feudal system ways.

A feudal wall does exist around most towns—not discernible, of course, and very easily scaled, but a wall, nevertheless—that separates the influence of "living" in one small town from the living in another. A small town is very much an entity in itself. It tries to be self-sufficient and it succeeds to a remarkable degree. Its people are intensely loyal to the community; bound together by school districts, civic improvements, small-town society, local pride. For all of today's modern miracles of transportation, people live most of their lives day in and day out not very far from their own doorsteps.

This may make small-town citizens sound provincial, but actually they are not. They do travel to the big city; they do shop for the finer luxuries in smart stores. Their desires are fed by television commercials and four-color ads in national magazines. They know what is going on in the world outside; they understand how the other half lives. They can become oh so very cosmopolitan.

But people get used to trading in a community; it becomes a convenient habit. It's easier to just go downtown and get it. Or to run in from the farm ten miles out.

Besides, Hank in the clothing store is always giving good deals. And, "I saw in the paper this week he's got boots on sale."

I cannot tell you what your trade territory will be, or the size and length of your wall. Yours may be next to a thriving city, geographically it may be cut off from some rich area, you may have a smaller town nearby with a paper of its own. The size of your town's wall will undoubtedly be different from mine.

I can tell you this one advertising truth, though: Help your merchant concentrate on his immediate area; he'll pay less for drawing customers from the immediate area than from another one. For every person you lure from the outlying district you are paying for many, many others who never come. A popular fallacy among businessmen—particularly those in smaller towns—is believing they can find as many customers outside their trade territory as in it. Yet if the merchant could lure back 25 percent of his community's customers lost to the mail-order business, he'd need to hire more clerks.

Keeping trade territories close to home is important to you because your newspaper's real strength as an advertising medium is its ability to attract from the immediate area. Nothing can match the pull your paper exerts on the merchant's customer. So insist he keep his advertising in his own backyard where his—and your—strength is.

★ SALESMANSHIP

All this talk about advertising is not much good if you can't sell it yourself. Salesmanship must convince the merchant on advertising, on having a good ad, on keeping his trade territory saturated, and on using your newspaper to do this. It takes *sell* to do the job.

Salesmanship is the one profession community newspapering shares with all other types of business. The art of selling is everywhere in the business world. You sell by knowing your product, by being interested in it and in your customer, by being enthusiastic, by being courteous and pleasant, by showing your customer why your product will do the job for him, by knowing how to clinch a sale. That's the way you sell advertising in the newspaper business, too.

If you've never sold before and haven't read one or two of the best books on salesmanship, do so right now. If you have sold before, or even if you are a salesman now, read them again. You'll never learn all there is to selling.

Assuming your interest in selling advertising has taken you to the library for a fresh—or refresher—course, I'll pass on some additional tips I've picked up beating the bushes along a few Main Streets.

They Must Be Sold. People must be sold. Talking with the merchant without a sales pitch won't sell advertising. Your presence in the store doesn't mean he's going to take a half-page ad this week. You must sell him that space. Always make a sales pitch for something on an ad call. All the cups of coffee you buy an advertiser are just cups of coffee unless you talk advertising, sales, circulation, trade territory—unless you sell between gulps. Make your pitch continuously when you're on ad calls.

Once my wife and I raised some chickens and wound up with so many eggs every morning I decided to peddle a few. I lined up about five people on Main Street who agreed to take some farm-fresh eggs instead of the grocery store's. Every Friday was egg day. I peddled about seven dozen eggs each week and had a great time. Then the winter temperatures froze up my hens and production nose-dived. Embarrassed, I went through that first eggless Friday not saying a word about my lack of eggs. I was amazed to find no one else did either. Store eggs were good enough if no one was selling farm-fresh ones. I finally understood that eggs, like advertising, take selling. It isn't enough just to go around and say hello to the customer. *You must sell him.*

Sell Early. Make your sales pitch early in the advertising call. Don't feel you must chat with the merchant for ten minutes, working up softly to your selling message. Make it right away. Sell first, chat afterward.

Let me show you several reasons why:

• Your time is limited. Yet you can't take priority over another customer coming into the store. The merchant can't be blamed for interrupting your conversation to wait on a paying customer. If you haven't made your sales pitch for advertising by the time the customer walks in, you must wait. You can't walk out. You have to stand for an unproductive length of time until the merchant is finished. If you had given your sales message, got an answer, or worked already on the ad, an interruption wouldn't have mattered. You could have left for another call, knowing you had finished your business.

• Why wait to spar with the merchant anyway. He knows why you're in his store. He unconsciously keeps avoiding the subject of advertising himself because he feels it will cost him money. So he seldom brings it up. You should sell as soon after you say hello as you can. Make your minutes with the merchant count. You can be neighborly and interesting and pass along small-town talk. But it's the advertising that goes in the paper, not all that small talk!

• Chances are—and this happens many times to me—the merchant who says "no" right off will soften before you take your leave. Let's say you talked advertising and couldn't twist his arm. You accept his refusal. Then you spend five minutes on other subjects, staying away from advertising. As you're getting ready to move on, the merchant changes his mind. You'll be surprised to find how many times you'll come away with an ad if you give your sales message early enough. Let your pitch simmer for awhile, don't hurry it or push too hard. Give the "no" time to turn into a "yes." If you wait until the end of your conversation to make the initial pitch, this won't happen. He'll get rid of you because you've wasted your first fifteen minutes in idle talk. You won't feel you can waste much more time and he won't either. A "no" actually terminates the call. The merchant is offered an easy way to say goodbye. So give yourself time to sell by selling early in the call.

• The salesman who doesn't appear to back into an ad call is more positive, gives a better impression than if he tries to sneak up on a merchant. Have you studied the out-of-town drummers? The good ones burst through the door and start on you right away. They don't squander time talking about the bad roads until the call is over. They don't waste their time—and they don't waste yours. I'm not legislating against engaging in small-town talk with your Main Street merchants. You will have much in common, you'll want to exchange ideas. If the call is for advertising, make that its prime purpose. Sell—then talk.

They Can Afford It. "Never think they can't afford to buy it." An exceptionally successful car salesman explained his philosophy of selling like that to me once. "I used to worry whether the customer could afford a car I was selling them. I don't wonder anymore. They can afford it. They're making the decision to buy it—not me. They'll go without something else to buy it if they want it. Or if I don't sell it to them, they'll go to someone who will. Underselling people is just underselling yourself."

Avoid the "No." Don't say anything where "no" will be the easiest answer to give. "You may not want an ad this big" pleads for a negative answer. "You probably don't want anything this week since it's too long before payday." A "no" comes quickly to that one! "This isn't exactly what I wanted for you but . . ." is sure not to be what the merchant wanted either. Be positive.

Sell the Help. Sell to the help as well as the boss. Building customers among the secretaries, bookkeepers, salesmen, and clerks is shrewd business. When you've made friends among them, they'll help you sell the boss. They'll say things like, "So and so will be here for this ad today. What do you want me to tell him." Or, "We should advertise these in the *Standard* this week." Or they'll help you get through to the boss when he's "too busy" for salesmen. They'll tip you off on what is going on or what the competition did. They know what is moving and what isn't, or what should be said in the ad copy. A surprising number of them do the actual buying, especially of bookkeeping supplies. Operate on the principle that everyone is important—and everyone is a customer.

People Like Being Sold. People like to be sold. I know I like a salesman to convince me how good a product is. After I've convinced myself I want or need an item, I like a salesman to tell me how right I am. Or if I'm fighting against buying something, the salesman who shows me I'm wrong or can save me money earns my gratitude. Your merchant will be the same way. He likes to be sold.

A List Helps. Make a list of the potential advertisers in your town. All of them. Keep track of how many times you make a call on each one. A simple sheet of paper will do; a 3-by-5 card file is more complete. Whatever you use, unless you're already an exceptionally hardworking salesman, will have many blank spaces. You'll be surprised how many advertisers you miss! They're out of town or you had to skip them because time was short. Or the guy told you to come back later and you forgot. You haven't been as consistent as you thought you were. When you miss regular calls you miss potential advertisers. In this weekly business, *you go see* the advertiser, he will not come to you. Advertising is not sold like a pair of pants. The ad merchandise comes to the customer's door instead of the other way around. Our merchant-customers wait for it to come!

I learned this the hard way. I never seemed to get down to see a filling station account at the edge of town. I was either too far behind every week or the boss wasn't in once when I stopped and I was another month getting back. The station seemed a long way out of town. One Thursday the station ran an ad in the competition throwaway, and this really burned me up. Why in heck did he go in there, I thought. He knows we sell advertising. He knows what the *Standard* could do for him. All he had to do was call or let me know he wanted an ad. When I confronted him with this do you know what he told me? "I must not be big enough for your outfit. No one ever comes down to see me. I never hear from you. Apparently I don't count with you guys."

So he went with someone who gave him the impression he did

count, the guy who was calling on him. We not only lost some advertising, we lost some goodwill.

Show Interest in Accounts. The worst advertising pitch you can make starts out, "What are you going to advertise in the paper this week?" Such a weak opener shows how little you've thought about this merchant's account. You haven't given him any ideas. You've shown carelessness, lack of thought, neglected planning. Your lack of interest in both the merchant's account and the advertising in your paper is apparent. That isn't selling—it's merely picking it up.

Publishers as Ad Salesmen. Should publishers sell advertising? This isn't a question at all on some papers; it's a necessity! A publisher often has no choice but to hustle the ads himself. Some publishers prefer to sell and generally can sell better than their ad managers because the hungry salesman sells best. A publisher faced with mortgages at the office and a high standard of living at home is generally considered hungry enough. He has the highest stake in seeing that ad lineage remains up. He may also know the town and the Main Street better than his staff. He is more enthusiastic about his paper than anyone else in the world, and enthusiasm is a contagious selling asset.

I have sold advertising for other publishers and for myself and I'm always amazed what an advertiser will say to an ad salesman that he won't say to the boss. The advertiser tends to browbeat the salesman or criticize the newspaper. The merchant takes out his frustrations on the salesman more readily than he does with the boss. A merchant can say "no" to the salesman much easier than to the publisher himself (who is a fellow businessman). Ad men have found out that the boss can reconcile a dispute, sweet talk a balky buyer, and smooth over differences that harass the ad manager.

On the other side of the coin, ad selling is demanding work and most publishers would rather someone else did it. A publisher on the street gets twice the interruptions a regular ad man does. A merchant wants to talk about the school board or what to do about taxes instead of advertising. He takes the opportunity of seeing you in his store to seek your advice or to give you his.

The publisher goes stale, too, just like anyone else. After a few years he may start to undersell, to neglect accounts. If the paper is understaffed—and which one isn't at times—the publisher begins to cut the ad calls because they take too much time.

The pros and cons on this question balance each other. The publisher can usually sell better, is more enthusiastic, has the greater stake; but the ad man brings a cooler appraisal, fresh ideas, and more time.

Layouts. The most neglected "extra touch" in advertising selling is preparing a layout for the advertiser. Here is the only time a merchant can "feel" advertising, to hold it in his hand, to see beforehand what it would do for his store. A layout helps make this intangible product become more tangible to the merchant. Making a layout also stimulates you to think more about the account, to concentrate on what this merchant is selling, then prepare a better ad campaign for him. You will sell better if you can show an ad layout to the merchant since selling an intangible is every bit as hard as buying one. The more tangible the approach the smoother, the more polished your salesmanship.

Know the Clincher. One author of a salesmanship book pointed out that the best approach, the cleanest appearance, the most attractive product, the most detailed sales message fails if the salesman doesn't know how to clinch the sale. More sales are lost, says that experienced author, by salesmen who can't put on the clincher, who can't get the customer to say yes. "The thrill to me in this business," said another salesman friend who understood this, "is when I'm putting the bee on a guy, the time when I can visibly see the guy give in."

Make sure you can "put the bee" on your customers, too. Observe yourself; listen to your own sales pitch. If you're not convincing enough in the clincher stage, practice until you are. The customer wants convincing, he wants to be pushed over the edge. Be around to do the pushing. Keep selling your paper, your own product, all the time. Tell the merchant how good your newspaper is, how many people it reaches. Never assume he's remembered the pitch you made last year.

"What should I say when he says . . ." Practice being a capable salesman. Have the answers. Learn how to stem a heated conversation with a witty remark. You must be sure of your sales pitch and deliver it with ease under most circumstances. Your apparent confidence helps the advertiser's confidence in you and in advertising. If you appear flustered or are stammering, if you can't handle criticism of your product, if you can't answer the questions merchants think up, your selling suffers from lack of drive and enthusiasm. Below are some of the commonest questions you will hear and some answers you can give to each.

"The cost of the last ad didn't pay for the sales we made."

"Advertising can't be measured on a week to week basis. You don't measure wages day by day. Sometimes the sales won't pay for the clerks either. But you still must pay them whether they have customers to wait on or not. Wages are a fixed expense of business. So are the "wages" of this salesman you've hired to go out and tell people about your store. The ad this week may have sold someone who'll be in your store six weeks from now. Or six months. Measure the success of your advertising on your year to year business."

"Why should I advertise? I have more business now than I can take care of."

"I never saw a businessman yet who had too much business. If you're busy now, your advertising buy is the most economical. Advertising when you already have customers buying actually costs you less per customer than at any other time. You're making better profit because your cost to draw the customer is less. It is much cheaper to handle extra business when you're busy. For the same fixed expenses you are taking in more revenue."

"Everybody knows what's in the store anyway."

"If you wish to speak in generalities, yes, it's true people know you carry furniture in your store. But do they know the price of this chair? Do they know it has guaranteed construction for three years? Do they know its color? Do they know you can provide matching draperies at a discount? You can leave the general information about your store to the sign outside. But you must be specific about what's on your shelves inside. You should be specific in advertising."

"I use my store window to advertise."

"And I think you should, too. But your store window can't do the selling job alone. You need someone to sell those people who don't come downtown, who won't walk past your window. Or who walk on the other side of the street. Your store window may sell those people who are downtown; advertising does a selling job to those people who aren't downtown."

"People never mention the ads I run."

"A person doesn't have to mention an ad to be a buying customer. He can buy something without ever telling you why he came into the store. You don't demand that other customers tell you why they came in to buy something. Yet you are demanding this explanation from the customers you 'advertised for.' Advertising cannot be measured accurately by the number of times someone says he saw it, but by how much that person is motivated to buy something from your store. The ad about shoes may remind a man he needs another shirt or the woman that her purse needs replacing."

"I never read the ads myself."

"I suspect you're like most other businessmen who never read kid's clothes ads. You don't buy kid's clothes, your wife does. But who does read ads about cars, tires, new suits, guns, boats, ties, the taste of a new beer? All of us are customers. I know railroaders who read typewriter ads and farmers who read sale bills. The ads that appeal to our wants, we'll read, sometimes unconsciously. Like trade magazines. We'll devour the trade ads to see new styles, new ideas for fixtures, or more efficient cash registers. But the special price on tomatoes? Who buys tomatoes?"

"It's too expensive. I can't afford it."

Advertising cost should not be figured on individual ads any more than cost of selling is figured on individual clerk's sales. Do you compute a clerk's cost day by day? Year by year, don't you? The same with advertising. Every dollar you spend on legitimate advertising returns dollars to you in increased business. If you can afford new business, you can afford advertising."

"I never know what to say in an ad."

"What would you say to the customer if he were standing right here? How would you sell him this article? Your ad should be written the same way—as if you were selling the reader. Just sell this article to me right here and we'll put that same sales pitch in your ad."

"How come your rate is higher than your competitor's?"
The best answer is classic: "My competition knows
the value of his product much better than I. If he
thinks it's only worth that much, I'll take his word for it."

Calls and More Calls. A secret to selling is persistent calls on the customer. In door-to-door selling, as we newspaper ad men must do, the salesman controls the calls, how many and how often. It's up to the salesman himself how much he hustles. The merchant sits in his store and waits to pounce on a customer. The ad salesman must go out and do the wrestling himself.

Make your time on a call profitable. If the merchant won't take advertising, sell him job work, or a new adding machine, or make a pitch for your paper and its circulation. Sell during as much of the calling time as you can. Come away from the call with something!

A regular call on an extremely small account is time-consuming for the revenue obtained. See if you can't tie this merchant to a ten-week program, using ten different ads you've laid out in advance. One call—ten ads. And the advertiser receives something for his money as well.

At Christmastime you could lay out a four-week Christmas advertising program and sell it in late November or the first week in December. Both you and the merchant have more time to plan a good campaign early in the holiday season. His anticipation of the Christmas business surge will help your selling.

When a customer wants a dodge against buying an item he's looking at, he invariably says, "Well, I'll be back." "When a customer says I'll-be-back to me, I know I've lost a sale," one merchant told me. The customer in the store is worth 100 out on the street. It's the same with advertising. Take the business this week, not a a promise for next. "Come back next week and we'll run it then," is often like the customer who says, "I'll be back."

Those "Old" Customers. If a merchant is lulled to sleep each night thinking about all his old customers who don't need advertising to bring them in the store, our sleepy merchant has his head under the pillow! Economists estimate one-quarter of the people in your town will change every five years. Someone is constantly moving in or moving away. New managers arrive, new help is hired, businesses are sold to out-of-towners, relatives return, transfers happen. Every town has a constantly changing population, and the merchant who isn't trying for this new business, those new customers through his advertising program, is missing sales. He should let advertising make the introduction for him.

★ THE AD IN THE BACKSHOP

How profitable will this ad you sold be when it gets to your backshop? Most young ad salesmen don't pay much attention once the ad is sent to the frowning floorman in the back. As you're in advertising more—and if you've ever been on the floor yourself—you begin to see that money is unnecessarily wasted on the ad stone.

One way for an ad salesman to learn about advertising is to work on the floor for two weeks, setting the ads he laid out. Suddenly the complicated boxes, the fancy mortises, the type set at an angle disappear. The ads become more functional, they're easier to set, they look better, they sell better. Most of those artistic devices that are supposed to make the ad "look" so good don't usually make it "sell so good."

Look at the profit picture of a 2-by-5 ad. Its mark-up is comfortable. But each time a floor man must stop and cut off pieces of border or mortise into a fancy box, the money you're making on the ad, the actual net profit from it, is decreased. Complicated offset paste-up is the same principle. More doodads are possible with offset and easier to do, but the extra fooling around costs more time and money. If all this extra work makes the ad sell better, unhesitantly I would advise you to do it, no matter how many dirty looks from the backshop crew. But it isn't a question of pleasing a floor man who doesn't want to set your masterpiece. Instead how much money out of your pocket does this cost? The frills often don't make the ad sell better. The fancy doodads often don't accomplish any more selling punch than the straight ones, if as much. Upside-down ads, or ads that lead the reader through a maze of illustrations and hidden copy, don't help the reader grasp the sales message quickly. They cost more to set. Remember, the reader isn't looking at the ads in the paper to see how clever you are, but to see what merchandise is for sale. The ad should seek to sell the reader in the easiest way.

When laying out an ad, try to remember that if attention is drawn to the ad rather than to what it is selling, the ad hasn't been successful. If someone says to you, "I liked that clever ad this week, you know, the one with the funny boxes," you can be nearly certain you failed to put across the sales message. It is like saying to the clerk, "I could listen to your pleasant voice all day. It even makes me forget what I came in to buy."

★ AD CORRECTIONS

A typographical error in straight matter is embarrassing; a typographical error in an ad is not only embarrassing—it costs you money! So watch the proofreading.

Most mistakes seem to be made in correction lines or in failure to make a correction marked on the proof. Insist on rechecking the ad corrections themselves. One of the baffling parts of weekly newspapering is how often an operator will set the correction line *exactly as it was before*. A handset price is often overlooked in the rush to get the machine set lines in, or the correction line pasted down in the wrong place.

You'll find most mistakes in ads can be prevented if the corrected press run proof or pasted page is checked against all the ad correction proofs. Don't let the same person who makes the corrections or puts them in do the final checking. As sure as not, he'll make the same mistake again. Front office personnel, not the backshop or paste-up men, should do the final checking because it will be fresher to them.

When You Make a Mistake. Try as you will, mistakes will happen in ads. Wrong prices, typographicals, upside-down illustrations, competitors' ads facing—we've all suffered through them. If you discover the mistake before the merchant does, beat him to the phone. Tell him what's happened, make your apologies, offer to make some restitution. Don't let him land into you first. Unfortunately the printed word, mistaken or correct, lasts for a long time. You'll soothe your wounded merchant by telling him yourself.

Publishers differ on how to handle the make-good. Some make an allowance for the mistake. Some rerun at a discount. I prefer to offer not to charge at all for the ad, particularly in serious mistakes. At least I want to make that offer. Depending on how bad the mistake, the merchant himself will often propose a compromise. This is better than my doing it. You'll make friends by offering to run the ad over free. Nothing burns up a customer so much as a merchant refusing to make good defective merchandise. In your case, you're the merchant and the businessman is the customer. He may tell you the mistake wasn't worth a complete rerun, but he'll appreciate your offer anyway.

A paper is not required to make up the difference between the advertised price and the correct one. If flour comes out $ .35 for 10 pounds instead of $1.35, you're not obligated to pay the extra. When you're new on your main street you'll be so shaken over mistakes you may be tempted to offer it—but don't. The advertised price was wrong, that's all a merchant need say. He doesn't have to sell a product at your advertised wrong price.

★ NATIONAL ADVERTISING

The most ill-treated part of the weekly newspaper is the national advertising. An ad agency executive once made a speech about the bewildering amount of mistakes the weeklies make in running national ads. Insertions are missed, made on wrong days, run twice. Signatures are wrong or left out. Added lines are ignored, ads are buried, or reproduction is unbelievably lousy. Weeklies consistently make about every mistake in the national ad that can be made in running an ad.

Why the indifference? Because this advertising comes in over the transom for the most part. The weekly ad man doesn't hustle it. His state press association or his national advertising representative does that. The advertiser is too far away to do much complaining. They don't reach for the phone and abuse your tender ear like the local boys. The early copy from these ads can fill up copy-poor first runs.

We abuse it, then we charge a higher rate to "pay for" an ad agency's hustling and layout. It's a gravy source of revenue, yet we treat it as if it were a poor relation. It's no wonder national advertising has gone elsewhere.

★ WANT ADS

If you ever need a testimonial of what advertising can do, turn to a three-line want ad. You'll find examples enough to convince even the most doubtful. Want ads have sold all kinds of merchandise for everybody; they have been consistent "salesmen" since the first want ad was ever published.

Some rules that might help increase your want ad business would include:

1. Try to have the advertiser include price in all want ads. Results will always be better if price is given.
2. Encourage reruns by lowering the rate for second and third insertions. Always try to sell multiple insertions: "Do you want us to run this twice?" Not—"Do you want us to run it just once?"
3. Put "sell" into want ads by using good selling words—a *reupholstered* chair, *snow* tires, *overhauled* engine, *roomy* camper.
4. Use separate classifications for want ads, e.g., For Sale, For Rent. Use larger type for classification headings.

5. Run small stories of good want ad results: Mrs. Harry George sold all three chairs she advertised in a *Chronicle* want ad and "could have sold more."

How to Use Better Want Ad Words. Writing good want ad copy means searching for the adjective that gives the selling object more attraction, and finding the one feature of the selling article that makes it a good buy.

Carpeting in a house that's for sale is the obvious asset usually mentioned. But so is an extra bathroom, a *brick* patio outside, a *double* garage, a *wood paneled* basement, a *tiled* game room. These details immediately create additional interest. The more you can describe the article for sale, the better your chance for results.

When you're taking an ad, find out as much information about the item as you can. Ask your customer to sell his house to *you* first: "What would you say if you were selling the house to me?" The ad then writes itself.

★ YOUR OWN ADVERTISING

We editors practice little of what we preach about advertising. We run house ads less than we should. Though we know what advertising can do for others, we seldom think of it in terms of doing something for us. Even if we do start an advertising program, it seems to depend on whether all the news will go in first. It's easy to preach about getting house ads in regularly, setting up a schedule as if they were someone else's paid ads. But in practice if the paper is tight the house ad is left out, and if you do have enough room you usually aren't ready with a prepared ad. Instead, some poorly done ad is thrown together to fit the empty space. We seldom plan what we want to sell. In a burst of righteousness we may start a program, but it's the first type to go into overset.

It is not enough to let the product speak for itself every Thursday morning. A gradually improving newspaper that polishes its news coverage, enlarges its pictures, and spruces up its appearance usually does it over a long period. The change is gradual enough to be overlooked, like a growing child. Your readers (including your advertisers) need to be reminded they are reading a good product.

Radio does an exceptional job of selling itself, much better than newspapers. Radio is constantly telling its listeners how lucky they are to be tuned to such an outstanding wave length. "The friendly sound," "the good guys," "news *as it happens*"—many times a day radio puffs out its chest and lets the buttons pop. They keep saying,

"We're the best, we're the best, we're the best," until the listener begins thinking, "It's the best, it's the best, it's the best."

There is nearly always a surge of public good will toward a paper when it wins a national or press association contest. The public is delighted about it. They are following a "winner"; they're on the bandwagon. Advertising your product and thereby creating this bandwagon psychology for your newspaper is important to you. People follow the flock more than they will ever admit. They want to be associated with winners, to be identified with success, to belong to the "right" side. The merchant has similar feelings. He, too, wants to be with the winner and if he gets the impression your paper is such a winner—an opinion that can be nurtured by your advertising program—selling advertising becomes a much easier job.

Advertising creates a feeling of permanence, a belief, a positive approach. If you're enthusiastic about your product, so others will be. If you're convinced of its power, you will convince others. You don't need to propagandize or stretch facts or invent claims to sell your newspaper. Your paper can advertise enough legitimate good points, enough obvious advantages, to attract buyers.

Weekly newspaper promotion should promote the newspaper first—the display advertising, want ads, readership and subscriptions. If you sell office supplies at your newspaper, you'll have an understandable urge to merchandise this department before pushing the newspaper. It's easier to advertise a typewriter than reasons why a merchant should advertise with you. A price and picture of a new office chair is quicker to lay out and takes less inspiration than a series on your newspaper's circulation and coverage. Ads about letterheads can be masterpieces, and office equipment ads can go to 1,000 possible typewriter sales instead of just 100 active advertising merchants.

However, more money can be made in advertising than by selling typewriters. In terms of money in your pocket, don't skimp in promoting display advertising. It's a newspaper's most productive, money-making department.

Promoting advertising has an important by-product. It's what the radio capitalizes on—when you tell an advertiser he should be advertising in your newspaper, at the same time you are also subtly selling other readers on the importance of reading your advertising. You're reaching the reader of the ads as well as the advertiser. It works with the advertiser himself. For the merchant to see your ad in the paper may sometimes be sell enough. He can't help reasoning that if he saw an ad addressed to him, his housewife customer will see an ad addressed to her.

Create classy advertising for yourself; really outdo yourself. A good promotion program not only advertises your paper and its

TABLE 6.3. Percentage of Sales Invested in Advertising

Amusement, Recreation	3.51%
Apparel and Accessories	1.94
Auto Dealers	0.86
Auto Service	0.95
Banking	1.25
Credit Agencies	1.42
Drugstores	1.35
Eating and Drinking Places	1.27
Electric Companies	0.40
Farm Equipment	0.54
Food Stores	1.22
Furniture, Home Furnishings	2.83
Gas Companies	0.29
General Merchandise	2.67
Hardware Stores	0.54
Hotels, Other Lodging Places	2.46
Insurance Agents	1.13
Liquor Stores	0.52
Lumber	0.54
Miscellaneous Retail Stores	1.33
Motion Pictures	5.16
Real Estate, Insurance, Loan Combinations	1.89
Repair Services (Except Auto)	0.64
Savings and Loan	0.10
Security Brokers	0.24
Service Stations	0.63
Subdividers, Developers, Builders	2.83

Source: *Advertising Age,* from Internal Revenue Sources, April 1972.

readership, but your ability as an advertising specialist as well. The sharp, well-constructed ad is saying: "We have the experience and the knowhow to get advertising results for you, too."

The best self-promotion program balances circulation, advertising, retail sales, job printing, want ads; all should have a turn in proportion to each department's contribution to the gross.

Table 6.3 shows percentage of sales invested in advertising for various types of businesses in the United States. The list includes advertisers as well as nonadvertisers. It also includes all "advertising" as the companies themselves classified it, and is not necessarily purchase of time and space, so it is off mark slightly. The progressive merchant will invest more in advertising than these percentages. The chart is a guide, an indicator rather than gospel. But I have used it to help start an advertiser or to push a good merchant just a little more.

★

CHAPTER SEVEN

I Gave It to the Other Guy

THEY copied all they could follow, but they couldn't copy my mind,

And I left 'em sweating and stealing, a year and a half behind.

RUDYARD KIPLING

★

ADVERTISING is a quick, sometimes soft, way to make money; unfortunately it's sometimes a quick, soft way for the other guy, too. Thus competition is born, and many of your troubles.

The free enterprise system at work in America is worthy of editorial comment; at work on you, it can cause ulcers! If you're in a busy, bustling town where the merchants know merchandising and advertising, you'll undoubtedly have to share this good fortune with others. You can give the pitch for your newspaper only to have another legitimate paper doing the same thing down the street. Or maybe a cheap throwaway starts up, or a radio station broadcasts all day long, or even a local television station. All make their basic money on advertising. In addition, your town's Main Street can be flooded regularly with the ad salesmen from nearby dailies, or the guys who sell matchbook cover advertising or pencils or calendars. There are businessmen who switch to circulars for house-to-house distribution or put their advertising messages on postcards or billboards. You may even end up selling ads against the high school yearbook staff or the country ladies with the recipe book.

It's rough on the constitution to lose accounts to smoother salesmen or to watch your merchant overspend with someone else and then cut you. I neglect to call on a spasmodic advertiser, then I discover his half-page ad in the competition sheet. A loyal business account changes hands and I have to fight to keep the new man from shifting elsewhere. I spend time talking a merchant into advertising a chair only to see the ad come out, not in my paper, but the competitor's.

For all this grief and personal discomfort, competition probably sells more for you than it takes away. The more people carrying advertising's message to Main Street, the easier it is to sell advertising. As I've said, one of the hardest jobs is not so much selling the small-town merchant space but selling him on the idea of advertising. Competition helps do this.

Having someone to sell against is better than selling against yourself. Pride enters here as much as the money involved. Some of us don't sell well against a space quota or "topping last year." We do better against a warm, breathing, talking competitor. If you're selling against a competitor, you won't neglect calls, you'll see everyone as often as you can, and you won't slide as easily. This makes your advertising sales program better even if the day by day struggle seems worse.

Although competition is peculiar to each area and each town, generally your three toughest competitors will be another legitimate newspaper, usually a weekly but on rare occasions a daily; a radio station; or a free circulation throwaway or shopper.

I have pounded the pavement selling advertising against all of these competitors, and from the advertising point of view I can rate their toughness. The radio station in your own town is the easiest competitor to face; the competing weekly newspaper is the next easiest; and the free-circulation throwaway is the hardest.

The other competing weekly can be the most frustrating from an editorial point of view, but two weekly newspapers in the same town compete on the same basis for the advertising dollar. Your weekly competitor is selling the same strengths you are and must admit to the same weaknesses. A good fighting weekly, competing on news breaks, pictures, and editorial comment, can make an editor's life miserable. From the advertising position, he is selling one newspaper against another.

The radio station doesn't have the advantage of printed word advertising. Air waves can be active competitors but they can't compare with black type.

The free circulation throwaway combines your basic strength, the written word, with hard-to-refute free distribution. The throwaway has newspaper's strongest asset, published advertising, but doesn't have to provide the dozens of free services of a legitimate newspaper. It can devote more time to making money by selling advertising. Its overhead is often much less—invariably they start in someone's bedroom or garage. The throwaway has an astonishing ability to get advertising results, especially on sale or bargain advertising results. (If you've never faced one, you won't believe how entrenched a throwaway becomes.)

★ RADIO STATIONS

Radio stations are everywhere and not without success. The local station becomes a personal friend to a community. The small-town populace sees a local radio station as a sign of modern progress. They are proud of it, they are grateful for radio's ability to follow the team on football and basketball trips. They like the personal interest radio takes in telling its listeners exactly where the fire was minutes after the whistle blew. They insist on weather forecasts, "up-to-the-minute" news, and lots of music.

Radio can plug sale items within the next fifteen minutes. An advertiser doesn't have to wait for a publication day. If he wants to knock down the price of bed sheets, radio can broadcast that information immediately. Or if the town's big community celebration is rained out or postponed, the radio quickly carries the message.

But radio doesn't use black type. It must rely on the ear, not the eye. Though its message is instantaneous, it is heard only once. Though radio tries hard to produce the quality communication of black type, most radio stations are still thought of as providers of music and weather by most listeners. Black type still provides more, sells better.

Radio's Pitch to Advertisers. Radio ad salesmen are fond of two terms: "blanket coverage" and "saturation." Both are glib ways to describe radio's pulsating, throbbing signal on the air waves of the trade territory. They mean taking a heavy pencil and drawing a big circle around your town, to include all the trade territory and many fringe areas of other trade territories, and putting that glowing signal of the local station in the middle.

Radio utilizes this "blanket coverage" idea to impress the advertiser with radio's potential listening audience. Radio likes to tell how they "saturate" an area and supposedly, within this black circle are thousands of customers eagerly awaiting the advertiser's spot announcement.

Any advertising medium can make this same statement—any newspaper, throwaway, store or business can draw exactly the same circle on a trade area map. A newspaper's potential audience—counting families who read the same paper, friends who pass it around, the well-thumbed copy in the cafe, the occasional pickup on the newsstand—is in that same black circle. So is the throwaway's scatter circulation. So is the billboard's potential readership on the highway; so is, in fact, the advertiser's store window, for every person in the trade area is a potential passerby.

To radio ad salesmen's credit, they have been able to make this blanket coverage idea seem an exclusive radio sales advantage. Don't let them. Point out that every medium has similar potential. The trick is not in the reaching out so much as in the reading, the hearing, the seeing: making the potential customer turn on his radio, and then listen to it; pick up the newspaper, and then read it; drive by the billboard, and then see it.

Radio has successfully sidestepped this correlation and pitched its appeal on the saturation of the area.

Radio also points out the number of radios owned in the area, invariably winding up with more total radios than people (one in the car, one in the kitchen, the console in the living room, the transistor in the kid's room).

Radio is very successful, too, in selling advertising contracts that tie up an advertiser for a period of time, committing him to a certain amount of money. The contract helps create a steady advertiser by making him think of his radio advertising, even plan ahead on it. The steady, regular advertising over a period of time allows radio a chance to prove its selling ability and creates more talk by the advertiser's customers. Those magic words, "I heard your ad on the radio," even if only three people say it (and this works the same for the newspaper), is the most impressive testimonial an advertiser can hear. He is always grasping for something tangible by which to judge advertising. Radio is good at enlisting such support from people, particularly if radio is new in the town and it isn't old hat yet to hear familiar names coming over the air waves.

Sponsorship of sports events, especially when teams go to district or state tournaments, is a shooting-fish-in-the-barrel kind of advertising for radio. Teams never seem to lack for sponsors. (You can't sell against such advertising without appearing to be against broadcasting the games, which you're obviously not.)

National advertising has shifted in many areas to radio, especially regional radio, trying for the shotgun effect instead of the concentrated one. Here, too, radio has succeeded in appealing to advertisers on their "blanket coverage."

Radio points to its "instant advertising," the ability to put advertising on the air within the hour if necessary, as a big sales point—and with justification. Even the daily paper can compete on this point much better than the weekly which must wait for Thursdays to dawn.

Radio's Weaknesses. Selling against the weaknesses is easier than competing in a competitor's strong area. But you don't want to "knock your competitor" either. The shrewd way is to stress those strengths of your newspaper which point up the weaknesses of your competitor.

Subtly working the following points into your selling will make an impressive case for newspaper advertising while at the same time weakening radio's sales pitch:

- Black type is the world's best, most popular, most productive medium of advertising.
- The customer chooses his time to see my newspaper ad, he has no choice with radio advertisements.
- I can tell you exactly how many people will receive my paper this week. I cannot tell you how many will read it. But the radio station can tell me neither how many people are going to turn on their radio nor how many are going to listen.
- A newspaper ad can be read and reread, checked and rechecked, studied and restudied, pondered, and remembered because it can stay around the house for days. A one-minute radio spot lasts for one minute.
- Did you ever hear anyone say: "I wish I could remember what the show is tonight? I think I'll turn on the radio and see."
- It doesn't really make much difference on which page a newspaper ad appears. But radio has "prime" time and an awful lot of "not so prime" time.
- The newspaper concentrates on the immediate trade territory much better.
- At night, after supper, do you really think anyone is listening to the radio instead of watching television?
- An advertiser is trying to reach women shoppers. Radio ad men always talk about the housewife who listens to radio while she does her work. What about all the women who work? Or the women who go to club meetings? Or watch daytime TV? Or the teen-agers who are in school?
- Radio seldom has an exclusive on the air waves. It must share the listeners with other stations nearby and far away, and it takes only a twist of the dial to change.
- You can lay down a newspaper and go put the dog out. But a minute's time on the radio never comes back.
- How many times have you heard someone say: "I just caught part of the news but I thought it said. . . ." That snatch of radio information, half-obtained, could have been your ad.

You Can Supply the Details. I've always gotten a kick out of the cartoon of the radio announcer sitting in front of the microphone reading from a newspaper in front of him. He's saying very importantly into the mike: "And now for the local news."

No matter how much radio boasts of its quick coverage, newspapers must still supply the details. This is as true in advertising as in the news.

Use the full page idea to show an advertiser the scope of newspaper advertising. Tell him: "Look what I can do for you in a newspaper. I can set seven (or eight) columns of type for you in 8-point if you wish. Or give it some variety with 10- and 14-point. You can have your main items in 24- or 36- or 48-point with a big type figure. I can put pictures or mats of your merchandise to show your customers exactly what you're selling. I can describe in detail every item with a before and after price no one can mistake. I can put "sell" into every inch of the 140 or 160 inches. Ask radio to do this for you and then ask what that much radio time would cost!"

More Use Classifieds. Bureau of Advertising records show that in 1972, $418 million more were spent for classified advertising in America than for radio advertising. This was just classifieds, not display. Mentioning this to a wavering advertiser often produces results. Advertisers hate to do something other advertisers have rejected. They like to appear as wise and shrewd as the next businessman. They want to be going with the crowd. The idea that others aren't using a certain advertising medium is often enough to decide them against it.

Beat Them with Better Ads. Small-town radio is the world's most prolific user of poor institutional advertising. "Go down to Joe's for your tires," or "Miller's has the most complete stock of furniture for your buying pleasure," or some such lackadaisical advertising copy comes from radio speakers all over the country. The ad pitch is generalized more times than it is specialized on radio, and specifics sell. Newspapers fighting against aggressive throwaway advertising soon learn that you won't sell merchandise by telling everyone that Joe has a lot of tires or that Miller has a good buy. The price of Joe's tires sells, so does the quality, so does the free installation—but not just Joe's large stock.

Your Trade Territory. Radio's brag about its "coverage" should send you to re-examine your trade territory. But keep in mind you can't crack a new trade territory without additional expense (frequently prohibitive expense). When a radio talks about "going into new areas" remember it costs a larger and larger percentage of the advertising dollar to attract out-of-trade-territory buyers. An advertiser shouldn't pay for this dead weight. He should concentrate on his own trade territory. That's when his advertising dollar is spent most economically.

Outside Radio. You may not have radio station competition in your own town, but an aggressive station in another town may be hoping to include your area in its "trade territory."

Combating an outside radio station can be easier; it must share its coverage, and sales staff, with other towns. You can sell on your merits of exclusive coverage to your town (which the outside radio can't offer) and very effectively point up the divided allegiance an outside radio station must assume.

The outside radio is weaker because it competes with other radio stations. The residents of your town can dial any number of stations. The so-called "blanket coverage" is diluted again.

When your advertising medium reaches people who aren't your customers, i.e., people outside your immediate trade territory, costs are higher per potential customer. For every dollar you spend to lure a customer outside your territory, you could actually bring in several customers in your immediate area. Radio's costs—particularly outside radio's costs—are therefore much higher.

"Tell Me What You Just Heard!" I watched a smooth newspaper ad salesman puncture radio advertising one time in an unforgettable lesson. The car dealer he jumped on won't forget it either. The gist of the dealer's complaint was that more people listen to radio than read the ads in the newspaper. In the background a radio was blaring about something, seeming to give weight to the dealer's statement. But the ad salesman, instead of ignoring it, pounced on it.

"Tell me right now, right now what that radio just said. Quick. No, don't try to listen now. Tell me what the announcer is talking about and what he just finished saying."

The salesman turned to the parts man nearby and asked him. Then he asked a customer who'd followed the conversation, and, as the ad salesman knew, not one could tell him what words had just come out of that radio! He wound up with: "Was that your ad you didn't hear?"

★ ANOTHER WEEKLY NEWSPAPER

Although the days of two-newspaper towns are rapidly vanishing, some towns are still strong enough (or grow strong enough) to support two weekly newspapers with advertising. In such cases this is real competition—competition in all departments, not just the advertising. You'll get scooped on news stories. You'll snap a picture of the homecoming queen with her eyes closed while the competition gets a wide-eyed, beaming smile out of her. You two will choose up opposite sides editorially on a bond issue and your side gets trounced. Job printing will drift to the other paper and so will subscriptions; so will office supplies if you sell them.

If all this isn't enough to fight over, you have to share the advertising of the business district, too.

But the advertising and the circulation, the pictures and the news all tie together. If you try hard to be strong in all departments, you'll be strong in advertising. The paper with the largest circulation reaches more potential customers for the advertiser (and can get the best ad response). The paper with the livelier pictures, the more alert news coverage, the more stimulating editorials draws more readers, creates more "customers" for the advertiser, and in the long run sells more ads. Since both papers are selling the same advertising medium, it follows that two legitimate newspapers are competing on the basis of which one reaches more potential customers for the advertiser. Be sure your paper does.

In facing another weekly, at least you compete on the same grounds. You don't have to fight the misleading claims of radio. You don't have to fight the unfairness of a throwaway pretending to be a legitimate newspaper. Your competitor in the legitimate weekly has the same troubles you do, fights the same weaknesses, enjoys similar strengths.

An ad salesman, no matter how aggressive or talented, is handicapped by a poor newspaper. Publishing a good newspaper is imperative in meeting and besting competition. You must sell a good product yourself. A well-edited, solid newspaper, alert and active, is the best offense against any kind of competition. Be on top of your competitor from the first. Force *him* to the defensive. Let him apologize for any defect or weakness.

An advertiser is a reader, too, and a good newspaper can attract him just as it does one of his customers. An advertiser who is presold on your newspaper is receptive to your advertising pitch, too.

Concentrate on your circulation. It must surpass the competition not only because your figures become more impressive, but because the odds on generating ad response are in your favor.

Make your paper drastically different. Don't be a rubber stamp of the competition. Help the reader know which paper is which immediately. Make your front page, typeface, and picture coverage distinctively your own.

Pictures (the larger the better) make the quickest impression on a reader of two weekly newspapers. In a small town you'll be forced to take many of the same pictures (at the same time) as your competitor. But try a different angle, rearrange the subjects, attempt another approach.

★ THE THROWAWAY

I've always thought those of us who've had to face throwaway competition should band together in a fraternity where the emblem of official membership would be something not unlike the Purple Heart. For if you have to bleed, a throwaway or shopper administers the wound quicker and deeper than any other.

Nothing quite equals its ability to skim the net profit cream, to make itself almost invulnerable to your competitive efforts. A sharp operator on a throwaway can make life miserable, because he is not only beating you to the circulation advantage, but beating it with your strongest asset, black type.

A throwaway emphasizes once again how powerful the written word is. We tend to think of the finely shaped textbook type or the Ionic of newspaper columns as the molders of public opinion, the purveyors of information. But the throwaway shows us you don't need a fancy, well-printed sheet to influence a reader. A typewritten mimeographed sheet is just as powerful. A sweep or two of an ink stick reaches out in the same way your 24-point Gothic does. Typewritten copy is readable; even hand-lettered lines carry a message.

So the throwaway shares our strength, then it proceeds to cut our circulation to ribbons by scattering the sheet by the hundreds. The radio talks about blanket coverage; the throwaway nearly succeeds in getting it. Boys deliver the throwaway like regular newspapers every week. The cafes, drugstores, and coffee counters receive extra copies. No one pays a penny for it. Everyone gets it at about the same time. It's mailed to rural boxholders; frequently sent to rural stores in big bunches. Its readership is astonishing. If you've never watched a throwaway in operation, you'll question that statement. It's sadly true.

Its resemblance to advertising circulars is a strong asset. Its very appearance and shotgun circulation mean *bargain* merchandise. The reader instinctively reaches for it as a bargain sheet, and what is more baffling, the advertiser just as instinctively advertises sales merchandise and cut-rate bargains in it. Many advertisers know how to advertise in a throwaway, but *not* in a legitimate newspaper. You'll cry real tears over this problem if you face a throwaway. Why would a merchant who deals with bargain hunters every day fail to appreciate the advantages of advertising bargain merchandise in his legitimate

newspaper ads? Why does he insist on institutional ads in the newspaper and then throw a big sale and advertise it in the throwaway?
The answer may lie with our neglect to be good ad salesmen and
merchandisers ourselves throughout the years. The throwaway's pulling power hits us in a long-time weakness.

I once compared notes with an ad salesman from another news-
paper-and-throwaway town, and he was still fuming over an incident
on his Main Street the month before. "I service a privately owned clothing store in my town and the old guy who runs it is a fairly steady advertiser. The other day I picked up the poop sheet and here was a
big 25 percent off sale ad in there from that guy. Prices, big descriptions, good bargains. It looked headed for a smashing success. Do you
know what he had given me that week? A mat on some girdles. Now
which ad do you suppose gave him the most kick that week?" he
asked disgustedly.

You'll face the same problem. Merchants don't understand good
advertising. We should show them how to include advertising in
their merchandising. But the throwaway does this big job of selling
ads by its very existence. To the advertiser the throwaway means cut-
rate. He advertises that type of merchandise in it, especially when
he's trying it out. All advertising is not for cut-rate or bargain merchandise, of course. You can sell more girdles by advertising them
than by not. But the cut-rate connotation opens a merchant's eyes to
other types of legitimate advertising, to the advantages of talking
about the products he sells, and talking about the store in which he
sells them.

People come into his store for the advertised merchandise in the
throwaway. They talk about his advertising. It follows that the
merchant who saw good results from a throwaway's ad is going to
believe in that throwaway for future advertising.

The advertiser may feel the kick from the throwaway. He will
receive outstanding results in a regular Thursday morning newspaper,
too. But the advertiser doesn't always give us the chance he does the
throwaway. Two lines of type in a service station ad will remain with
me forever. Johnnie's Texaco gave both of us an ordinary ad about
Johnnie's station and how wonderful the service was. When published
that next Thursday, the ads looked about the same—except for an
extra two lines of type in the throwaway ad. Down at the bottom of
that ad in the throwaway, above the signature, Johnnie had put in:
"One pair of used pickup tire chains, 700 x 15. You can have 'em for
$5.50." In this farming community of ours, if Johnnie didn't have ten
to twenty calls on those chains, I'll close up shop. Even I was interested, but the size was wrong.

Why did Johnnie put his chains for sale in the throwaway instead of our paper? We got the same ad, but we didn't get the "sell" part. Just the existence of the throwaway had probably convinced that service station owner that if he wanted to sell a bargain pair of tire chains, he should go with the throwaway.

Results build more results. If an advertiser reads the throwaway looking for outright, shameless bargains himself, that's the medium he turns to when he has a bargain of his own to sell. One of the early mistakes publishers who face throwaway competition make is not to take the throwaway's drawing power seriously. We are late to realize the throwaway is beating us on results because the advertising of specials, bargains, and cut-rate items is the kind that gets quicker results. A throwaway's results are more tangible than the long haul program about a store's services or its fine line of Chippendale. When an advertiser obtains results, you can't blame him for wanting to play the game again on the same card.

However, the throwaway keeps few, if any, of your newspaper obligations. He doesn't cover council meetings or bother with correspondents, social events, or sports. Most throwaways are content to skim the surface, to publish only what it must, either to fill space or keep up appearances. Once in awhile you'll find an energetic pusher who uses pictures, news, even editorials. If you do, your Purple Heart gets an Oak Leaf Cluster for extra punishment under battle. For the most part, the throwaway doesn't pretend to be a newspaper. Most are devoted to advertising, and their high readership attests to the fact that people like to read ads.

A throwaway operator goes in for distribution of other circulars, too. He agrees to include a regular circular from a clothing store or a hardware store or maybe the theater calendar, stuffing it inside his throwaway. The charge may vary from two to four cents for each circular. Thus, if he can't get the ad himself, he still picks up some revenue for distributing it. His distribution system, because it's in operation every week, is usually superior to any you could arrange in a hurry (unless you, too, have newsboys). He's already paying boys for regular distribution so what he makes is nearly clear profit.

No great mechanical investment plagues the throwaway. No labor force, little overhead, few taxes, sometimes not even rent for downtown office space. It's a small investment operation with an ample amount of brass but little training. It can be published anywhere in town, even at home (just room for a mimeograph machine will do). A man and wife can run it. Most throwaways in small towns have a Multilith, usually a 1250, but some go bigger. In larger towns it is sometimes a larger offset operation, with more legitimacy and an increased tendency to go for news and pictures. Some owners publish a different shopper for each section (or trade area) in town.

The shopping guide can also be a competitor in your office supply department and your job printing efforts. Both are natural fields for the throwaway to enter, and it can mean more competition for you.

A Tough Battle But Not a Losing One. Facing throwaway competition is a long, hard battle, but not necessarily a losing one for you. The throwaway can still be beaten—maybe not eliminated, but beaten —with advantages it once enjoyed cut down. A legitimate newspaper has the distinct advantage of already being established. Its resources, by comparison, are limitless. The weekly can increase mechanical abilities, employ more help, get more equipment than the beginning throwaway (or the beginning weekly, for that matter). The strength in competition lies with the already-established newspaper. It can entrench itself more solidly in the community than the beginning competition can. It has the financial resources to keep going despite severe competition.

The throwaway is at a disadvantage on money-making possibilities. The publisher of a throwaway is not in the business for love of the game. He wants to make money. If his efforts don't produce the lucrative return he'd hoped for, beating the bushes for advertising begins to look bleak. You, as a weekly newspaper publisher, should keep trying to cut down this "lucrative return," to chop it, to make him struggle for the extra buck, to make him earn it. When the return on his investment of time or money becomes too little, the throwaway usually folds. If you allow him too much foothold, he may be around a long time. If he doesn't make money, he won't stay. That's your objective: to cut down the revenue that flows into his pocket. The money doesn't necessarily need to flow into yours—but don't let it flow into his.

Approach the throwaway competition from this angle, again assuming you have built up your paper. If you haven't done a good job of publishing before, start now. Your good newspaper is your sharpest weapon.

Distribution. One advantage a throwaway enjoys is its impact upon the community on publication day. Everybody gets it at the same time and can look at it on the same day. The merchant feels this impact. Twelve women burst into his store Thursday morning looking for the sheets he advertised in the throwaway. Twelve people still may come into the store for blankets the merchant put into his newspaper ad, but some arrive on Thursday and some on Friday and some Saturday, and maybe the last blanket is sold Monday morning. There's the impact from a newspaper, but not the immediate impact that impresses an advertiser. The throwaway's "results" from that first day are a real advantage, especially on doubting advertisers. It helps build the throwaway's reputation as a bargain seller. If a newspaper uses postal service to deliver its word, people don't read a paper at the same time. Your immediate impact is diluted because of staggered mail service.

Newsboys aren't the easiest people to organize, yet I know of no other way where your distribution can neutralize the throwaway's timing any better.

Circulation. Work hard on your circulation, not so much to top a competitor's exorbitant claims but for results for your advertisers. I can't stress too much how the advertiser grasps for tangibles in his advertising program. He craves remarks from customers.

Work on your classifieds for the same reason. Want ad results impress an advertiser. They help a merchant trade up to regular advertising. Want ads produce astounding results and a competing throwaway can clean up on them. People will begin to think of the throwaway first for their classifieds simply because they see more of them (with more bargains, possibly). Make them think of yours that way.

Your Rate. Your rate should be high enough. I don't believe in underselling your competitor with a lower rate. Outsell him on quality, service, and circulation. Be sure your rate is at least equal to his and preferably above it. If your competitor's rate is higher than yours, he is making more money for the same work as you're doing. You might as well make as much, or more, than he does. He'll pay for results. If one medium costs more than the other, human nature's perversity makes the advertiser think it is better. Which leads us into the second reason for having a higher rate: the Cadillac impression. No matter how much a businessman wants to save money, he is still impressed with expensive or high-priced merchandise. If it costs more, it must be worth more. Don't compete by underselling your ad rate. You're denying yourself a legitimate return. And you're letting your competition outsmart you on the impression of quality advertising.

Strike Where They Ain't. Concentrate on what the throwaway doesn't have. Pictures, for instance. Blow them up, scatter them all through your paper. Good news coverage is a must, because normally the throwaway publisher doesn't have it. You can always point out: (if the throwaway is the usual 10-by-15 or 8½-by-11 size) "I can put all the news and other information he has in that sheet into *one* page of my newspaper." If the merchant doesn't think in terms of your service to him or your newspaper's service to the community, make him conscious of what you do every Thursday and have done Thursday after Thursday through the years.

Paid vs. Free Circulation. The classic debate of the weekly versus the throwaway is which is better, paid or free circulation. Paid circulation has tremendous power in a community. But so does well-handled free circulation. Again, as it was with the radio, stress those strengths of yours that point up the weaknesses of the throwaway.

Point out, for instance, that paid circulation is "wanted" circulation. People plunk down a dime or 15 cents for a paper because *they want it.* They look forward to it and call if it isn't right on time. It's delivered (if you're not using newsboys) by postmen so there's no loss; none of the papers ends up in some culvert or scattered on the back lot. Remember this effective argument: "I don't know how many people look at billboards. Or how many listen regularly to the radio week after week. Or how many read the stuff that's thrown on the front porch. But when a person lays down a dime for my paper every week, pays out hard cash for it, by gosh I know he wants to read it!"

Impress upon the merchant that "distribution" is not "circulation." Circulation describes the legitimate list of subscribers who regularly receive a publication. Distribution has no such list, and not necessarily any regularity. The throwaway distributes its publication; you circulate yours by name. The merchant can understand this readily. He won't think of it himself; usually you must bring it to his attention.

When talking circulation, don't try to fool the merchant by including all those single wraps and out-of-state bundles into your trade area circulation figures. If you have 700 out-of-town subscribers and 1,700 others, don't call your circulation 2,400. It's not that much for the merchant. He wants to circulate his ad within the trade territory, among his customers, not all over the world. The former resident in New York who subscribes isn't going to come to Indiana to buy.

You must realize the competitor is telling the merchant you are including these figures in your circulation. The smart way is to beat your competition by telling the merchant, yourself, first. Be honest with him. Strike out those out-of-town customers. Tell him how many papers you sell inside the trade territory, then work with those figures. I discovered that being honest with my merchants from the start saved me accounts I might have lost.

Pass your own ammunition, too. If your throwaway competitor is true to form, he'll come up with some fantastic "circulation" figures.

He'll carry a little squib about his sheet reaching "10,000 people every week." Only 8,000 people may live in the entire county, but he couldn't care less. He knows that merchants, small-town ones especially, never count up the actual people they serve, so he isn't afraid to exaggerate.

Find an accurate figure of how many families live in the territory. The list of boxholders and all the rural patrons is available from your postmaster, or use the number of water meter taps as basis for the town. Then consistently point out to the merchant how many people live in the trade area and how many you reach. He'll learn quickly and appreciate your honesty.

"Newspapers." Draw a distinction about "newspapers." Don't let the throwaway seep into an advertiser's thoughts as "another newspaper." Label the sheet for what it is—a shopping guide. Then publish the best newspaper product you can. The better your paper, the more obvious the distinction.

Your Own Throwaway. The best way to combat a throwaway is to publish your own. This may seem like giving in to the enemy, and you may feel you are bruising your principles on paid circulation versus free, on newspapering versus throwaway. You may have preferred to lick 'em with the ammunition of newspapering instead of joining 'em, but with your own throwaway you are invading your competitor's territory with two superior products—your free shopper and your newspaper. This two-barrel approach creates the strongest position you will ever have in your community. You have all the strengths of your competing throwaway and all the advantages of your own paid circulation newspaper under one roof and one management. The combined punch can really produce. I am so convinced of this "paid plus free" invincibility that I've started free circulation shoppers of my own in conjunction with a newspaper, not only to discourage any future throwaway competition, but to give my newspaper the force it needed to be a superior advertising medium.

I found that my two publications blanketed my trade territory completely. I didn't have to apologize to the advertisers for those people who didn't take the paper. I suddenly stopped worrying about not producing for a merchant because maybe we were weak in this part of the county or weren't covering this or that neighboring community. Or that the newsstands weren't selling enough. I *was* covering it now, either paid or free or both. I just stopped apologizing for maybe not giving the merchant enough readership. The advertiser could no longer say, "Well, your newspaper just doesn't go to enough people because that ad didn't sell anything last week." I now could say, "It went there all right, but either you or I or both of us didn't do our job with the ad itself."

What weakness one had the other made up for. Paid circulation was around the home for a weekend. Free circulation hit the community in three hours. Paid subscribers were my strength but I no longer missed the nonsubscriber. Most communities have people who are not within the reach of paid circulation. All the transients, all the seasonal workers who move in and out before settling down to a paid subscription to my newspaper, the summer influx of new faces—these were now within the grasp of my publications and my advertisers. Potential customers in outlying farm communities were now all in the "family." Neighboring towns, which had no tie with my own town as far as local news or school activities, had a tie with the shopping district and my advertising.

I also found my shopper sold the newspaper as well as itself. I had enlisted a brand new active salesman, and a potent one.

Want ad coverage showed immediate new health. I was covering a new bunch of people regularly with the bargain hunting concept of the throwaway.

Production under web offset was a snap, and it looked superior. Ads were lifted from the regular paper and just repasted into a throwaway, plated up, and run.

I took the initiative away from my throwaway competitor and I discouraged anyone else from looking at my community. And I was able to make more money with the higher ad rate!

If you want to start your own throwaway, here are some tips:

1. Don't back into it gradually. Come out strong right off. I first crept in with a partial coverage throwaway, then we increased its circulation more to just those "who didn't take the *Standard*." Finally, we went total coverage which is what we should have done in the first place. You want your shopper to be better than his; as soon as you limit it, you limit your effectiveness.

2. Sell your paper and your shopper together. Don't say the rate is $1.25 for the *Standard* and then 25 cents an inch for the *Sun*. This is inviting the "no" again. Sell it as $1.50 and "this puts your ad in both the *Standard* and the *Shopper*." The advertiser doesn't have to take both; he is not being forced into a combined rate. But your sales pitch is stronger if you combine it into either one "yes" or one "no."

3. Go first class. Really put out a good shopper. Make it a sharp publication.

4. Don't apologize for it just because you've always believed in paid circulation so strongly. Don't second rate it. You have a good thing going and you should capitalize on it.

★ OTHER COMPETITORS

Although other weeklies, radio stations, and throwaways are the main competitors, others will covet the advertising dollar. The billboard salesman hopes to convince advertisers their messages should be alongside the highway. The matchbook salesman wants to print the same message on a fancy matchbook. The high school kids are sure their annual will sell refrigerators. The fast-talking ad manager from the nearby daily makes regular trips to your area to smooth talk the advertiser, particularly for those special editions. The community cookbook women need funds from advertisers, the gimmick salesmen push their pencils and calendars, the sweet-voiced gals sell the Yellow Pages, and the list goes on and on.

Outselling these "fringe" competitors is not the desperate weekly struggle the other three competitors cause. These are gadfly irritations and you will never eliminate them completely. You can help the merchant say "no" to them and give him some needed backbone by pointing out:

1. That much of this "fringe" advertising is donation.
2. That if you measure advertising cost by the number of customers reached, some of it is high cost indeed.

The merchant should hope to reach the largest audience possible with the least cost. When you consider how much real "sell" is in a book of matches or how many customers read a cookbook ad, you can begin to calculate the exorbitant cost per customer.

Advertising money is dear to any merchant. If his program is limited, he shouldn't be spending money for high-cost advertising. If you approach the problem from this angle, i.e., saving the advertiser money on a cost-per-customer basis, he'll thank you for it. Sometimes they just need someone else to supply the gumption for them to say "no."

They don't think of their advertising dollar in terms of customers reached. Break down the cost of advertising so the merchant readily can see it. Take the postcard example. Let's say your trade area circulation is 2,000 families and your open local rate $1.00. If your paper reaches 2,000 families and your rate is a dollar, a 2-by-4 ad will cost the businessman $8.00. The merchant can expose his sales message to a potential audience of 2,000 families for $8.00.

If he were to put that same message on a postcard and mail it individually to all 2,000 families, the postage alone could cost a considerable amount and he'd have to pay the expense of printing the postcards (or mimeographing them). Then he'd have to address them all! Work on the cost-per-customer-reached basis and you'll find a receptive audience among merchants whenever you talk about saving money!

Help the merchant draw the line between "donations" and "sell" advertising. If the merchant insists on donating by advertising this way—and many, many times the pressure from good customers or good customers' children is too great—talk him into increasing his yearly advertising budget to take care of the "donations" and still have enough money left to undertake an intelligent advertising campaign.

We've come down to the only real trouble these additional competitors can cause you. They take money from legitimate advertising budgets, and your paper is one that may suffer the cut! The merchant doesn't consciously advertise with these extras in preference to you. He often understands their value and also recognizes their deficiencies. High pressure salesmen (both professional and amateur), greediness for more customers, or a prosperous time of year all work on the merchant. Then at the end of the month or the year, when his advertising money is shot and his financial conscience is stricken, he lops off your advertising share.

★ DON'T KNOCK YOUR COMPETITOR

Don't be tempted to tell a merchant he's wasting his advertising money and the advertising medium he is using is lousy. You will only lose by it.

I'm not talking about "setting the record straight." Diplomatically, you can point out the obvious circulation tall tales. But don't criticize your competition's actions or his methods. Knocking a competitor to an advertiser is virtually telling the businessman he has no judgment and is spending his money foolishly. No one likes to be told that. You can cite advantages with great confidence, brag shamelessly about your own product, and, as I suggested previously, stress those strong points of yours which point up the weak points of the competition. Don't spend your time with an advertiser telling him how punk the competing sheet or radio station is. Talk about how good your product is, instead.

Don't whine all the time about your misfortunes; the merchant doesn't want to hear it. The ad salesman or newspaper publisher who consistently whines about the competition loses ground steadily.

So don't knock your competitor. It's not good business in any business.

CHAPTER EIGHT

Ink on Your Hands

THE Master's Eye will do more Work than both his Hands.

BEN FRANKLIN, *Poor Richard*, 1755

★

I'LL NEVER FORGET one night in the preoffset days, after the rest of the force had gone and I was finishing up the final half of the pressrun. It was hot summer and the back door near the press was open to draw in some of the cooler night air. I knew that those people walking by in the alley, hearing the bed of the press rolling back and forth, the paper whirring and whishing as it came off the flysticks, would think to themselves, "Well, they're getting the paper out tonight." And I enjoyed thinking about that. You can feel very close to a newspaper on a night like that, alone, with a press underneath you.

And I thought, too, about how many times I'd been on this same old press feeding four-up sheets of newsprint into it, feeling the pressure of the Wednesday seeping away as the job's end came closer. Knowing this one week's struggle was winding up in the rhythmic pick-the-sheet-up, feed-it-in, pick-it-up, feed-it-in. How many sheets have I put through this old press, I wondered? How many times have those grippers with their gaping jaws come up to take the sheet from my hands? How many press revolutions in a year of Wednesdays? And how many times has this old press turned over for someone else in its lifetime with the same sound I was hearing now—the same thump as it came back off impression, the clatter, the hum of the rollers across the form?

Alone, with that single bank of lights over the press, the night air drifting in against the heat of the shop, the last sheet not far from my fingertips now, I was grateful to have the final touch to all I'd written.

As I stood up on that press, flipping one sheet after another, I briefly knew what it meant to those printers of older days who were everything to their papers—writers, typesetters, press feeders. It was truly their creation. They had done it all. It was theirs.

That night it was mine.

The first man to print words for others to read was working in the backshop. From our compatriot Gutenberg's time to the present, editors have had to have printers. Once the printer was also the editor; nowadays the editor is seldom the printer. My generation of editors grew up in the backshop, many of us moving to the editor's chair after serving an apprenticeship as printers. Even in letterpress's waning dominance, this printer-editor dependence was declining in the weeklies. Offset came along in the 1960s to administer the coup de grâce. We no longer dabbled in the ink barrel as we once did. Our printer's aprons hung on the hook for longer periods. We were busier editing than printing in a profession that was once busier printing.

When offset arrived with its promises and its white collar respectability, being a printer ceased to be so important. I would not want to go back to the harsh days of weekly letterpress publishing even though I confess to have enjoyed it while I was there. In a profession demanding talents of the head, the tongue, and the pen, I found real satisfaction in the part that demanded work of hands as well. To place a piece of type in its proper place in a form, to control the paper and ink, the speed of the press printing that form against the blank sheet—this part of newspapering did provide solace.

I accepted the challenge of machinery and the learning of its complications. I loved knowing the profession down to the final 2-point space. There was pleasure in the smell of scorched mats and hot metal, the sight of hanging negatives twisting in the light or metal shavings bright on the floor. And there was always the familiar inky atmosphere of all backshops.

But editors cannot be dependent upon a backshop. It drained us. Past production failures still haunt me. Finding operators or someone to set the ads was a constant worry. This backshop dependency forced us to make the mistake of looking at newspapering from the backshop view, not the editor's chair. I'm not sorry to see that old familiar backshop gathering dust in these days of offset.

To dismiss the backshop, though, is not so easy. Many smaller offset weeklies need letterpress help. Much job work is still letterpress because that is the most profitable way to do it in that particular shop. The size of your newspaper will determine how much you tie on that printer's apron.

If your paper is small and you're doing everything, backshop and front office become the same. On my weekly, my newspaper thoughts have not always been catalogued into front and back, whether in the old days of letterpress or these new days of offset. I do not try to separate them. Weekly newspaper life as I have lived it is not one or the other, but a mingling of the two.

I've stopped setting ads to go take a picture. I've spent a Tuesday night putting a typesetter back into operation. I've thought of editorials while I made up or pasted up inside runs. I've stopped writing a story about a flood to help a shorthanded backshop crew. I've padded a job someone forgot, cut scratch paper "just so" to fit a private memo pad holder, talked to a customer about a full page ad while I watched a job press run, and closed a deal on letterheads while feeding the second run. In a week's time I may have had to help a beginning press feeder put on a new tympan, a new cameraman shoot a tough halftone, mix a week's supply of fountain solution, shoot a half-dozen offset negatives, hand set a batch of headlines, set corrections, reposition a cockeyed picture, coax a stalled vacuum pump into working again—all this sandwiched between a picture, an ad, an editorial, a news story.

All weeklies, large or small, have a similar life cycle. In varying degrees we are caught up in the pressure of backshop as well as front office. Generally, there is little, if any, departmentalization; the weekly publisher or editor does more of everything, even when he sits up front. He finds himself squeezing under several hats, and the backshop is closer than he knows. We weekly editors cannot always write it, forget it, and wait for the presses to roll. Even if we never go back to a darkroom or sidle up to a stone, we must still see that someone else does. If we do not always have to be in the backshop, we must still know the place.

I am not concerned about how much time you spend as a "printer," but I think we both should know about printing. Knowledge of production is a profitable investment. You can work people better if you know what they're doing. Pricing, advertising, and job printing all make more sense approached from both ends. Buying, selling, and trading machinery become more profitable; purchasing more efficient; editing more positive. Management should know what it is managing.

I would urge you not to avoid a backshop education, even a "paper" education. Some prospective editors, encountering the strangeness of this new world and those printers already in it flee back to the comfort of the front office. They never do learn enough about a backshop. They miss the cog in newspaper publishing that ties the words to the ink. Mechanical, then, becomes suspect, and the printer gains a needless superiority.

You can learn much of the printer's craft just being around it.

You may feel out of place standing around in your business shirt, but the knowledge seeps in from one Thursday to the next. You rub elbows with layouts, negatives, and jars of red opaque until you're comfortable friends. You learn to speak in ems and 6-points. You anticipate the printer's thoughts and understand his jargon.

Some knowledge cannot be absorbed so easily. You can cast a wary, sidewise glance at a Linotype as you walk past it year after year and still never be able to operate it. That knowledge comes only after you apply the seat of your pants to a Linotype chair. You can look at a thousand illustrations of halftone negatives and not really see one until you hold it, wet and hypo-streaked, up to the darkroom light yourself. Not all of us have the kind of time, sometimes not even the opportunity, to become moonlight printers. If you can't actually be a printer long enough to learn printing, at least plunge into its theory to achieve enough knowledge about printing to manage without ever actually doing.

★ THE PRINTER

Understand the printer first.

His life is involved with production; yours with creation. He will want to see the practical side, not the esthetic. He will worry more about how long a job takes to set, not how much money it will make for the shop. Because *his* hands must shape the ad or the job, he will resent your creations that may make it harder for him. He will want to make an ad look as nice as it can, but nice "his way" and not so much "yours." He will seldom have to deal with the customer, so he will not understand why the customer has more power than he. He resents, even though he may not want to, your front office chair, your education, and your white shirt, which is why you must be very careful of all three in whatever relationships you have with backshop men. He will try to foster, most of the time unconsciously, a division between backshop and front office. Besides being a human failing, this push of wills protects his position, because unless you prove otherwise he will not believe you know anything about his printing domain.

He will cross you for these reasons, but he won't cross you all of the time. He will become an invaluable asset, a partner, a confidant if you just take the time to understand his point of view and, I'm convinced, if you take the time to know what he is talking about.

One of the reasons I'm so insistent on acquiring backshop knowledge, even if only in theory, is to prevent a misunderstanding between the practical, production-conscious backshop personnel and the editor or publisher who wants to be professionally competent, make money and be boss. I think we head off those confrontations if we both speak and understand the same language. Moreover, I believe a good editor (since he looks at the backshop from a different direction) can improve efficiency and production.

Give the printer due credit at the outset. He does know what he is talking about, and before you discard his theories, try to look at them from his viewpoint. I've discovered I am too quick to push aside a suggestion from the backshop just because it comes from the back. This professional snobbery has blinded me more than once. I still find it hard to remember the printer is thinking about his backshop and printing and production all the time. He studies it day by day; I only briefly consider it as part of the overall newspaper. I have seen the backshop right too many times to make a blanket condemnation of all they suggest. You cannot help but sympathize with the printer's problems once you have suffered them yourself.

Uninitiated front office help who view the backshop crew as an ill-tempered, scowling bunch don't realize what irritations the front can cause the back. Printers run by routine—the type is set, carried to the phototypesetter, to the paste-up table, to the camera, to the press. The backshop man tries to speed the process as much as he can, meeting as many deadlines in his work as the front office man does in his.

But consider what happens to this efficient backshop routine when lack of news copy idles the machines on Monday afternoons simply because I didn't clean up my hook. Or when the copy comes to the puncher mistake-riddled and dirty, forcing her to decipher. Naturally I can't expect the usual setting speed. If ads arrive late, a floor man or paste-up gal is ready to make up ads for the first runs and discovers there are no ads to set. If I send down an ad improperly marked or poorly laid out an hour's extra work results.

Backshop routine is spoiled when proof straggles back while a page is waiting to be filled, editorial copy stalls up front for some flash of creativity, or the operator changes to a new font or point size to set one bunch of cutlines and then some more trickle in later and she must change again. Efficiency lags when the job printer is ready to go with a bunch of letterheads and no one has ordered stock, or he holds a press an extra hour because I forgot to pick up a proof, or he prints all blue ink in the morning, changes over to black and I come running in with another blue job I've mislaid. He may have an easy Thursday because the job work is light, but Friday is hectic because I discover a bunch of jobs in that heap on my desk.

No wonder the printer scowls!

★ YOUR OWN EFFICIENCY

As the above examples point out, you must make sure your own efficiency is unquestionable before you're too quick to criticize the backshop for inefficiency. Have copy to the machines *before* they run out. Keep copy clean and copyread carefully; no operator should be expected to be a copy editor, too.

Concentrate on one run's needs at a time. All first-run copy should take preference over the second, second over third, and so on. Not monitoring what the operator is punching can give you three galleys of front page news set and proofed, but no copy for the next run.

Routine work—datelines, resetting standing heads, pasting down the legals, casting new border, casting pigs—should be done early in the week, not delayed until just before it's needed. Lines can be drawn, page numbers put on, and standing ads ready to go before Wednesday. Throwing in and "putting back" should be out of the way early.

Don't set straight matter copy in preference to ad copy. Machines setting ad guts keep two or more people busy on the floor or on paste-up.

Don't do anything that doesn't contribute directly to getting the newspaper out. Job work shouldn't be started in the middle of getting out the newspaper unless your facilities are big enough to do both.

The sloppier the office, the less efficient it will be. Lost tape or scissors, standing heads and reruns not pulled off, untidy pasting tables or ad stones, all contribute directly to slow production.

Insist on deadlines—the first run off the press on a certain day, certain pages pasted up first, all ad copy set on the machines at a certain time, want ads closed off, display ads all in. Deadlines set an even pace.

Don't wait for Wednesdays to publish. Publish all week long.

★ WHAT TO LEARN

You won't have time to learn every detail of printing, but then a total course isn't necessary for what you and I need to know as editors and publishers. You do need to know the basics: typefaces, how a Linotype casts slugs, how impression works, what pages print where.

You should learn darkroom techniques and principles since this is where much of offset's work is done. And to carry this one step further, concentrate more on the offset part of printing since newspapering's trend is to offset.

You should learn how to set an ad into type, either hot metal or cold type or both.

You cannot understand job work properly until you know paper. So you must learn the weights, kinds, and characteristics of printing papers.

If you can learn a few things by setting up job work and making halftones, you will improve your basic knowledge.

Start with Your Darkroom. Your darkroom work will go much easier if you first set standards for exposure and development just as you did with your photography exposures. You must calibrate your camera or enlarger, i.e., determine the exposure and development of a normal negative or a normal print. From this basic exposure you can increase or decrease the exposure to compensate for light or dense negatives or for gray or too-contrasty prints. Without this standard at the beginning, you'll spend most of your time finding a point of beginning. Without a normal exposure index, you must go through the tedious process of elimination to discover your mistake. If this happens each time you go into the darkroom, you can become very discouraged.

★ MAKING HALFTONES AND PRESCREENS

When switching from letterpress to offset, publishers usually find halftone or prescreen shooting the hardest to do right. Spectacular photography reproduction is one of offset's advantages, so failure to turn out good halftones or prescreens (screened prints) after leaving letterpress is frustrating.

Halftones (screened negatives of the photograph) require more careful work than prescreens (positive screened prints of the photograph), but the dot principles (which I will explain later) are the same in both. In halftones you work with a reverse (a negative); in prescreens you work with a positive. You will undoubtedly be using more prescreens than halftones. Prescreens are easier to do since you eliminate the tedious developing and drying time in the darkroom, and they are quicker to make because you run them through an automatic processor. You do not have to strip them into the page negative; you lay down the finished prescreen right on the page paste-up. You can match cutlines to pictures more accurately because you can see what the picture is.

But consistent quality of the good halftone is unbeatable. When you want your front page pictures or job work to be exceptional, you will probably rely on the quality of a halftone.

To make good halftones and prescreens you must understand dot structure on the screened negative or print. An exposure of the halftone negative puts a dot structure over everything, but the proportion of light is not accepted equally by the blacks and whites. You must compensate for the unequal absorption of light by three different exposures (usually only two are needed in prescreen shooting).

In shooting halftones these exposures are:

The *highlight exposure* to give light to all areas but primarily to the white areas of the photograph.

The *flash exposure* to give additional light to the black areas of the photograph.

And, if needed, the *bump exposure* to give additional light to the white areas of the photograph.

The proportion of time for each exposure varies with the calibration of your camera and darkroom and the contrast of photographs you are screening. But the proportion will probably be something like this:

> 80 percent for the highlight
> 15 percent for the flash
> 5 percent for the bump

The black area of the photograph is clear in the negative. The good black or shadow dot is a pinpoint black on a clear field.

The whites are the solid areas of the negative, and a good white or highlight dot is a pinpoint clear on a solid field.

Figure 8.1 is a good photograph. A normal halftone negative should look like Figure 8.2, and it would print like Figure 8.3.

Fig. 8.1. "March Lamb" shows a "good piece of photographic copy."

Fig. 8.2. A good line negative. Notice dot structure.

Fig. 8.3. Printed halftone from Fig. 8.2.

Fig. 8.4. Highlight dot, white   Fig. 8.5. Pinpoint   shadow
pinpoint on a solid field.   dot, black on a clear field.

Light exposed to the highlight area of the halftone builds up the white to the proper pinpoint shown in Figure 8.4. This is the highlight exposure.

More light in the clear area of the negative "builds up" the dot in the halftone to be like the dots in Figure 8.5.

Building even more light to the highlight area (as in Figure 8.4) makes the highlight dot "drop out." Now the halftone will print brilliant white on newsprint. (Actually, there is little or no dot there at all.) The tinier the highlight dot, the whiter the area prints. I prefer this dropping out of the highlight since it not only builds on the white to make it whiter, but builds on all the middletone and gray areas as well. You can sometimes achieve this brilliant drop out dot with just the highlight exposure, but it may take the bump exposure to get more whites.

You must remember that all exposure is proportionate. The additional highlight may build the flash up too much. This is because light is put all over the negative. In both the flash and the bump, the light is selected for either the shadow areas (the flash) or the white areas (the bump). More light to the highlight in an attempt to drop out the highlight dot may build too much light on the shadow dot. The longer the halftone flash exposure, the grayer the black areas become.

You do not want a gray look to your highlight (white) areas of the picture. If your white portions of the picture are printing gray (not brilliant white), your highlight dot is too big. You should go to more of a pinpoint highlight.

Or if the black parts of the picture are too gray, your flash dot is probably too large and not a pinpoint.

You want pinpoint dots at both the black and the white (Figures 8.4 and 8.5). The gray areas of the picture (the middletones) will then take care of themselves.

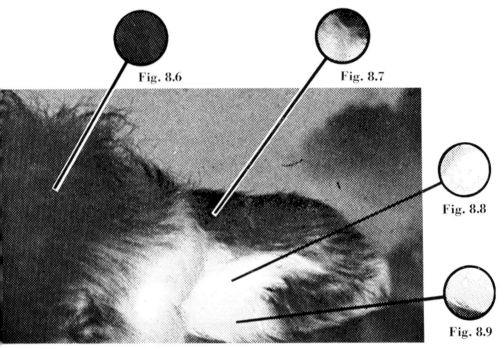

FIG. 8.6. Good pinpoint white dot (from lamb halftone).
FIG. 8.7. Dropped out highlight dot (from lamb halftone).
FIG. 8.8. Weak flash dot (from lamb halftone).
FIG. 8.9. Good pinpoint flash dot (from lamb halftone).

Figures 8.6 through 8.9 are from an enlarged portion of Figure 8.2. They show various parts of the dot structure and how they appear when you look at them under a magnifying glass. Figure 8.6 is a good pinpoint white dot. But the real white portion of the picture has dropped out in Figure 8.7, and this is the way it should be. Dropping out the extreme white areas of the picture lightens all the rest of the white areas. In Figure 8.9 the pinpoint flash dot is fine, but it was not enough in Figure 8.8 and this area will print solid black. In a small portion of black like this one it is not noticeable, but not having a sufficient flash dot in a large area of black would ruin the halftone.

You can compensate for a photograph's faults in halftone screening because you control the amount of light to any one area of the negative. You can compensate for a grayer picture, for instance, by bumping which forces the grayish highlight to print whiter.

You can correct a picture with too dark shadows by increasing the flash exposure so the shadow dot prints grayer.

I don't drop out the highlight dot too much when I have a picture with a predominance of white such as a white uniform, light buildings in the background, or a light sky. These dominantly white areas will go completely if you push the highlight dot too far. Your grays will be light, but you lose the whites, create pasty faces, and wipe out detail. You can drop out the highlight more successfully when your white areas are smaller (a white shirt collar against a dark suit) or when the photograph has equal amounts of blacks and whites. The checkerboard effect holds up extreme highlights and allows gray areas to lighten more.

You will lose detail if you don't have a strong enough shadow dot, yet you don't want it so strong it will print gray. The shadow dot is the detail dot. A weak shadow dot (where the dot hasn't "built up" to a pinpoint dot) causes the picture to print fuzzy and the black areas to fill in.

Since job work halftones (which will be printing on finer paper) are more critical, I don't drop out the highlight dot quite so much and I make sure the shadow dot is a definite pinpoint.

Your negative should develop for two to three minutes and you should inspect it during developing. Inspection developing guarantees that a slightly wrong exposure will be corrected or weak developer compensated for. Only about one-fourth of the developing time takes any skill. The first three-fourths is only rocking the tray back and forth. But be alert after the negative starts to darken and the three-fourths stage approaches. If you jerk the negative out too soon, the highlight dots are underdeveloped and the shadow dots are too weak. Dallying too long washes the whites completely out and increases the shadow dots too much.

Use a magnifier to watch the highlight dots in this last-quarter stage. You can observe them by holding the negative up to the red light. Always look at least once *before* the dot is completely formed, maybe just past the three-quarter stage. Your perspective is established if you can see the highlight dot larger than you want it, and then, on successive inspections, watch the dot diminish to the pinpoint stage. Look quickly and don't hold the negative out of the developer for long intervals; it may develop unevenly if you prolong looking at it.

Watch the highlight area, not the flash—the white area of the photograph, not the black areas. Of the two, the white area in the print is more critical to the halftone than the black area. A shadow dot can lean towards the gray and not detract from the printed picture so much. But an underdeveloped highlight dot makes the entire picture too gray. I always coddle the highlight dot.

Temperature must be constant. A higher or lower temperature acts as an increase or decrease in exposure.

Your screen must go tight against the film. If your halftone has one spot or section that developed differently, you probably had a bubble of air trapped under your screen during exposure.

Your halftone making will be easier if you can establish a constant product in the darkroom photograph. As nearly as possible print the same tones every week. A constant standard in the print means a constant standard in the halftone shooting. Print the photo the size you want the halftone. One-to-one shooting is much faster.

Prescreening. The principles used in prescreening are exactly the same as in the halftone negative. The dot structure is built up the same way, by establishing a white and a black (highlight and flash) exposure; but now the exposures are reversed. The main exposure builds on everything, mostly on the black, and the flash builds additional dot into the white.

In a prescreen, the black dot is a pinpoint white dot in a solid field (the reverse of Figure 8.5); the white dot is a pinpoint black dot in a white field (the reverse of Figure 8.4).

There is one important difference in prescreens and halftone negatives. The prescreen dot structure may have to be grayer than a halftone, because the prescreen has to be developed *with* the page negative, not separately as the halftone is. You must adjust the prescreen dots to correspond with your page negative development. Normally, the rest of the page will take longer to come up than the black and white dots in the prescreen. Your prescreen will look grayer than your normal halftone. But in the development of the page negative the prescreen develops out until it looks exactly like the halftone. In fact, it *must* look exactly like a halftone or it will print with all the faults of a poor halftone.

Experiment to find what the dot must be in your prescreens to be right when the rest of your page negative is done. As long as you recognize a good halftone dot, you can see what the prescreen should look like in the developed page negative.

First establish your exposure and development times. Check them for several weeks to make certain you have them correct, then, believe in them. Don't be changing back and forth to new times, new materials, new chemicals.

If you don't recognize black and white densities, consult the many different kinds of published scales and density charts. Or you can use a densitometer.

The standards you have for your darkroom rarely are the same as someone else's darkroom. I listened to too much advice in the beginning. I tortured myself with a half-dozen different systems and methods until I realized I had to find my own (based on the knowledge gained by trying the other systems). Other darkrooms can be a guide, but you probably will have your own times that work best for you. Your camera may be a different model. Your water system may provide better or worse conditions. The film you use, the way you print your pictures, your enlarger—all these affect the normal time settings.

As I tackled each new product or process, I set up the basic exposure for it until no matter what the work was—printing a picture, making a page negative, shooting a prescreen—I knew then what the basic exposure should be. This became our darkroom standard and no matter who went into the darkroom, the procedure was the same.

An exposure may not come out right because of a wrong camera setting, a temperature too hot or too cold, using a new film without calibrating it first, guessing at exposure, or being sloppy with your timer. If your basic exposure has been successful for several months and suddenly goes wrong, start troubleshooting through the entire darkroom. Something will be out of whack; it seldom is the basic exposure.

Good Photographs. Give a cameraman a good photograph and he'll give you a good halftone. If you ever shoot halftone negatives yourself, you will take more pains to make better photographs in the darkroom.

If you pick out photographs of similar contrast, you can shoot these together satisfactorily. But you can't shoot an extremely black and white photo with a gray one and have the two come out like they should. One may be right; the other won't be. Three seconds more flash on one picture will gray out the blacks; three seconds might be just right on the other. I keep a pair of scissors near my developing tray, and many times I'm able to clip out a slower developing negative from a bunch of ganged ones and push it just a little further.

The most frustrating part of making halftones is not always being able to speed the process much past this one-at-a-time pace unless you are willing to settle for reduced quality.

★ **SETTING ADS**

Setting up ads for letterpress requires more printer skills than does offset ad make-up. Any high school student can paste up offset ads, but a layman fumbling around a printer's stone is lost among the leads and slugs, upside-down type and 1-point spacing. In offset you don't need to maintain the strict measurement from side to side, top to bottom. Casting, routing, sawing, and cuts are eliminated, as are mitered borders, justification, and filling space with leads and slugs. In offset you use scissors, a pastepot, and some grade school pasting skills to put the ads together. Offset's easier ad setting is one of the first improvements you notice when you switch to offset, maybe even the biggest benefit of the change from letterpress.

In offset ad setting, put the border down, then illustrations, followed by display and body type, then the signature. After this go back to straighten and align the entire ad.

Laying the border down first is a great help. If you don't have the border in place, you create more work for yourself. The border shows your available space so you can lay everything down fairly accurately the first time. This is especially true of the side-to-side spacing. With border in place, your eye automatically aligns the line within the ad and you see how much space you have for the copy. Without the border you are floating the ad guts too much. The blue lines of the layout sheet don't visually show you quickly enough where you are.

After the border is in place, you can space your waxed illustrations, body type, and display lines as you go; but don't do the final straightening until the ad is complete. If you take the time to put each line down accurately and then find you must do it over, you've lost time.

Efficiency is much better if you can work on the ad at a tipped surface rather than a flat table. You can look at the ad as if you were holding it in front of you instead of bending over.

A light table isn't necessary to paste up ads. With a light table the make-up person tends to be too fussy and often takes too much time straightening individual lines. The diffused light prevents him from seeing the entire ad. Without the confusing backlight, you can "back off" and look at the ad as one unit, not one straightened line after another.

Do all your cutting at once. The material for your ad will come up in one bunch or scattered on a couple of sheets. Cut everything out then lay the cut apart copy to the side of your worktable where you can quickly pick it up to work with it.

Putting all the pieces at the edge of your table or trimmer so part of each piece sticks out and can be picked up easily is a real time-saver. You can see the pieces quickly; you're not hunting all over for a stray line. They're not sticking on top of one another, and they're not lost.

Put copy down lightly at first; don't press it permanently until you've inspected the ad at arm's length. Then roll it firmly so pieces won't fly off in transit.

★ **MACHINERY**

If you are a typical weekly newspaperman, I know newspaper machinery is almost as foreboding as the old printers. But from one who didn't know anything about machinery before he became a weekly publisher, let me assure you it is possible for you to keep things going, too.

Machinery, close up and torn down, isn't as mysterious and

baffling as it appears from the front door. Its neurotic tendency is to break down when needed most. It may take coddling and pampering through one Wednesday after another; still you can "boss" it like you do other help. You may never become a machinist; yet by borrowing some patience and keeping the instruction and maintenance manuals well thumbed, you can limp along until you're able to turn the responsibility over to someone else.

You have three sources of help when machinery goes haywire— your own shop, a local repairman, the manufacturer.

Most of the time you will be able to fix it yourself. Usually only a small adjustment is needed or a part needs tightening. Sometimes it just needs oiling, but don't let oiling become a crutch. For a long time if my machinery didn't work, I'd oil it, just on general principles. I know now that everything didn't run better because of my oil-it-first principle, but in spite of it!

The secret of fixing things is not to jump to conclusions. If something isn't working, don't take something else apart. Figure out how a piece of machinery works. What turns what? Why does this piece do this? Trace the movements through. You may spot why a part is hanging up.

Look for excessive wear such as a shiny spot that would indicate friction. As silly as it may sound, look under everything for a dropped screw or bolt or spring. Pieces fall out regularly. Do the obvious first, even if it seems ridiculous. Is the switch on, or a breaker tripped?

Before you take anything apart, ask yourself: Will this tell me what I want to know? Look carefully to see if you really need to take a screw out or a part off to reach the trouble spot. I spend most of my "fixing days" putting back together some piece that was not part of the trouble.

Keep instruction books close at hand. Read them, know where to look for troubleshooting help. The book usually has the answers, but it takes looking. Sometimes an answer to another problem can solve the present one. I've always believed in instruction manuals. I do recognize their limitations and I've been exasperated more than once by what they *didn't* say, but they've helped me to understand how a machine was supposed to work. I've noticed most printers have an aversion for instruction books. They're always sure the book is wrong. "Those guys at the factory don't know what they're talking about," they'll tell you. You must recognize this attitude as an expression again of the printer's independence. He doesn't want an outsider telling him something he thinks he already knows. He would rather fight it by himself than admit a book would have the answer, or that you could find the answer faster than he could. The printer who goes to the book is far ahead. The book's knowledge and information, coupled with the printer's natural mechanical ability, is quite a partnership. I'm dwelling on this to prevent you from being seduced by the average printer's insistence that instruction books should be burned. They can be a big help.

Maintenance manuals are in the same category, and most of the time they're just as neglected. Insist that they are followed closely. Oil and clean religiously, just as you would with your new car. Clip those maintenance checklists you see published in trade publications and tack them up somewhere. Old machinery, with proper care, can outlast the printer.

If you can't find the answer yourself, go directly to the manufacturer. He is always willing to help. A phone call can save you hours of looking and start you on the right track. I have fixed machines by having the technical representative or repairman "talk me through" a repair job over the telephone.

Often, the printer seems reluctant to call on those "other guys" for help. As we move more and more into the electronic age, our dependence on technical people becomes greater. We should be shedding these kinds of prejudices.

You can always ask for assistance from the local repairmen or machinists in your community. Every small town seems to have one genius who has devoted his life to fixing things for his neighbors. I can think of a couple in my town I almost had to put on the masthead with the rest of the staff.

Invest in proper tools. Don't stumble along with just a crescent wrench and a pair of pliers. It is battle enough fixing machinery; and improper tools make the job longer, your patience shorter.

Don't abuse machinery. Don't pound on it or ram-jam it around. Losing your temper at a stalled machine inevitably causes more damage than the original breakdown. Don't fight machinery and don't be afraid of it.

I've found if I keep track of how I fix a machine once, the next time is easier. When I was keeping a set of Justowriters going, I typed up what had been wrong after each breakdown and how I fixed it. I then had my own troubleshooting list which really worked, not only for me but for anyone else who had to work on the machines.

★ MEASUREMENT

2 coppers	=	1 brass
2 brasses	=	1 lead (or 2 points)
3 leads	=	1 slug (6 points)
2 slugs	=	1 em or 1 pica (12 points)
6 picas	=	1 inch (approx.)

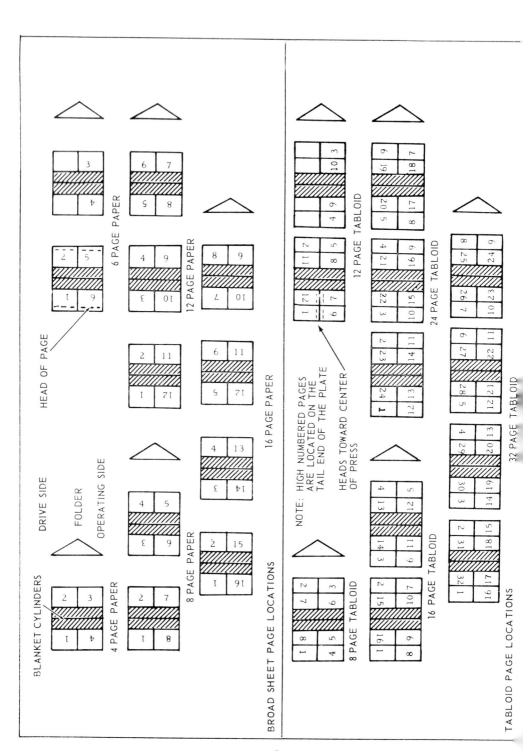

BROAD SHEET PAGE LOCATIONS

TABLOID PAGE LOCATIONS

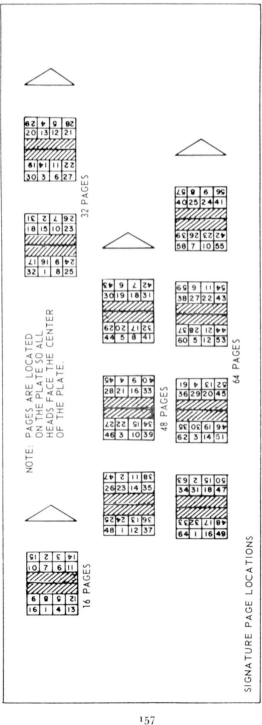

SIGNATURE PAGE LOCATIONS

Courtesy Goss Division, MDG Graphic Systems.

FIG. 8.10. Page locations for broadsheet, tabloid, and signatures.

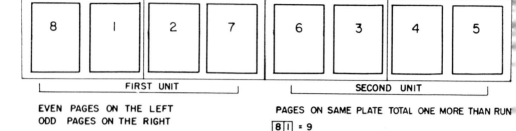

Fɪɢ. 8.11.   (Broadsheet) eight-pager on the make-up table.

To find the approximate number of picas in a certain number of inches, multiply the inches by 6, e.g., $6 \times 8 = 48$ picas.

To convert per-column-inch ad rate into agate line ad rate, divide 14 into per-column-inch rate ($14 \div 91¢ = .065$ line rate).

Page Positions. If you are confused about page locations for press-work, study Figure 8.10. This chart shows page and plate position for a web offset press. You can also use it for page layout guides by lining up the pages on a make-up table as in Figure 8.11.

★ STAY IN THE FRONT

Don't become too fascinated with the backshop. It's no place for an editor. He must stay in the front. As much as you may become absorbed with backshop work, as much as you might actually enjoy working in back rather than dealing with the public up front, as much as you know you can job print better than some guy you hire; as fast as you can operate—stay in the front. Your newspaper cannot be run as successfully or properly if you manage from a Linotype chair instead of the front office swivel.

Keeping up with the news takes time. There are pictures, editorials, and columns to produce; advertising to be planned and sold; competition to be met and conquered. All this means hard work and squeezed time. Competition is too varied nowadays, advertising dollars too fickle. Your readers, educated by increased national circulation of improved dailies and magazines, expect more from your paper. They are not content, and rightly so, with just any sort of Thursday publication. They want a newspaper. It takes a long, long week to give them one. You must spend much of that week in the front office or out hustling to make your paper better, and more profitable.

No editor ever made as much money operating as he could have made selling. If you've ever been forced into a long stint in the back-shop, you can understand how your allegiance changes. The boss on the press is a different boss. You approach work differently than you do from the front. Pressure comes from another direction. A possible sale is an interruption, a potential customer an irritation. You're not trying to produce more business, only to take care of that in front of you. Your attention becomes focused on the ad to set, not the account to develop; on the job to finish, not the layout to originate.

But knowing the backshop is knowing all of newspapering. Though you stand a front office's length away, you will profit by what you know about the backshop.

If I Wanted It Tomorrow, I Would Have Brought It in Tomorrow

The body of
Benjamin Franklin, printer,
(Like the cover of an old book,
Its contents worn out,
And stript of its lettering and gilding)
Lies here, food for worms!
Yet the work itself shall not be lost,
For it will, as he believed, appear once more
In a new
And more beautiful edition,
Corrected and amended
By its Author!

BENJAMIN FRANKLIN, *Epitaph for himself,* April 19, 1790

★

THURSDAYS and Fridays, those immediate days "after the paper is out," have long been hallowed job printing days for the backshop. With our newspaper out, and in the midst of our front office Thursday holiday, we are ready to tackle the pile of job work.

Commercial printing, if you want to use the fancier name, no longer dominates weekly newspapering as it once did, because we are not so dependent upon it. In fact, the newer generation of editors seldom learn it or pay it much attention. Because they don't understand it well, they leave it, like many other parts of the backshop, to the printers. Newspapering has taken over the weekly publisher's attention and this is the way it should be.

This change of allegiance is ironic because country newspapering owes its beginnings to the backshop's job printing. Our newspapers were job shops at first more than newspapers. The generation of weekly newspaper editors just before mine were still mostly old-time printers who remembered those days of scarce advertising. Job printing kept the place going. Because they were printers, they could do the work themselves "after the paper was out," so labor costs were cut. Job printing was not a product they had to sell; it walked in the door. It was steady and took a minimum of equipment to produce. Besides, these early-day "editors" understood printing and enjoyed doing it. Printing established a tangible, businessman-to-customer relationship. There were no problems of measuring advertising's pulling power or a newspaper's influence. The reason so many weekly newspapers were dull and lifeless for so long was because printers produced them like a piece of job work. This dependence on job printing held back the growth of actual newspapering and exaggerated printing's importance. Its influence and domination of a weekly newspaper's philosophy of success is only now fading.

But fade it must. As an editor and publisher who worries about the finances as well as the esthetics of this business, I must remember job printing is a newspaper sideline, not a business competitor. The profit on a community paper is in the newspapering, not the job printing. Mark up makes the difference. Making money with anything depends on the dollar spread between the selling and the manufacturing. In job printing this spread is not very high—not nearly as high as the spread in advertising. Two thousand 9-by-12 sale bills are priced in the Franklin Catalog at $29.45. Yet this same sale bill, running as an ad in your newspaper, would bring in $48.00 at $1.00 per column inch rate. The same amount of labor and nearly identical cost of stock is involved in both. Multiply this advertising versus job printing profit ratio by ten or twelve or sixteen pages and you can see my time is better spent selling extra advertising than promoting something on a job press.

I don't want to dismiss the importance, or the attraction, of job work. It isn't all a matter of profit and loss statements. Nor do I intend to sound callous to the editor with the artistic bent who enjoys putting the sharp blackness of ink to the smooth finish of an enameled paper. If you're fascinated by layout and design, job printing is the natural outlet for your talents. If you appreciate fine work—the delicate balance of type to copy, the dignity of a printed job—you cannot but value the enjoyment job printing gives.

I've always been concerned about spending too much time on job work, because newspapering is our prime concern. It's our livelihood, our profession, and it demands much. When we neglect our concentration on it for distractions like job printing, the newspaper must suffer. The continual problem in weekly newspapering is where do I put my energies to best use? Unquestionably, I must advise you not to put too much of your time into job printing. There are only so many hours in an editor's limited week—so many hours for newspapering, so many for the business side, so much for yourself. You end up doing what you like to do best and maybe if it is job work, that's as good a therapy as digging in the flower bed. But time spent on job printing has to be considered less money returned to the business for the hours put out.

Whatever time you do spend with job printing, make sure you are consciously making money from it. Your prices should be competitive and fair, yet high enough to return profit. Production costs should be cut. Presses should not run extremely low profit jobs "just to keep busy." Labor costs should be carefully watched.

If I seem preoccupied with the profit angle, I do so intentionally to impress that job printing must return a profit. Let's realize some return from job printing if we must become involved with it.

Besides the actual profit, the commercial job department contributes in two other ways:

1. It provides work for your backshop crew at the end of the week when there's no newspapering. You generally cannot hire part-time printers, yet on many weeklies, newspapering does not make a full forty-hour week for the backshop men. This is especially true with offset papers. Job printing fills out the week and helps carry the printer's wages.

2. It utilizes machinery that would otherwise be idle. On those days when newspapering is not using Linotypes or presses or paste-up facilities, we can recapture part of our investment in them by running job printing.

Giving up or neglecting a job shop may invite competition by another printer who solicits job work. If you're already in a competitive situation, legitimate job work flowing to a competitor hurts you twice, once because you don't have it, and once more because he does.

Printing is often a companion to advertising, a sale bill that also runs in the paper, a direct mail promotion from an advertising campaign. It can also be a foot in the door to a prospective advertising customer.

Job work does make a contribution to our business; but you must understand its limitations as a profit maker, recognize its potential drain to your energies and your time, and remember we weekly newspapermen are not printers anymore.

★ SELLING JOB WORK

In job work you will make money if you sell it aggressively and thereby increase the amount of sales; and if you can cut expenses, increase efficiency, and watch the pennies. One is income, one is outgo. To be successful, you should concentrate on both. Let's take selling first.

Three things sell job work—ideas and creativity, quality, and service. Our job printing customers expect that we know how to create a form or job for him (or that we can take his idea and make a printed form out of it); that we will make it professional looking or, as he will put it, "make it look nice"; and that we will provide him service by delivering the job on time, trimming, folding, and padding to give him the best finished product.

Promoting ideas and creativity means going out of the office to increase the business. If you have the personnel and feel job work deserves this extra attention (without lessening the push for additional advertising) you can increase your job work gross by hustling. Making consistent calls is the most vital part of job work hustling. You have to be out in the bushes to find new business (or to keep the old, if you're up against an aggressive competitor). It takes "sell" here just like everything else we've talked about.

Commercial printing has an advantage that once it's sold, it can become steady repeat business. Many forms you do for customers one year will turn out to be the same next year. In a sense you only sell it once. When it returns to the shop the next time (with the form up or the negative all ready) you have extra profit. But keep these old customers satisfied while you're promoting new ones.

Specific job work ideas always produce more printing sales. Create new business by selling a person on novelty work. An insurance agent once grabbed an idea from us for printing a continuous order of simple scratch pads. The pads had his name and address on them and a plug for life insurance. What sold the order was the fact he had his *picture* in the lower right hand corner, too!

Design a matching letterhead and envelope; dream up brochures, advertising matter, mailing pieces, and business cards. Go after four-color work. Promote No Carbon Required (NCR) forms. Keep pressure on the local government offices, the city hall or the courthouse. Look to colored paper, fancy finishes, and more striking inks to convince a customer he should be off that old black-ink-on-white-paper habit.

You encourage future business, once it is sold on the street, by giving the customer the professional job he expects and by giving it to him without undue wait. Delivery is the "after selling" to the customer and you should deliver as soon as you can. It's not good business to print a job, wrap it and then leave it on the counter for a couple of weeks waiting to be picked up. Once the job is finished, pad it or cut it or have the holes punched as soon as possible, then have someone deliver it either on an ad call or make a special trip. Customers who must keep calling or coming back about their orders aren't happy customers.

If you have a chance to talk to your customer about the finished job, be sure to tell him how nice the job looks. He will be greatly pleased. It is his now; he "owns" it and he will appreciate hearing from you that what he has is a good product. It is very easy to say to him, "Didn't this job turn out well?" Or, "That blue is certainly a good color." This "selling" after you have made the sale hooks the customer for the next time.

The professional touch sells. If you can point out an improvement he hasn't considered, like a perforation in a salesbook or NCR paper, he will become confident of your shop's capabilities. Suggest colors in stock or ink, or offer a sharp sketch that will intrigue the average customer and convince him he was right in coming to you. You must give life to the customer's raw idea. The finished job should be the most useful tool the customer could have purchased.

You can sell by showing the customer savings, too. He should be encouraged to buy more for his dollar by the savings on additional runs. A customer will order 500 when 1,000 would have been a more economical order. He should be shown the cost per unit savings as he increases his order.

The 250 per unit cost is about *twice* what the 500 per unit cost is. The 500 per unit cost is about *twice* what the 1,000 per unit cost is. The 1,000 per unit cost is about *twice* what the 2,000 per unit cost is. Around 3,000 and 5,000 the unit cost starts to level off and remains constant from then on.

A customer may order 1,000 sheets of a form three times a year. This small quantity ordering costs him extra money. Point this out to him by some simple arithmetic:

$$
\begin{array}{rl}
1,000 \text{ at} & \$25.30 \\
1,000 \text{ at} & 25.30 \\
1,000 \text{ at} & \underline{25.30} \\
& \$75.90* \\
3,000 \text{ at} & \\
\text{one time} & \$43.65*
\end{array}
$$

* From an actual sample in the Franklin Catalog.

He could have saved $32.25 by ordering just once. This is the kind of business he will understand.

However, if one of my customers frets about whether he should take advantage of the big run or whether to experiment with the form first, I always encourage him to go with the smaller run. He invariably changes the form. Then when he runs out in a short while, he's back with the changes and the decision to run more.

Always ask the customer how many sheets of a form he will use. You don't want to oversell him when he doesn't use many. If you talk him into twice the amount he would use in a reasonable time, he will think dark thoughts of you every time he sees that pile of unused forms.

Sell job work from the front, don't sell it from the back. If a customer wants red ink, print it red; don't try to talk him out of it just to save the washup. The salesman who thinks like a printer never sells very well. He is more likely concerned with complications in producing the job instead of selling it.

Producing Job Work. The hardest part of job printing in weekly newspapering is the actual producing. Job printing is not that difficult to sell—actually most of the "sales" walk in the front door. But the producing creates the problems, the holes in your profit. Unless our production is tight and very efficient, none of us will make much money at commercial printing.

Your profit in job printing will depend greatly on your personnel. What kind of machinery you have isn't so important as what kind of a printer you have. I've seen some poorly-equipped job shops make more profit than big ones with fancy presses. Many a printer has made good money on a 1250 Multilith and little else. But even with only average help, you can develop a good, profitable job shop department if you institute an efficient and systematic method of production.

You must have some control of the job as it flows through the place. You have to hover over it without actually being there. You have to make sure the job doesn't bog down as it goes through the several pairs of hands in the backshop. The job must be done with a minimum of expense, time, or mistakes. It cannot be allowed to wander around the backshop. Every time this happens, the shop loses money, and because you cannot watch the job yourself, you must devise a system so others will.

How to Take a Job. You can eliminate many problems if you take the job right in the first place. Many jobs are doomed in the first fifteen minutes in the shop. Sometimes it's as if the job was just tossed on the counter and found there the next morning. We haven't asked enough questions about the job, we didn't find out what the customer wanted so our technical know-how could improve his original idea, or perhaps our customer was vague about what stock to use and so were we.

If you are vague about details from the first, so is the printer later. Is it padded or loose? Punched or not? We may give a price quotation and forget to mark it down, thus creating another bottleneck at billing time. Maybe the job ticket is incorrectly filled out; sometimes not even complete. If we give misleading information about the delivery date we will probably end up with an irritated customer.

Develop control over the job during its first minutes in the shop.

Filling Out the Job Ticket. Your best partner is your job ticket. It will go everywhere you don't. Make it a working partner. It should be so complete no questions need to be asked by anyone handling the job, not the printer, not the bindery gal, not the bookkeeper.

Use an automatic checklist for the most necessary information.

Check for—quantity
       —size (of the sheet)
       —color (of ink)
       —stock
       —padding or binding
       —delivery date

This list answers the basic questions. If the job is more complicated, more details must be supplied.

If the job is numbered, for instance, be sure to find out the starting number. The customer may want to continue with his present numbering, not start with 01.

If the customer will file it in a ledger, what size should the holes be? How far apart?

If the form is to be bound in books, what kind of binding should it have—a commonly used tag binding or should it be more durable? Bound at top or side?

What forms stay in the book? Should the others be perforated?

Does the customer want to see a proof?

If the form is printed on the back, will the form be work-and-turn or work-and-tumble?

All this information must be put on the job ticket to prevent a break in the work flow.

My staff sometimes becomes exasperated when I ask questions like these about a job they took. "Why didn't I ask that," they wonder. It's only because they didn't look at the job from the customer's viewpoint. We should think about how this job will be used. As we have it ordered now, will it be the best job the customer can get? If it were my job, could I improve the customer's basic idea? Is there anything we can supply that the customer never thought about?

Be specific in filling out a job ticket, and don't guess at the stock—know it.

Including a sample of the job with the job ticket helps the printer understand what the customer wants. Include a layout, the more accurate the better, of what you want the job to look like. This gives the printer a solid start. If it's possible, read over the customer's copy while he's still around. Whatever questions you can ask him will save the printer asking you later.

If you've given him a price, mark it down on the job ticket immediately, not on some scrap of paper someplace. This insures he will be charged the same price he was quoted, and it saves confusion at billing time.

If he wants the job mailed to him, include these instructions and give the mailing address.

Any special billing instructions should be marked down when the order is taken, not at billing time. (I put all my figuring, my layout, customer copy, and comments in the job ticket so I always know where it is.)

Put only one job order per job ticket. Don't bunch up jobs on one ticket. To avoid confusion, each job should have its record and its own place on the assembly line. The only exception would be on combination orders, like envelopes of different sizes, letterheads with different officers' names, or any similar jobs that are natural go-togethers.

All special instructions must be on the job ticket. As an extra precaution, tell someone else everything you learned about the customer's wants. You are the only person he talked to, and if you're not around no one else will be able to answer questions.

Check the Stock Again. While still taking the job order, I urge my staff to check once more on the paper to be used. Before the customer leaves, I like to make sure that my idea of the paper needed is the same as his. When he says "make it heavy" does he mean six-ply cardboard like I assume, or ledger which may feel substantially "heavier" than bond to him. If I say it will be on a "pebble finish," does the customer understand or is he expecting a smooth, enamel-like texture? Don't hurry through your explanation of the paper to be used on the job. Make sure your customer and you are thinking alike.

Do you have the stock in your inventory, or will you have to order it? Here is another place we stumble. We don't always follow through with the paper after we take the order. This is not something we need to do while the customer is still around, but don't let the job get very far into the backshop before the paper is—or will be—there waiting. Whoever is responsible for ordering job work paper must make certain all jobs are covered by an adequate supply.

Time and efficiency are lost when a job is at the press but the paper isn't.

Delivery. The customer should understand when the delivery date will be. Don't mislead him. Don't promise more than your shop can deliver.

When you and your customer have agreed on delivery, mark this down on the job ticket, too. This gives your printers a definite delivery date. It establishes the job's place in the work flow. Your printer will be arranging his work to a great degree on what jobs have to be done first. With the date on the job ticket, he won't have to guess (or ask you again) what you and your customer decided.

Every job cannot be a rush job. Few things embitter the printer as much as overpromised job work or the editor who puts RUSH on everything and then can't understand why jobs bog down in the back. Every rush order squeezed into the flow of work slows down production, and rush jobs you don't deliver on deadline don't make friends.

Overpromising often happens when the editor overestimates his backshop crew's capabilities. Every staff member who takes a job wants that job given priority. He feels personally responsible for its delivery. The printer, on the other hand, will have his own schedule of work and won't be overjoyed to find his day's work riddled with rush jobs from the front. I have not let the backshop decide which of my customers I want to give preferential treatment, but I have become very stingy with rush jobs. The backshop has little conception of the pressures developed between the customer and the business. To them, a job is a job. To the boss, it might mean future business, an accommodation to a good account, a selling tool, or just plain selfish profit. The trick, I think, is not to use fast service as the dominant sales factor. Give your backshop some leeway *when you sell the job*. Ask the customer if you can have a little bit of time on the job, and let him agree to a week or more. Establish right at the selling point when he would like the delivery date to be. You will find most customers will be willing to take their turn. But if you sell on an I'll-have-it-for-you-tomorrow basis, the customer takes this seriously. What you are doing by selling fast delivery is convincing the customer that one of the best things about this job is having it in his hands tomorrow. If you have the shop and the work force to do it, this is great; most of us don't. You can tell him the shop will begin work on it immediately. But give everyone as much leeway as you can. Save those rush promises for customers who demand it or when delivery date is the reason you got the job.

To Help It Run Smoothly. A sharp front office can help a job run smoothly. You should eliminate bottlenecks, not create them. It's not good business, for instance, to lay out jobs in off sizes. If the customer asks for a 6-by-9 job on bond paper, talk him into either the 5½-by-8½ size or 8½-by-11, both of which cut out evenly from 17-by-22 stock. Don't send back 10-by-12 signs to run on white six-ply cardboard when an 11-by-14 sign cuts out of 22-by-28 stock with no waste. As you begin to understand paper better, these decisions will be helpful to both customer and printer.

Anticipate your printer's problems with the job. If your customer doesn't care whether his job is printed blue or red, don't choose red when you know another blue job is running the same week.

In manifold work, stick to a basic sequence of colors (white, canary, pink) or, in NCR (No Carbon Required) paper, don't pile up a large stock of Coated Front and Coated Back in all kinds of colors. Keep your decisions basic. Don't volunteer unnecessary work.

Whoever handles taking job work orders should make certain the job ticket moves back to production as soon as it can so the printer will know how the day's or week's work is shaping up.

Don't sell fancy, rough-surfaced offset stock to a customer and then expect your printer to do a good letterpress job on it.

Give the printer a good layout to follow. Read the copy over and make sure you can understand it before sending it back to the printer. Recopy if necessary, or make a new layout. It won't be wasted time. As a general rule I don't send the customer's scribblings to the printer. Though I may have understood when the customer told me about it, it will be cold to the printer. There are fewer errors and more efficiency if the printer has a good layout.

Proofreading. I insist someone in the front office do the job work proofreading. The printer shouldn't be expected to read proof on the job he sets. Let someone read it who is seeing it for the first time.

All job work *must* be free from errors. You can't deliver an incorrect job. In the shortness of every Wednesday you may be able to excuse newspaper typographical errors, but such an error makes a letterhead useless.

Read all job work twice, once with copy to make sure the printer didn't leave out something, the second time for any typographical errors you might have missed the first time.

Don't volunteer proofs to customers unless you have a finicky customer and you'd rather give him the responsibility of okaying the job, or if it's a particularly difficult and complicated form and you'd feel better if the customer would share the load of getting it right, or if it's a layout job by you or your art department and the customer hasn't seen it yet. (These layout proofs are not always final proofs; sometimes the layout is sufficient.) Otherwise, don't volunteer to show proofs. Running back and forth to the customer involves loss of time. Normally he trusts your judgment.

If you do show proof to a customer, always proofread the job yourself beforehand. Mark your corrections on the customer's proof so he can see these mistakes were caught and will be corrected. Don't count on the customer to catch typographical errors, because he's not trained to spot them. If you don't read the job yourself first, you'll find a half-dozen glaring errors the customer missed.

Layout. I believe layouts should be pasted down on the same size sheet as the finished product will be. Here's the procedure we use for the best results:

Tape a piece of unmarked white paper the exact size as the job on a piece of larger faint-ruled layout paper. Tape it square with the blue lines. Then paste up your job on the unmarked paper using the blue lines of the layout sheet as a guide (Figure 9.1). By pasting up on the unmarked paper, you can see exactly how the type will appear in relation to side space, margin at top, overall appearance without the distraction of the blue lines. Yet a pica pole laid across the layout and onto a blue line gives you a straight edge to follow in aligning the type.

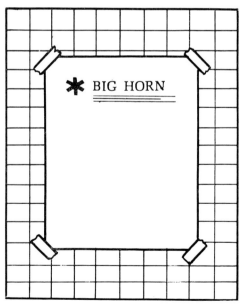

Fig. 9.1.   Unmarked paper taped down on layout paper.

Fig. 9.2. Layout put down on black background on camera copyboard.

Then place the layout on a black background on the camera copy-board and make a line shot (Figure 9.2). By using the black background, the white layout sheet shows up black against the clear negative (Figure 9.3) and you have an exact size negative for stripping. This makes stripping much easier since you have four exact corners to match to the red lines of the masking sheet. It shows the printer the proper placing of the copy on the sheet, sideways and up and down. You

Fig. 9.3. The negative looks like this.

don't have to have a copy of how you want the job following the printer around; it's all there on the negative.

Our experience shows that whatever extra time and film is taken
in the darkroom is balanced by speeded up stripping and more efficient presswork. Layout work itself is better since the paste-up person can see the paste up on the sheet.

★ PAPER

Paper is the single most important part to understand about job
printing. Without a knowledge of paper or "stock" you cannot sell
job work well. You can't fit the customer's desires to a finished
paper product because you won't know what to suggest or what
would look better. You will be unable to price it properly or make
job printing move through your shop profitably. You don't have to
be a printer to handle job work, but you must know about paper.
   Several people have asked me, "How can I learn about paper?"
I don't know that there is an easy way. Being around paper and
printers is the way most of us learned it. Mistakes probably taught
us the rest. We handled it, ordered it, watched it run through a
press until it finally made some sense. It's not a hurry-up-and-finish
education, but if you're impatient, you may be able to understand
it quicker if you'll put paper into these groups:

   Bond and Offset—the workhorse stock, the easiest to print, the
cheapest to buy. Bond is also the paper I chose years ago as my
"basis." I learned about bond and then established it as my point
of reference. A paper was "twice as heavy" as bond or "three times
as expensive" as bond. Most of the letterheads, office forms, mailers,
stuffers, and booklets I've done have been on either bond or offset.

   NCRs (No Carbon Required)—bond papers that are chemically
coated to receive or transfer writing without carbon paper. Writing
pressure on the original sends the message to the duplicate which
in turn can send it on to the triplicate, etc.

   Book Paper and Enamel—slick-finished papers with similar characteristics to bond, but used where quality is important (magazine-
type stock, four-color work, fancier booklets with critical halftones).
These papers are more expensive to buy and require more careful
presswork.

   Ledger, Bristol, Tagboard, and Cardboard—heavier stock for use
where bulk is important. Ledger has more body, will take more

punishment than regular bond (the kind needed in a bookkeeping system). Index and printing Bristols are stiffer yet. Most general work requiring heft and bulk (index cards, cheap covers) will be printed on Bristol. The Bristol most often used is 110-pound index. Cardboard, mostly six-ply, is stock for signs, posters, anything that must have thickness. Tagboard is similar to Bristol and is used for binding booklets.

Text and Cover—paper with special finishes and textures, striking colors and designs for fancy printing. This paper is used for booklet covers, menus, and advertising pieces. Text is not as heavy as cover, and it runs easier. These papers are the most expensive.

Specialty Paper—envelopes, business cards, wedding and social announcements, gummed paper, safety paper for checks, bumper sticker stock, tags. These items are made for special jobs.

Within each paper stock listed above are the "Chevrolets and Cadillacs," the low-priced and the high-priced. In simplest terms, you have to buy quality paper to print quality. You can get by with a no-rag content paper on one customer but maybe not on another. Generally you will buy more inexpensive than expensive paper.

Basic Sizes. Every kind of paper has its basic size. This is the size that is sold by the manufacturer and it also determines what kind of a cut you can get. The basic bond paper size is 17-by-22, for instance, and you can cut four 8½-by-11 sheets out of it evenly. You must memorize and learn each of these sizes.

Substance. Substance is the weight of 500 sheets of a paper in the basic size of that paper. The manufacturer hasn't helped us with this. Instead, he has adopted one substance for one paper, and another for something else. You just simply have to memorize and learn this, too.

In bond paper, a 16-pound substance is used for duplicate and triplicate (since it's lighter weight than the original). Letterheads are 20-pound substance. Ledger has 24-, 28- and 32-pound categories. In index paper, 90-pound substance index is considerably thinner and lighter than 140-pound substance index.

Cost Per Sheet. One of my earliest foundations was to establish how much paper cost per sheet. I found that once I had listed all the various papers and how much each sheet of each kind of paper cost me (with approximate freight added), I didn't have to refer to the paper catalogs so much. I was quicker at figuring prices. I had better knowledge of how paper costs were affecting the job. It also firmed up one basic kind of stock (one index, one bond, for instance) and a basic size. I wasn't confused with the warehouse full of available paper, and my decisions were easier.

You must add freight to this basic cost list. A carton of paper, regardless of the kind, weighs about 125 pounds. This means that you can have 3,000 sheets of bond in a carton, but only 300 sheets of the heavier six-ply. This freight cost, unless you're luckier than the rest of us and have it coming in freight free, must be added to the per sheet cost. It won't be as much for bond paper (3,000 sheets in a carton) as in the six-ply. Cost per sheet *delivered to your plant* is what you should list.

Grain of Paper. In ordering and cutting paper, you should have a basic knowledge of grain. Grain is the direction in which most fibers lie, which corresponds with the direction the paper is made on the paper machine.

Grain is either "short," lying with the short way of the sheet, or "long," lying the long way.

It affects the way a sheet will run through a press, whether it curls up or not, and how it scores or folds. Normally, you will order your basic size the same, time after time, until you (or the paper house) won't bother with grain instructions. In some odd cuts or in cover stock, grain may be a big factor.

You can recognize grain in heavier stock simply by folding it. If the job was run with the proper grain, it will fold smoothly. If it wasn't, the paper will break and crinkle along the fold.

Consult the Paper Catalogs. To understand paper further, pore through the sample catalogs. You can learn much about paper from them by actually seeing what a pebble finish is or feeling the smoothness of an enamel. The samples will also show what a wide range of covers and texts exist, how many different colored bonds and offsets there are. Going through paper samples always charges my enthusiasm for printing. I keep thinking, "In all this variety and color of paper there just have to be jobs in this old town to match." It's a great stimulant.

Learn from Your Own Shop. Your own backshop will be the best place to learn about papers and printing. When you go back there, keep your eyes open. Know what is going on. Absorb every remark a printer makes about paper.

How to Cut Paper. You won't be physically cutting paper, I hope, but it helps to understand cutting (Figure 9.4) when talking about basic sizes and the ordering of paper. It's very simple, but I've watched beginners have trouble. The procedure is:

1. Find the size of the printed sheet desired (8½-by-11)
2. Put it over the basic sheet size (17-by-22)

$$8\frac{1}{2}\text{-by-11}$$
$$17\text{-by-22}$$

3. How many 8½-by-11s can we cut out of 17-by-22?
4. The 8½ goes into the 22 two times. The 11 goes into the 17 one time.

$$8\frac{1}{2}\text{-by-11}$$

$$17\text{-by-22}$$
$$1 \qquad 2$$
$$1 \times 2 = 2$$

Two out this way.
Try it the other way.

$$8\frac{1}{2}\text{-by-11}$$
$$\downarrow \qquad \downarrow$$
$$17\text{-by-22}$$
$$2 \qquad 2$$
$$2 \times 2 = 4$$

Four out is correct and saves waste.

5. Then divide the number you want printed (1,000) by 4 (for the 4 out) = 250.
6. You'll need 250 sheets of 17-by-22s to print 1,000 8½-by-11s.

★ MAKING IT PROFITABLE

Job printing's low markup makes good management imperative. Printing profit can vary from shop to shop. In my place I may have a crackerjack printer who can produce faster and better with a minimum of wasted time. You may be limping along with a mediocre man. Yet we both would probably charge the same for an 8½-by-11 letterhead job from identical Franklin Catalog pages. You may have an offset press with many ruled forms on plates. I may be printing them letterpress with the down rules requiring extra composition and an extra run. Your freight may be no factor, mine might be. You may be in a competitive situation while I could be exclusive in my town, charging higher prices.

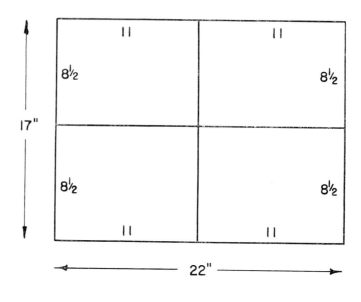

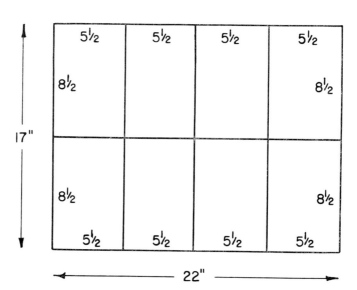

FIG. 9.4. Seventeen-by-twenty-two sheet cuts evenly in 8½-by-11 and 5½-by-8½ sizes.

Printing profit fluctuates from week to week within our own shops. Two different envelope jobs of 500 running right after one another are more profitable than running either job singly. They would have the same setup, same make-ready, same ink distribution yet both are charged at the same price. Running jobs together, all blue ink runs the same day, several envelope jobs in a row, or 8½-by-11 runs consecutively make a more profitable Thursday and Friday than if you had a manifold run of 1,000, two letterheads of different color ink, a ticket job, a complicated Class B ruled form, and maybe a statement job.

You have to be more conscious of all this with job work than you do with advertising. It takes tight management.

Ordering. Don't create extra costs in ordering. Try to bunch your orders in four-carton and sixteen-carton price breaks, not only for the savings per sheet but the freight cost savings, too.

Never order two-thirds of a ream since the broken ream price breaks at this point. You can buy a full ream for the same price as two-thirds of a ream at the broken ream price.

If you only need twenty-five sheets of some expensive cover stock, you need only to order that amount. Even though the penalty cost per sheet is high, you save money in not having an odd lot of paper around. The customer should be charged at the actual cost price so he pays for the penalty.

When you are undercapitalized and find yourself short of cash, do not invest in large quantities of paper. Let the paper houses do the warehousing. You can usually have paper shipped to you in such a short time that your money doesn't need to be tied up in a large stock of paper.

Jobs for Your Competitor. You can make more money on some jobs if your competitors do them. Don't fill the shop with work unless it is profitable. If your competitor's price on a certain job is barely above your costs, don't reduce yours just to take the job away from him. Wouldn't you rather he took the loss?

Or if the customer has a form that is complicated by rules and perforations—or if it's a company form mass-produced in the city someplace—don't take it just to have some business in the shop. You can make more money on an idle press than on one printing a job at a loss.

Farming Out Job Printing. Farming out job work to bigger, better-equipped plants has cured many of my printing ills. Letting another printer do the jobs I can't handle profitably or quickly makes good business sense. I can't buy a press for every job. The investment difference and upkeep cost difference in an 11-by-17 offset press and one that will take a 10-by-15 sheet is considerable. If I tie up my shop with a complicated, long-running form, some other jobs must wait. If I spend extra money on stock I don't always keep on hand, on a folder to handle a multifolded job, for employees working over-time, it all means more production costs and less profit.

The big boy in the next town or off in the city usually can furnish the stock, do the job, send it back to me and still allow me a good profit.

Farming out job work is especially effective with offset work. A small-town editor can even shoot all the negatives and do the strip-ping. The city printer then only has to run it.

It's time to consider sending your bigger, more complicated jobs outside the shop if you're running behind; if it's a job requiring pin-point quality which you can't provide (like four-color work); if it's extremely complicated, or if your profit will be lower by doing it yourself.

You should be able to send out these jobs and make more money delivering the smaller runs and normal repeat business.

Using Specialty Houses. Few small-town printers can produce jobs like wedding invitations, business cards, snap-apart forms, and regis-ter tickets as economically as specialty houses. As the years have gone by, I've shifted an increasing amount of this business to a specialty house, with happy results. Wedding invitations that we used to spend considerable time trying to produce are now done more professionally by a specialty house. They look better than ours, the customer has a wider, more attractive choice, and we make more money!

Raised-letter business cards are the same story. We can't buy the stock as cheaply as one outfit can supply us the printed card.

The one disadvantage is the delay in delivery. Production is out of your control. You can't find room for a wedding invitation "needed Friday" when the job is out on the West Coast.

Usually a custom form, like on a plain business card, can't be done as easily as it can in your shop (or done at all by some houses). Yet overall there is lucrative business in using these print shops to produce some of your more complicated jobs.

Pad Up the Scrap. Keeping scrap around is like saving pieces of string. They're either too long or too short. Scrap gets dirty and disarranged unless you wrap it. And if you wrap it, you've invested more time than it's worth. I've seldom found the right size in the scrap pile, or if I found the right size, I never had enough sheets to wrap. Unless you can find specific jobs for it regularly, cut most of the scrap pile for scratch pads. You can sell them for a nickel apiece and forget the frustrations of the paper heap.

A Good Job Ticket. As the job ticket moves on through the shop, it should keep telling you all you want to know about the job. The printer's time and work, how much material and paper were used, how the job's price was figured, the bookkeeper's posting. Finally, the job ticket should be filed under an easy-to-find system.

Here's what I think a job ticket should tell you:

> *General information*—This is a place to put all the basic information about a job (quantity, size, color, stock, padding or binding delivery date) plus any special instructions (folding, numbering, order of pieces) when you take the order.
>
> *Time spent producing*—Actual time spent producing the job, how long composition took, how long to run, is recorded here.
>
> *Paper schedule*—Add information about the kind and size of stock used, and the number of sheets actually cut for the job.
>
> *Billing information*—Enough space should be provided to itemize individual charges (engravings, extra postage, etc.), total price, tax, and any special billing instructions.
>
> *Remarks*—Enough room to write special comments.
>
> *Number*—Each job ticket is numbered.

You can add more refinements. Who took the job? Who proofread it?

I encourage my printers to use the back of the job envelope for the cutting schedule. He has to figure his paper cut on a piece of scrap somewhere. I'd just as soon he'd do it on the back of the job ticket. The rest of the paper information is there. Having the cutting information there, too, is just another check.

All this information on a job ticket insures better control of the job while it is printing, an accurate picture after it is finished. It's an easy step from here to cost accounting.

The job ticket should be big enough. I've used both the open end regular No. 11 or No. 14 envelope and the 9-by-12 size, and I prefer the bigger one. I like a ticket big enough to hold all the copy, notes, and last year's samples.

The ticket should wind up in a good file where it can be easily found. I like the cross-filing system where a card numbered the same as the ticket is filled out with the same basic information as on the ticket (date, number wanted, kind of job, price). This card is eventually filed separately by account. The card gives the shop a cross reference and an easy way to find the main ticket number. The job ticket itself is filed numerically. The plates and negatives (with a sample of the job) can be filed by account, e.g., all Jones Drug Store jobs in one filing category. The card can also serve as the basis for a production board, where the card moves along the board from camera, to press, to bindery.

A Job Book of Your Own. Those wedding order books and stationery printing catalogs have always been models of how simple and easy it is to order printing. If we weekly editors had something similar, we could sell printing better and probably sell more. One bottleneck we all have is the printing ignorance among our front office people. They don't know paper, they can't price a job, and they are embarrassed to show how little they know so they hustle the customer on to someone else or make the customer come back "when the boss is in."

We need a formula, a system, for helping our employees sell and price job work. I have borrowed on the wedding catalog idea by working up price sheets for the commonest kinds of printing: envelopes, letterheads, stationery, business cards, simple bond paper forms. These price sheets are arranged to show price for various kinds of paper, amounts, extra color, and padding. Sales tips are given for each section (e.g., sell matching envelopes, "window" statements save time, $5\frac{1}{2}$-by-$8\frac{1}{2}$ are not as good as $6\frac{1}{4}$-by-7 letterheads). Samples of work done by the shop precede each section. In the back I placed one sheet of all the common bond papers and labeled each one: "This is 20 lb. Hammermill," "This is 25% rag Neenah Bond." The customer can actually see and feel this paper in comparison to other papers.

These catalogs are bound with a plastic binder so individual sheets and samples can be added or replaced. A three-ring notebook would work just as well.

What we had, eventually, was our own "wedding order" book, complete with samples, prices, explanations, options. It made ordering printing in our shop easier and simpler for both my customers and my employees. And it took from me the constant load of pricing, taking orders, and explaining.

Job Machinery. An amusing country saying is that you can tell who is boss in the farmer's family—the farmer or the wife—by which is bigger, the barn or the house. A similar situation exists with job printing machinery. I have seen shops with an old newspaper press, outdated type, or a badly used saw right beside a shining job press or a purring perforator. You can tell at a glance which that editor thinks is "boss."

It's an occupational disease among editors to fall in love with new printing equipment. We seem to be especially vulnerable to job printing machinery. Thousands of machinery salesmen are in business because editors can't resist a new job press that "goes faster" or one that will "handle a bigger sheet." But like new typewriters that don't write better editorials, new job equipment doesn't always increase job profits. The editor who understands that he cannot buy a press for every kind of job sleeps better nights.

I certainly won't try to make rules about what kind of equipment you must have to run a profitable job shop, but it's not hard to make a list of "don'ts" when it comes to investing in job machinery:

• Don't try to cover every job with new machinery. If you run only six 11-by-17 jobs a year, why invest in a press capable of taking that size? Would a rotary perforator save money or could perforating rule on the press take care of current needs? Do you need a bigger folder? Your volume will answer many of these questions. If you're in doubt, go to your job tickets. Let them tell you what you did in past years and how many times you could have used new equipment.

• Don't be impressed with how fast a press will run. A press that runs 7,200 impressions an hour doesn't do much better than a clunker at 1,200 if the job is only 250 sheets. The same principle is at work when a printer insists on trying to run a press at top speed and then fights stoppages, balky feeding, and poor inking so much he loses his impression-per-minute advantage. At 2,400 hourly impressions, every five-minute stop loses 200 sheets.

• Don't underestimate old machinery that is still usable, still workable. The old 10-by-12 open press once handled nearly all the weekly's printing before today's increased volume and diversification, and it's still a welcome workhorse.

Pricing. You have to learn pricing and if you live with the Franklin Catalog for awhile you can speed the process. It's the most comprehensive, the most valuable book on job printing pricing around.

An editor years ago was either enough of a printer to know what it actually cost him or he figured by the seat of his pants. Nowadays we editors have the Franklin Catalog, and no homemade formula can be as easy or as consistently accurate for all kinds of jobs as this "black bible" of printing.

The Franklin Catalog can be adapted to any community. You

can use it to back up your own straight cost-plus-profit method. It shows you exactly what you should charge for padding, for numbering, and it helps you understand paper. It's an education by itself, really.

For consistency I teach my staff to be dependent upon the book. Most job printing orders received on the street invariably end up with, "Now how much is that going to cost me?" Don't try to quote a figure from the top of your head. Wait until you can see the book. You'll either quote it too high, which could scare off the customer; or too low, which will lose you money. I may offer a round figure as approximate, but I do my pricing back at the office with the book in front of me.

Charge for everything. Don't give away anything, don't donate the extra charges like engraving costs, art work, better quality paper. Pass these costs along to your customer. He won't mind paying what the job is worth. While we're talking about price, it's a good place to point out that most people won't come in for job printing on price alone. Quality, the "good-looking job," is important to customers. They want their printing to look "uptown," and they want service. Both quality and service are ahead of price.

Don't underprice. Run your Franklin figures often to make sure the grade figures you're using are up-to-date. Recheck last year's prices if you're repeating them. Ask around with other printers to see if you're in line. Underpricing is an easy sin and cheats your shop.

Job work can be figured a couple of other ways than Franklin. One is by taking straight cost and adding the profit; the other is by estimating one-third stock, one-third wages, one-third profit. These are old printers' ways and you almost have to be a printer to make them work.

It is interesting to compare them, though. Take a 500 No. 10 envelope job and figure it all three ways.

Letterpress composition for the envelope job would take an average of 30 minutes, press make-ready is another 30 minutes; a press (take an automatic here) will run 500 in about 30 minutes; and stock will cost between $3.00 and $3.50. You've tied up actual wages (at $3.50 per hour) of $5.25. You have some $8.75 invested in these 500 envelopes. At straight cost-plus-profit (40%) you should charge $14.60. The three-way split comes out $15.75. And the Franklin Catalog says to figure it at $16.50 (work on small presses, offset catalog, 1972 price). I'd rather stay with Franklin. It's more accurate and much easier.

On repeat orders make sure the price this year is either the same or only slightly different (preferably higher) than last year. Your customer is suspiciously irritated when his prices wander up and down. Of all the complaints I had on a competitor once (from people who were transferring their business to us), the one most given was his sliding method of pricing—one price one year, another the next.

In bidding for printed jobs, I ask myself first: How much profit do I want from this job? Since bidding tends to drive the price down, the profit takes the cut. If you are forced to sharpen your pencil to get a job, you must be prepared to earn a lower than normal profit. I also ask myself if my shop is too busy to handle low-profit work. If my shop is just handling what we've generated locally, I hesitate to add low-profit work to bog it down further.

To arrive at the profit-I-want figure, I work with actual cost figures (i.e., cost of paper, cost of labor, cost of composition, negatives, flats, plates, presswork, bindery, misc.). Then to this actual cost (or as close as I can come) I add what profit I think I must have. Or you can use the Franklin Catalog and adjust the grade or the type of printing from Medium down to Ordinary, for instance.

I like to keep track of the bids and how much they brought. I file this successful bid away with my actual bid in case the same job pops up next year. It also gives me an opportunity to see how close I'm coming or how much I think my competitor lost.

★ LETTERHEADS

Letterheads and envelopes, more than all other jobs, are the customer's own trademark. No matter how small the business, usually the owner will want to have some printed piece distinctively his. A letterhead becomes his identification in the business world, and he wants it to look as nice as it can. Letterheads may take special care at first, but once you design one a customer likes, it is steady repeat business for a long, long time.

Sizes. Most letterheads are printed on 8½-by-11 stock. This is the regular boxed size of the various bond stocks. (The customer will call this size "full size" or "business size.")

The 5½-by-8½ size is too narrow to look right, but some will prefer it. Discourage them if you can; this is really too small. Others will want to turn a 5½-by-8½ into a half sheet 8½-by-11, making it 8½-by-5½. This can work out if the customer wants a half sheet, but it always looks out of proportion to me.

One of the most popular sizes in the smaller letterheads is 6½-by-7. This retains the 8½-by-11 shape but is small enough to be a note size. It fits in a 6¾ envelope, a good selling point.

You will get requests for a 7-by-10 letterhead, the Monarch size, which is slightly more personal than the 8½-by-11. Be careful, this size takes an envelope larger than the 6¾ regulars.

Color. Encourage the customer toward color. Color, either in stock or in ink, is distinction itself. Your customer may balk at color, thinking it too pretentious. If you sense he is going to be uncomfortable with anything but black ink and white bond, then don't force it. However, suggesting colors to other customers, especially the younger generation businessmen, may make real friends. Show color charts and the kinds of paper available.

An additional color, properly used, almost always improves a letterhead. Always suggest two-color. Even though it costs more, two-color takes the letterhead out of the everyday class. You can achieve the two-color effect by using a color stock along with a color ink. This is cheaper for the customer since it saves an extra run.

Be sure to point out the extra cost, but don't sell it on how much more expensive it is but on how attractive it will look. Always show your customer samples of two-color and ask him to visualize how the letterhead would have looked in just one color.

Use second color as sparingly as you can on the letterhead; too much kills the effect.

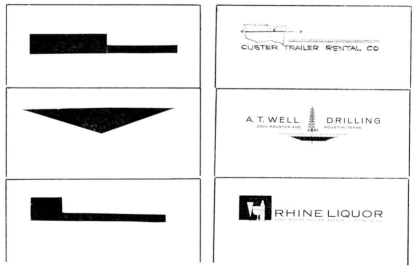

Examples are from the Fox River Paper Company's "Templa-Kit."

Fɪɢ. 9.5.   Several layout designs for letterheads.

Stock. Sulphite bond stock does not have rag content. It is very utilitarian, yet attractive enough for most letterheads. The bulk of all letterheads will be printed on this stock.

Rag content has some rag in it which makes it a better paper with a more distinctive finish. Your better customers will want this just for appearance mostly.

Erasable stock is preferred by some who like its easier-to-erase qualities. It is expensive, but again don't sell the price. Sell quality and distinction.

Layout. The new customer seldom has any idea what he wants or how he wants his letterhead to look. If he does, you're in luck. If he doesn't, don't panic when he says, "Design me a letterhead."

Layout is hard at first, but not the impossibility it seems. There are a few basic principles of all layout work; and even if you're not an artist you can place emblems, pictures, big type, lines, borders, until the letterhead looks different from the hackneyed name, address, and phone number.

Ask your customer what he wants on the letterhead, what kind of business it is, his name or the firm name, the address, and phone number. Be sure to get the right zip code. Ask if there are any em-

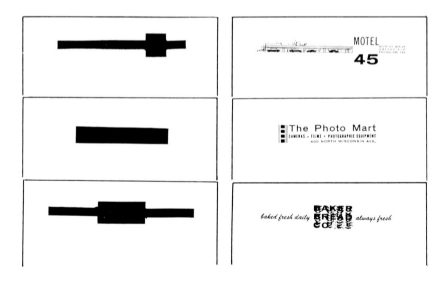

blems or pictures or identifying features of his business. This identifying feature may be the first step to building the letterhead design. Is there a letter, a picture, or one thing that symbolizes his business? Does he sell clothing, lumber, cows? Does the nature of the business lend itself to color?

Most letterheads fall into one of several basic designs. Figure 9.5 shows the commonest designs used.

Apply one of these basics to your customer. Look for your identifying feature. Choose type for the main line, then arrange the lesser information (phone, address, etc.). Try various combinations. Show it with additional color and without. Don't put too much on a letterhead; don't clutter too much along one side or the bottom.

When you're showing the letterhead to a customer, put it on a mounting like black paper or in a plastic sheet protector. Show the matching envelope at the same time, even if he didn't order envelopes. Be ready with the price. The best time to talk price is when the customer is seeing this layout for the first time. He's excited about his new letterhead, he is aware you have done extra work on it for him, and he is psychologically more prepared than he will be when next month's bills arrive.

All jobs are the customer's property. Print it like *he* wants it. If he wants to change to pink stock and purple ink, deliver just that.

★ ENVELOPES

Envelopes are one of the easiest jobs to print and easiest to handle. Nearly all of a letterhead's selling points apply to envelopes, too. Envelopes are sold not only as combination letterhead-envelope jobs, but also for statements, checks, vouchers, and on up to bigger clasp envelopes.

There is competition in envelope printing—including our good friend, the Government Printing Office. The GPO prints so cheaply none of us can compete on price, let alone counteract the stamp already being on the envelope! Numerous mail-order envelope houses can underprice us. We must contend with the rubber stamp business and those people who think a smudgy, slightly cockeyed rubber stamp imprint is a substitute for fine printing.

If you sell envelopes in combination with letterheads, put the main letterhead theme on the envelope. Omit all but the essentials to avoid cluttering. The phone number is not necessary on the envelope; seldom is the company slogan. You should always include the name of the firm; the one identifying feature of the business; the address, town, zip code.

Two-color envelopes are much more striking than one-color. So is colored or tinted stock.

If your customer wants more than one size envelope or letter-head, both sizes can be run at the same time at a slight savings to the customer. For example, 500 8½-by-11s and 500 8½-by-5½ letter-heads can be combined as consecutive pressruns. (Or 1,000 No. 10 envelopes and 500 No. 6¾ envelopes.) Only one small press change is necessary. The savings is small (Franklin says to deduct two dollars for two sizes of Class X envelopes), but it can be a selling point.

If you have a long, long run or special printing, ask your envelope company for a quote. They can probably print the envelope before it is put together much cheaper than you can buy the envelopes and print them.

★ BUSINESS CARDS

Business cards fall into a pattern that seems to be repeated over and over: One bold main line; three or four lines of telephone numbers, post office box numbers, street addresses and names; and a cut or company emblem.

The main line and the emblem or cut should dominate. In your layout put this line down first, then spot the other lines of smaller type underneath or in the corners around it. (The main line can actually go anywhere but usually it's in the center of the card.)

The emblem should identify the company or its product. Don't make this cut too big or it will be out of proportion.

If the emblem (or the main line) is in a different color, the card will look sharper.

Most cards are printed on an 88 or 88B size (1⅝ or 2-by-3⅜ or 3½). This size isn't quite such a horse blanket size, and fits a wallet easier.

The 63 card is 2¼-by-3¾ or 3⅞ and can accommodate more type, but it is an awkward size compared to the 88.

No matter how efficiently your shop can print business cards, the specialty houses may print them cheaper. It is true we can print to a customer's particular specifications, and we can print the cards faster. For the general run of business cards, though, look closely at your "deal" with the specialty houses. It can pay.

Cards can be round-cornered or square-cornered. The rounded corners are less formal, square-cornered cards a little more sophisticated. Vellum finish doesn't have the snap the smoother, plate-finish card has.

When you are printing with pictures (like campaign cards) choose the smoother finish.

Kromecoat is the smoothest finish of all. It takes more careful printing, but it has a brilliance hard to match.

Card stock can also double for tickets, passes, giveaways, or for anything where strength but not much type or size is needed.

★ CARDBOARD

The heavier papers of cardboard thickness have limited use so they are relatively uncomplicated. Signs and posters make up most of the work because these jobs require a paper stock that will take abuse.

Usually only two weights are needed, four-ply and six-ply. Six-ply has superior strength but creates some press running problems. If you can get by with the more flexible four-ply, you'll save your customer money.

My personal preference is to have the stock coated on both sides. In the old days many jobs were run off on a coated-one-side stock, but this one-side-white-one-side-gray looks old-fashioned anymore. The coated-two-sides speeds up printing and looks better in a window poster.

If you can, have your cut use up the sheet, especially in signs. Basic size is 22-by-28 so make your signs an even 7-by-11 or 5½-by-15 or 11-by-14. There's something traumatic about wasting part of a sheet of paper that costs 14 cents!

If the customer insists on an odd-size cut, charge him as if it were the next "right" size larger (i.e., 9-by-12 charges at 11-by-14).

★ SOCIAL STATIONERY

Social stationery makes use of two kinds of stock: a French fold sheet with or without envelope; or a special size card, paneled or plain, with or without envelopes. All social printing can be done on these two kinds of stock with various sizes of folders, cards and envelopes.

You must take extra care with this kind of work. A distinctive touch is the key. Choose fancy, flowery type and be generous with white space.

This is also the type of printing a specialty house does better. If your shop doesn't have a wedding invitation catalog, find an address from a trade magazine.

★ AUCTION BILLS

You should seldom sell a sale bill by itself. Here's one printing job that's a natural for a combination with advertising. If you don't talk advertising after you talk sale bill, you've missed a grand opportunity for profit.

Sale bills have always been notoriously dull printed jobs. We weekly printers need to jazz them up more, put more display, more detailed descriptions, more cuts (photos if possible), and more color. Sale bills already have great readership, we only need to give them more punch.

The trend is toward sale bills printed on some stock different than that old multicolored newsposter.

★ COVER STOCK

Cover stock jobs are divided into two sizes, 23-by-35 and 20-by-26. The 20-by-26 utilizes those 5-inch and 10-inch cuts (3-by-5, 6-by-10, 10-by-13); the 23-by-35 uses the 8½-by-11 base (5½-by-8½, 11½-by-17½).

Cover has such a wide variety of colors and textures you can have your choice of almost anything, but don't get carried away and fill your shelves with it. Pick out a basic stock, like a ripple, in several colors and concentrate average jobs on it. I keep a few kinds and colors of cover in stock, but not everything. When I want to splurge I have the fancy ones shipped to me.

Think color with cover and text stocks. There are some striking combinations.

★ BOOKLETS

Preparing a booklet job can be shattering. There's work in them; and the pile of copy, cuts, and blank pages often seems impossible to untangle.

Actually, it's not that tough. If you will make up a dummy of the booklet it goes easier. (Even a small generalized dummy will do; it needn't be detailed nor even exact size.) Mark page numbers on each page of the dummy so you can see what page number backs up the other.

Signatures are put together to make books and booklets. A signature is a number of pages printed on one sheet of paper; when the sheet is folded and bound these pages form a section of the booklet. A sheet printed with two pages on one side and two pages on the other, and then folded twice is a four-page signature.

The booklet has to come out in multiples of four. (A four-page, eight-page or twelve-page booklet.) If type won't fill the complete

Fig. 9.6.   A signature.

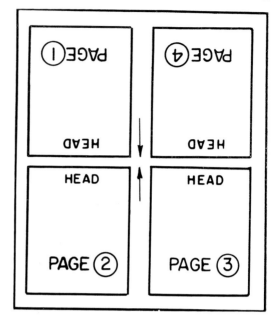

booklet, blank pages at the end must complete the necessary four-page signature.

Shoot the pages by signature if you can. Tape the pages together so stripping is easier. Always shoot head to head. Note the arrow in Figure 9.6.

Ask the customer if he wants a different kind of stock for the cover or if he prefers a "self cover" (stock the same all the way through). Many times you can sell him "up" to a better cover stock and a better job.

Don't overlook the two inside pages of the cover. On some jobs you can print on the two inside pages and save going to four more pages.

★ MANIFOLD SETS

When a job has more than one copy, or is in "sets," you have additional problems to consider. Order of colors is one problem. Traditionally in print shops, the original is white, the duplicate is canary, the triplicate pink, and additional copies either blue, green, or goldenrod. Your customer generally won't care if you stay with this "normal" order. It helps your stock supply since you won't have to keep as much around.

Binding is another extra consideration. You should always ask what the job is to be used for so you can know whether to perforate and bind in book form; or whether padding will be sufficient. Binding creates another question: Should it be heavy binding to stand some knocking around? If so, you'll use marbleboard. If the job doesn't need extra durability, you can use tag binding.

Perforations are also additional work. Be sure you and the printer understand which copy perforates and which copy stays in the book. If the job is perforated, it is probably numbered, too. When you are asking about numbering, find out which number to start with.

When books of manifold sets are made, carbons should be included in the back of each book. Your customers won't think of this, so you must. Bind them right into the book, perforate them so they are easy to tear out.

Stapling requires space; leave enough room on your form for the staples. This means off-centering the form, side to side or top to bottom. An extra half-inch will do. See Figure 9.7.

You should make sure your printers understand how the back

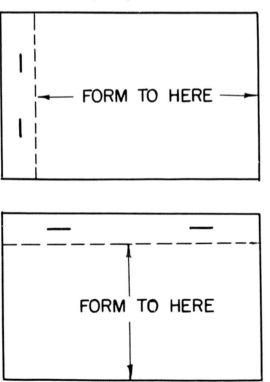

F𝚒ɢ. 9.7. Forms with staples at side, top.

If you print a form on
the back of this . . . .

..and you flip it over this way

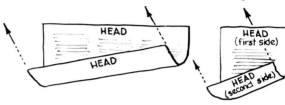

It is WORK and TURN

If you print both heads on top . . . .

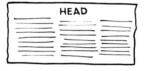

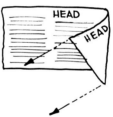

and turn it over from
right to left ,

It is WORK and TUMBLE

FIG. 9.8.   Work-and-turn and work-and-tumble forms.

of the form is to be printed. Learning what a work-and-tumble or
work-and-turn form is helps your instructions. See Figure 9.8.

★ NCR WORK

Manifold sets utilizing the NCR papers have unique problems.
Most important is making certain the coated sides of the papers

match (i.e., Coated Back [CB] going next to a Coated Front [CF], or a Coated Front and Back [CFB] in proper sequence). Backs must face Fronts or nothing happens.

Color sequence is even more important with NCR papers because the colors have to be coated right to be interchanged. If your customer wants a pink for the second copy it must be Coated Front and Back. If you have been using the pink for a triplicate, you probably have more CF pink on the shelf than CFB. In our smaller shops we can't stock all the various combinations without tying up money and risking loss of quality on the paper. So it is even more important to stay with "normal" sequence of colors.

You must explain NCR's sensitivity to your customer. NCR will not take punishment. The same characteristics that make it great (using pressure instead of carbon paper to transfer an image) creates a weakness in rough handling. A customer cannot write on the entire pad or book unless a piece of metal or heavy cardboard is slipped in front of the next set. Otherwise, the writing pressure on the top set goes all the way through to those on the bottom.

The best advice to a customer is to tear off the set from the pad and write on it by itself. Make sure he understands this. When it is impractical to do this (like in a book), show him how the metal plate or cardboard insert works.

You're a Businessman, Too

THE typical newspaperman probably won't take it as a compliment to be called an artist, a manufacturer, or a merchandiser. Yet, he is each of these, and he usually is all three at once.

EDMUND C. ARNOLD, *Modern Newspaper Design*

★

A COMMUNITY newspaper editor's busy day is not strictly newspapering, for he is also a small-town businessman.

The businessman, not the editor, pays the bills, signs the paychecks, agrees to the lease. The businessman invests in new equipment, watches the pennies, fires and hires. The businessman's instinct seeks price breaks, pays heed to freight rates, worries about taxes, keeps books, buys and sells typewriters and marking pens.

Newspapermen don't go into the weekly business to be businessmen, or because of the money involved. The profession calls, not the pay scale. Many editors would stay for less than they're getting.

But no newspaper can continue to publish the news, pictures, and advertising of a small community unless that newspaper also shows a profit. The editor brings his talents for journalism, his creative abilities to the weekly newspaper; the businessman's side of his nature, instinctive or acquired, brings the profit. It is a tribute to this distinguished profession that the weekly newsman can play both roles, striking this difficult balance of making a business profitable and a newspaper excellent and not have the two interfere with each other.

★ WHAT SHOULD YOUR NEWSPAPER BUSINESS DO?

Newspapering at the weekly level is an extremely lucrative business. You have one of the small town's best money-makers. The banker and some professional men like the doctor or the lawyer can make an income comparable to yours, but not many other businessmen will operate such a high profit business as your newspaper.

If your paper is between the $50,000–$100,000 gross volume class and is well managed, it should return a cash flow of approximately one-third of the gross. When you get to $100,000–$200,000 gross volume, the figure usually drops to 25 percent, according to Marion Krehbiel, Kansas newspaper broker and consultant.

In a National Newspaper Association survey conducted in 1966 among fifty-four newspapers with grosses from $36,000 to $222,000, the average net income including publisher's salary or draw was 17.9 percent.

The publisher of the average weekly newspaper, then, can expect to net approximately 20 percent before income taxes and after a decent management salary and 5 percent depreciation. Dailies do well to make 10–12 percent pre-tax as a maximum on the same basis, says Krehbiel, and semiweeklies will run 15 percent at best.

This kind of money for a small-town "executive" of any other kind of business is unusual.

The figures do not show another of your financial assets, the owner's license to write off some monthly costs as business expenses— the house phone, part of the gas, oil and upkeep on vehicles, certain donations, and other legitimate deductions which if you weren't boss you wouldn't get. It's all part of the publisher's take though it may not show in any statistical survey.

Why do newspapers make such good money?

• Advertising accounts for most of this profit making. With advertising we invest very little to realize high profits. Our creativity requires no monetary outlay. Our production expenses are fairly constant, but the amount of advertising that can be sold is seldom limited.

• We sell to the customer *outside* the shop. We go to him, not he to us. We exercise a control over our income most other retailers do not enjoy. They must wait for the customer to come in; we go to the customer ourselves. Our sales are limited only by our own abilities and energies.

• Newspapering sales are self-generating because we have a consistent, week-after-week reminder in the newspaper itself. Every

Thursday it appears from one end of town to the other. It is impossible to forget a newspaper that sells its importance every week. The crush of business that oftentimes appears on Thursdays is proof of this. My customers were reminded of a printing job, a subscription payment, an ad for next week by that day's paper.

• A newspaper is a quasi-public utility. Legal notices must appear in it. A paper is the best place for anybody to make an announcement. It is an authoritative, important part of the community.

• We have several outlets for profit making, not just one. We sell the basic subscription for our product. Then we sell advertising to put in our product. At the same time our shop can be manufacturing job work and selling it, buying office supplies wholesale and selling them retail. Finally, the law requires that certain legal notices appear in our newspapers. Statute sets the price and frequency and establishes our exclusive right of publication.

Making such money—and maybe more important, keeping it—isn't automatic. Management and business skill are needed. To realize and hold the profit a newspaper can make will depend upon your personal ability as a businessman, as a "good manager."

This sound business foundation is extremely important. No matter how fearless and courageous your paper is, no matter how brilliantly edited, black ink on newsprint depends on black ink in the cash ledger. Without financial security no newspaper can meet its Thursday morning. Lack of profit is the only calamity that can force a newspaper to miss a publication day. Hard-working, resourceful editors have cheated fires, floods, tornadoes, personal illness to get out a week's edition. But lack of money can still a press forever. We must make the business pay.

★ GOOD MANAGEMENT

The good manager is both a hustler and a miser. I have to figure out ways to make more money. At the same time I have to watch spending and hold down expenses. Both are important and dependent upon each other. If I sell more but spend too much in giving away color, hiring more help, or buying more machinery, I haven't helped my financial condition. If I hold expenses too tight on a potential sales force, or if I'm too cautious and too pessimistic, I may stifle a chance for good profits.

Good management requires the ability to see the possibilities of increasing the income while controlling the outgo. You're not managing properly if you concentrate on one or the other.

★ INCOME

Advertising dominates the income side of the ledger. In a 1966 national survey by the National Newspaper Association and Newspaper Association Managers, Inc., here is the way income was broken down on weekly newspapers:

INCOME	1965 AVERAGE	1966 AVERAGE
	%	
Local advertising	45.0	45.3
National advertising	5.3	4.5
Classified advertising	10.4	6.5
Legal advertising	3.6	4.0
TOTAL ADVERTISING	64.3	60.3
Circulation	10.4	8.2
Commercial printing	21.2	27.4
Miscellaneous (including office supplies, machines)	4.1	4.1
	35.7	39.7
TOTAL INCOME	100	100

Push Advertising and Job Work. The quickest, most profitable way to generate more income is to push advertising. Our fixed expenses of newspaper publishing create an ideal way to return high profit through advertising. You and I must pay the help whether they're setting ad guts or straight matter. Whether we have 40 percent ads or 60 percent ads in a 12-page paper, newsprint costs are the same. The rent goes on; electricity costs are unchanged. We don't buy any new material; we don't invest in any new stock. So when we run a 60 percent advertising–news ratio in a 12-page paper instead of a 40 percent, we've made ourselves some fine profit. (If an 8-column-by-21 newspaper has a one dollar rate, the additional revenue from this 60 percent 12-pager as against a 40 percent one is $403. It takes a lot of pencil sales in a week's time to net that much.) In selling office supplies or printing job work, we must spend more money to make money. We buy material to resell. In advertising our stock is there, waiting to be sold.

Job work is the logical partner with most weeklies. It dovetails with newspapering and keeps employees and machinery more productive at the week's end. There is money in it, but remember newspapering is king and job work should complement, not compete.

Office Supplies. You can make extra money if you put in a stock of office supplies—desks, chairs, typewriters, ledgers, bookkeeping aids, adding machine tape, papers. But I would do it only in desperation.

The office supply business is much like job work in being a low markup operation; but even more than job work, for the money earned you will inherit a disproportionate amount of troubles:

- You'll have to fight shoplifting and damage loss.
- You'll inherit retail business headaches that the rest of your operation won't have.
- You won't be big enough to take advantage of volume buying, freight shipments. (If you're that big, you'd better divorce it from your newspaper.)
- As a sideline business, when it draws too much of your time away from advertising and newspapering, it loses you money.
- You must wait too long for your money to turn over.
- Time is needed to order, to wait on customers. If you have to hire help just to take care of the office supply business, again you're putting emphasis on the wrong part of your operation.

Small newspapers who saturate small trade territories with advertising sometimes turn to office supplies as a boost for the gross. If you have an exclusive in your town (or if giving up what business you have will help a competing throwaway hang on), you probably can show a profit. Office furniture has a double-your-money mark up, register forms sold once will be repeat business for a long time, portable typewriters, adding machines and cut paper are steady sources of revenue. But it is tough work for the profit and it also takes you or your staff away from that always lucrative advertising.

If you do jump into the office supply business, you can make more money if you won't put your inventory too high. Turn a small inventory over more times, and order to take care of normal needs. Keep turning those staple items (typewriter ribbons, bookkeeping forms, adding machine paper) over and over. This involves more ordering and more messing around, but you don't tie up as much money and you don't get caught with shelves of outdated merchandise.

Always Keep Selling. Sell every chance you get, not only just in your paper. Put some "sell" on your subscription notices, in your front window. Never let the bills go out alone each month. Include some sales pitch with them. Twelve times a year a merchant opens an envelope from you; each time you should send along a message about your newspaper, job printing, office supplies.

Be conscious of your "store front" image, both outside and inside.

Don't let your front office windows clutter up. Put something in them that will sell and change it often. Break away from the old printing office stigma with the cluttered rolltop desk and the faded newspapers aging in the corner. Modern customers want to be sold by a modern business. It's all part of the selling.

This is a good place to point out that entering newspaper contests not only brings recognition for you and your paper's quality, but it helps "sell" the paper to the community. A newspaper's recognition is recognition for the town as well. If you're a winner in contests you gain new respect and new friends, besides the trophies.

★ EXPENSES

The National Newspaper Association and Newspaper Association Managers, Inc., which provided the income figures on page 197, also provided these expense averages from the 1966 survey:

EXPENDITURES	1965 AVERAGE	1966 AVERAGE
	%	
Office salaries (all except publisher's salary)	19.3	16.5
Shop wages	24.1	22.9
Materials (paper, ink, etc.)	15.7	18.5
Depreciation	4.1	4.0
Taxes (all except income)	2.3	2.6
All other expenses	22.2	22.1
TOTAL EXPENSE	87.7	86.6
Net income, including publisher's salary	12.3	13.4
	100	100
Adjusted net, minus publisher's salary*	7.6	8.2

* Modest sums, varying in each of six circulation categories are deducted to ascertain a true net income.

Just as one kind of revenue (advertising) dominates income, one kind of outgo (wages) dominates expenses. Almost half our outgo ends up in wages.

Wages are also the hardest expense to control and the one expense you cannot retrieve. If I order too much printing paper, I will eventually use it up. If I overspend on merchandise, I'll eventually sell it, even if at cost. Wages, though, once spent are an expense forever.

This is the reason I set a definite limit, a maximum per week for time worked by each employee (perhaps 35 or 40 hours). An employee has a human tendency to put in extra time unnecessarily. If he is on a limit of 35 hours and knows he will not be paid for any more hours, that's all he will work. He seldom volunteers extra time. If he's allowed to work as many hours as he likes, he will likely put in more time than he would under a set weekly time limit. Extra time is not often productive time.

Abuse of overtime stems from this same tendency to pad. An employee, knowing he can go on to overtime, will take a surprisingly longer time to do the job than if he has to be done by five o'clock at no extra pay. He'll make work in order to earn the overtime.

Unnecessary overtime costs like this and nonproductive extra time are the biggest expense drains a paper has.

The Time Clock. Going to a time clock was the best management move we ever made with employees. It gave the company an absolutely accurate permanent record of time worked.

Since time cards were figured on the minute basis, the time clock rewarded employees who came early and worked late. It punished those who punched in late and left early. It prevented all misunderstandings about hours put in. It developed incentives for good work habits among the employees. And it saved us money!

Time clock companies have an impressive direct mail advertisement which shows by a chart how much five minutes of "lost time" per day costs your company in a year. This chart shows that five minutes lost time per employee costs your company $850 annually if you have ten employees at two dollars per hour (based on 8-hour day, 5-day week, 255 working days per year, overhead cost taken equal to hourly rate).

Though you may hesitate at first to spoil your family-type operation, you'll wonder, after you put in a time clock, why you waited so long. It's invaluable to management.

If you don't use a time clock, work employees on a regular-hour basis as much as possible. People work better under a set eight-to-five or nine-to-six schedule instead of a loose arrangement of "be here some time after eight." The reason you lose on sloppy hours is because of the human tendency to start the day any old time but not to work past the whistle. The employee is much more miffed at working fifteen minutes after the whistle blows than coming fifteen minutes early. Yet technically he owes you the time. This bookkeeping of what time he owes and what he's paid is impossible, so it's better to set a regular time for him.

Wage Projections. The best control over wages is a projection of what you hope wages will be for the year.

At the start of every new fiscal year, I make as accurate a wage projection as I can, going back through the payroll records to determine how many average hours were worked, how long the employee has been at that wage, how the actual expenditure for wages compared to my projection of last year. I anticipate wage raises and estimate if the new year will bring an additional workload.

I break down this yearly projection into monthly pay periods and check these projected figures against the actual expenditures *every* month. This projection gives me an aiming point for my wage expense and rings the bell as soon as it goes over.

Breaking Down Your Other Expenses. The rest of the expenses can be broken down into separate categories. I detail expenses to keep track of expenditures by department. Here's the list I use:

> Officers' salaries
> Regular salaries
> Payroll taxes
> Other taxes
> Rent or lease expense
> Newsprint expense
> Merchandise expense
> Office expense
> Printing expense
> Newspaper expense
> Repairs
> Freight and postage
> Insurance
> Accounting and legal expense
> Utilities and telephone
> Automobile expense
> Dues and subscriptions
> Correspondents
> Donations
> Interest
> Travel and entertainment
> Advertising
> Miscellaneous

At the year's end, we add depreciation and bad debts, but we don't project these. With this breakdown we can prorate exact costs to various departments.

Under the "office expense" we lump all services or material which affect the operation of the office (i.e., towel service, cleaning, light bulbs).

Under "newspaper expense" we put those costs incurred in publishing the newspaper (i.e., materials, ad services, photography expenses).

"Printing" has all those costs of job printing paper, job inks, or actual costs to produce job work.

You can also group these by "fixed expenses" and "variable expenses." Those expenses which would depend on how much business was done (newsprint and printing, for instance), ones which you have some control over, would be variable expenses. Fixed expenses would be the rent and taxes, those which tend to remain the same year after year.

Expense Projections. Projections of these expenses are made exactly as I did the wage projections. First I obtain last year's exact expenditures, then estimate if this year's will be any higher or lower. After this is done for several years, a definite pattern evolves and you can accurately project a year's expenses. Projections give you a map to follow. Knowing ahead of time what you are "supposed to spend" tends to hold the actual expenditure to that.

Your expenses should level off except for those variable expenses like printing and newsprint which will go up in proportion to the volume. The less fluctuation in expenses, the more money you will make. A drastic fluctuation is a red flag—something is out of kilter.

Plug Those Holes. Money leaves a business in little dribbles; to have a good business you must plug the holes. Buy in quantity whenever you can. Take advantage of prepaid shipments. Paying for minimum weight shipments (50 pounds of paper shipped in the 100-pound minimum) is expensive.

Don't take money out of the cash drawer for personal expenses even though it may be your own money eventually. Treat the business money as if it were someone else's. Account for every dollar.

Discount your bills. That 2 percent cash discount by the tenth adds up. In a year's time, you can't earn $80 any cheaper than by discounting $4,000 worth of paper.

Don't be too generous about donating work or doing it for less pay. If you don't make money with it, it costs you!

Keep your ad rates up where they should be. Don't be caught with the same ad rate while expenses go up. Ditto for subscription rates and job printing prices.

Utility bills should be nearly constant year after year. Any sudden jump or fluctuation warrants investigation.

Periodically check your Franklin Catalog to make certain your "grade cost" on paper keeps up with current prices.

Consolidate orders. Spreading out orders to various salesmen costs money. If you want to split your business with them, buy in quantity, not a ream at a time.

Donate as you feel you should to the dozens of groups and people who ask, but don't be fooled into thinking that the "business is donating." *You* are shelling out, right out of your pocket.

Don't pay on too many installments at once. Credit buying is necessary for most of us but carrying charges, interest, and extra insurance costs compound.

Watch excessive long-distance telephoning. A letter is still cheaper than a phone call, and those phone bills can mount up. If you must phone and you're not sure your party is at home, call person to person; and remember direct dialing is cheaper than going through the operator.

Don't succumb to the new-machinery bug. Don't buy a press for every job, a timesaver gimmick for every task.

Keep in mind that supplies like darkroom chemicals and ink can be purchased cheaper in bulk quantities.

Find out from all your suppliers where the prepaid freight allowance is (e.g., ten cartons of envelopes may arrive prepaid).

Don't buy paper in broken package lots unless it's for a special job. You can buy one full package for the same price as two-thirds of a broken package. Consult your catalogs to see where the quantity price breaks are. Ten reams of $8\frac{1}{2}$-by-11 cut paper may carry a 30 percent discount, but twenty reams might be 40 percent.

★ EMPLOYEES

The best newspaper help you can find is you and your wife. That's only two, though, and unless yours is a very small-circulation paper, you'll need more hands than that.

This hiring of other people will bring more complications and cost more money in your newspaper operation than anything else. There will be times when 90 percent of your troubles would be over if you could only settle employee problems.

Newspapermen have the normal complications of other working people. Add to this misery the demanding work of our profession and the limited source of skilled help in our communities. Weekly newspaper help is not readily found or easily taught. Even though offset has cut down the amount of trained help we need, we still can't easily find ad salesmen, printers, photographers, and reporters. A small town has a constant pool of mechanics, hay hands, clerks, truck drivers, secretaries. To supply his staff, the weekly editor must often go outside the area for experienced personnel. Or he must start a local person in a long, expensive apprenticeship.

Deadlines and peaked workloads compound the problem further. You don't simply open the doors from eight-to-five Monday through Saturday. A week's work on the newspaper goes into three days. Enough help must be there for the peak; the paper can't wait for another week. It comes out this Thursday and the one after and the one after. It's Christmas rush and haying season bunched together from one Wednesday to the next, week to week.

We need good help—and we find it, surprisingly enough. But there is constant challenge to keep ahead of it, to eliminate the friction and the unpleasantness, to stimulate learning and progress and encourage stability among your employees.

Handling of personnel properly will be your biggest challenge in management. Here are some things you learn after being boss awhile:

• You cannot afford too much help. Being overstaffed cuts deep into the net profit.

• On the other hand, you can't afford too little or too cheap help either. Being understaffed is as expensive sometimes as being overstaffed. Untrained help may be lower priced, but lack of speed, mistakes, and slowing production for explanations all cost money. When you can't deliver the job or put out your kind of newspaper, your potential profit is cut, and you invite competition. You aren't producing for the customer. You may be tying yourself to unprofitable detail work when you should be selling. Overstaffing cuts the net profit to the business by skimming the top; understaffing cuts the profit by stifling it.

• When you figure employee costs, add the extras, too. You may hire a man for $100 a week but you'll also pay your share of his social security tax, workman's compensation, unemployment, and other taxes. If you have an employee's retirement plan or a hospital program, add that, too.

• Pay the help promptly. Pick out one day (usually the end of the week) to pay everyone, then don't forget. Don't make an employee ask for his check each week; it's embarrassing for the employee, and needless.

• Employees' problems are usually not about newspapering. They're personal problems—sickness, family problems, injured feelings, private troubles. Many times what appears to be insubordination is only an employee worried about something outside the office. You may find yourself as much adviser as boss.

• A boss cannot talk to one employee about another (foreman excepted) without creating friction. The employee who listens to a boss talking about a fellow employee isn't fooled into thinking the boss won't talk about him with someone else.

• Training help is costly. Some publishers refuse to do so. They search for trained help; pay accordingly. Most of us have no choice but to take the apprentice when we would have preferred the trained man. But hiring apprentices to save money is false economy. You are teaching newspapering when you should be running the business, and apprentices are notoriously rough with machinery. Until they're trained, they don't earn their keep.

• Don't chastise help in front of customers or other help. Whatever has to be said can be said in more private—and cooler—times.

• A mistake in the office by an employee should be presented outside the office as a mistake by the office, not by any one individual—"our" mistake, not "his."

• Pinch pennies, but don't be cheap. Employees become more upset over being denied some little convenience because of "economy" than in doing a little extra work.

• As boss, admit your own mistakes. The employees already know them anyway. Nothing a boss does is more foolish than to pretend he can never make mistakes.

• Keep overtime at a minimum; let help go home as soon as the work is done and they'll get it done sooner. Normally, employees would rather have time off than extra pay. They want more leisure rather than more pay.

• Let employees be part of the paper. Let them know what you're planning, what you hope to do. Encourage their participation; hold regular staff meetings.

• Encourage employees to learn new skills, to take more responsibility, to increase their capacity for production.

• Employees want good working conditions and responsibility more than high wages. More people quit working because of the boss, the office clique, the lack of stimulation than because wages aren't high enough.

• Insist employees take vacations, coffee breaks, and extra time off after night work.

• Don't contribute to a front office-backshop feud by taking sides. Don't encourage it among your employees.

• Give employees credit for knowing something. Newspaper employees like to contribute to the creative work of the profession.

• Listen to all ideas by employees. One of the most frustrating experiences of a newspaper employee is to have someone stifle his creativity. Encourage his interest and his ideas. "He never listens to my ideas," says an employee who has been cut deeply.

• Don't conceal your displeasure. Be honest with your criticism, and keep it current. Bottled up irritation shows in other ways; the employee is baffled by your curtness and sharpness without ever knowing why. He can't correct his mistakes if he never knew he made them.

• Don't be afraid to ask your employees' help. If they think they can help you personally or can contribute in a real way to the newspaper's welfare, they'll work harder. They take a personal interest in helping you.

• Don't cower before the knowledge of backshop personnel because they know the mechanical part of the newspaper better than the boss does. *You* should run the paper and *you* alone. Be firm in your convictions, but not bullheaded.

• Be aware of possible personnel changes in August and September, those traditional moving times.

• Don't mistrust advice or criticism just because it comes from an employee (particularly a backshop employee). The employee's practical knowledge about his job specialty makes him invaluable. Encourage his initiative.

• Recognize an employee's extra work. He won't mind the additional hours if the boss recognizes his after-hour efforts. It is frustrating when a boss is oblivious to your long hours.

• Don't be too lenient with employees. Be understanding and compassionate but be firm, too. They must understand you are boss.

• Check back on an employee to see if he is doing what you want done, or whether he has gone back to his old way. Insist the employee follow the method *you* want.

• Hiring more than one person from a family always causes complications. If you're dissatisfied with the son's work, the mother's attitude toward you is affected; when you let the son go, the mother may go, too.

• Hire good people and pay them more than they're worth. Pay help enough. Don't hesitate to financially reward their efforts to improve your operation. It depends on the employee. Overpay a good employee and you stimulate his enthusiasm and interest. Overpay a poor one and you indulge him.

• Encourage youngsters to work in journalism. You can observe child labor laws and still stimulate younger citizens toward journalism. A high school boy with an interest in journalism can someday wind up as your editor!

•Be tolerant; don't expect your help to work as dedicatedly and as hard as you will. Understand human failings and human feelings. Ben Franklin once penned some advice in *Poor Richard's Almanac* about wives which could go for employees too: "Keep your eyes wide open before marriage and half shut afterward."

★ YOUR BOOKKEEPING SYSTEM

Nothing else will tell us how our newspapers are doing like a good bookkeeping system will. You may think a small, one-horse book-keeping system is good enough for your business; but it isn't. Every business, no matter how small, needs a good set of books and a boss who understands what they are all about.

Nothing in your business can hide from good bookkeeping. At the same time, there is nothing that *can't* be hidden in a poor set of books. If bookkeeping isn't properly done, or if the system is shoddy and sloppy, you won't learn anything from it; from a good system, you can learn whatever you want.

A businessman will say, "I just keep books for Uncle Sam." He's wrong. He is keeping books *for himself*. I never used to think I had the time to mess with bookkeeping. I had books kept as a matter of record only. I didn't use them as a tool to find out if one part was losing more than another or to wonder about that large amount of cash long. I slopped through cash balancing, check numbers, posting totals. I had a record all right; but that was all, and I'm not sure now it was even a correct record.

A double entry bookkeeping system exercises strict control of your business. Errors are detected in posting, charging, and check writing. You are protected against wrong entry since everything must balance, and you get protection against misuse or theft of funds.

If you don't want to be deeply involved with bookkeeping or don't have the staff for it, you should let an accountant keep your books. After a long experience of doing it myself and teaching new bookkeepers (or changing over self-taught ones), I would advise pub-lishers of any size newspapers to turn over as much as you can to a regular accountant. I'm convinced it pays. He can free you personally from much strain. You will still have a bookkeeper to do regular bookwork chores, payroll, cash sheets, and tickets, but the professional accountant does the rest. He can eliminate that time-consuming de-tail work and the frustrations of trying to balance. He puts order in your office by insisting the books be kept up, the information he needs furnished on a set schedule.

A Checklist. To help you keep track of your business, you should regularly check the books. Here is a list of some important things to look for:

1. What was the income this year as compared to last year at this time? For each category?
2. How did the expense totals for each category compare with the projected totals? Was there any department especially out of line, either up or down?
3. Were the accounts receivable higher than last month?
4. How many past due accounts moved into the ninety-day-and-over status?
5. Was the cash on hand long or short? Was it off by a large amount? What is the total cash long or short for the year so far?
6. Were there any large paid-outs? Were the paid-outs out of line?
7. Did the total for the month's wages exceed the projection?
8. Did the accounts payable go down or up?
9. What were the overtime figures for the month?
10. What was the net profit or loss for the month?

If anything is out of line in these, you should be sharp enough to recognize the red flag when it goes up!

Regular Reports. Use bookkeeping's figures to show you how the business is doing. Every month, or at least every quarter, all the income figures should be compared with last year; all the expense totals should be run against the projections and the over/under computed. The expenses should be compared with last year. If your books are properly kept, you should be able to run a profit and loss and a current financial statement at the end of any period.

If you split your expenses as they should be and can compute your salaries by department, you can run a profit and loss statement for each department.

Your accounts receivable should be aged by current status, thirty-day, sixty-day, ninety-day-and-over, and in your hands by the start of each month.

Your accounts payable list should be brought up-to-date and totalled at least by the fifteenth.

Compare your lineage figures with last year's for the same period.

You should know what is in all your bank accounts at any time.

Keep the Figures for Several Years. You'll be interested in watching records of both income and expenses for several years back.

This record can be easily posted in a big ledger utilizing blue ink for the monthly totals and red ink for the annual totals. Just a glance will give you the income or expense picture for a three- or four-year span.

Accrual vs. Cash. Your method of accounting will probably be accrual rather than the cash method. Accruing expenses and income registers the amount in the month it was incurred, not when the actual money came in or went out of the business. You put in an ad for Jones Drug in March. Revenue from this ad was accrued in March, even though Jones didn't pay for the ad until April.

In the cash method you would have counted the income for the ad in April when it was paid, not when it was accrued.

Expenses work the same way. You buy some printing paper in March. This is a March expense, accrued in March. You actually pay for it in April. Under the cash method it would have counted as an expense in April.

The accrual method is more accurate since you know exactly where the business stands.

In the cash method if you don't pay your bills for ninety days this gives the business a false picture. You are actually behind on those expenses but they don't show until they are paid. When your accounts payable are current all the time and your accounts receivable aren't too far behind, it won't matter so much.

Just remember, with the accrual method you pick up the income or the expense *as it was incurred,* not as it was paid.

Those Pesky Debits and Credits. If debits and credits bother you in double entry bookkeeping, remember the jingle, "Debit that which comes in; credit that which goes out." In the Cash on Hand account, you debit all the cash received (that which comes in) and credit the deposits (that which goes out). In the Cash in the Bank account, you debit all deposits (that which comes in) and credit all checks written (that which goes out). For every debit in the books there must be a credit to offset it.

The accounts receivable total at the beginning of the month—plus the charges, less the received on account—*must equal* the total of the accounts receivable at the start of the next month.

The accounts payable total at the start of the month—plus the current accrued account payables less the paid on account—*must equal* the accounts payable at the start of the next month.

DAILY CASH and CHARGE SUMMARY

CASH

For _____, 19 ___

Amt. Received	Local Adv.	Nat'l Adv.	Merchandise (Taxable)	Merchandise (Non-taxable)	Printing (Taxable)	Printing (Non-taxable)	Want-Ads	Legals	Subscriptions	Tax	Other Income	ROA	Deposits	For	Pd. Outs Amt.

CHARGES

Amt. Charged	Local Adv.	Nat'l Adv.	Merchandise (Taxable)	Merchandise (Non-taxable)	Printing (Taxable)	Printing (Non-taxable)	Want-Ads	Legals	Subscriptions	Tax	Other Income
Combined Totals											

Cash on hand at start of day _____

PLUS Cash received _____

PLUS Received on account _____

EQUALS Total Cash received _____

LESS Cash deposited _____

LESS Paid outs _____

EQUALS Cash on hand at end of day _____

Your count of cash on hand _____

Long _____

Short _____

Fig. 10.1. A daily cash sheet that works.

Balancing the Cash. The cash should be counted and balanced by someone every day, if possible. See Figure 10.1 for an example of a good form. This checklist seems to help those who balance:

> Cash on hand at the start of the day
> *plus* cash received
> *plus* received on account
> *less* cash deposited
> *less* paid-outs
> *equals* cash on hand at end of day.
>   Your count of cash on hand: Long _____
>   Short _____

Keeping an Accounts Payable Journal. An accounts payable journal was too much bother before I started keeping one. Now I wish I had always had one.

Check all your invoices and bill totals, post every statement total in the accounts payable journal (even if you can't pay the bill that month), post every payment by check number, and keep a current balance of each account.

This gives you a complete picture on every account you owe, when accrued, when paid, by what check number, the balance remaining. When all balances are added, you have your current accounts payable total.

Keeping this up each month provides an easy way to run an accounts payable total and an up-to-date record of what you paid, what you owe.

Books You Should Keep. If you set up your own bookkeeping system, you should have:
1. An Income Journal to register all income.
2. A Disbursement Journal to show where the money went when the checks were written.
3. An Accounts Payable Journal to keep track of who you owe and how much.
4. A General Ledger where the monthly summaries from the above journals are entered.

Ask an accountant to help. He will have good advice.

Your Financial Statement. A financial statement gathers together all your bookkeeping information in one place and shows you the worth and business success of your operation. Figures 1.2, 10.3, and 10.4

THE WEEKLY PRESS
Financial Statement
July 1, 1971 – June 30, 1972

ASSETS

Current Assets

Cash on Hand   --Total from cash register

Cash in Bank   --Total in bank as per bank
                                            statement

Accounts Receivable   --Money owed by customers

Inventory   --Count of paper, ink, merchandise

Fixed Assets

                          Cost   Depreciation   Book Value
Machinery & Equipment
Furniture & Fixtures   _____   _____   _____
                          (A)   (B)   (C)

   (A) Total of what equipment cost you
   (B) What has been depreciated off this total so far
   (C) How much its "book worth" is after depreciation

Other Assets

Other Investments   --Your outside investments

Prepaid Taxes   --A year's insurance premium
                                            is paid ahead and used up
Prepaid Insurance   month by month. That por-
                                            tion still left is an asset.
                                            Same with taxes.

Goodwill   --Not usually included unless
                                            actually paid for at time of
                                            purchase

FIG. 10.2.   How to prepare and read a financial statement.

LIABILITIES

Current Liabilities

Accounts Payable --Money owed by you to trade creditors

Accrued Sales Tax --That portion of sales tax owed but not yet paid

Accrued Interest --That portion of interest owed but not paid yet

Current Portion of Debt --That portion of installment payments due within one year (as differentiated between total due)

Total Current Liabilities

Long Term Liabilities

	Due within One Year	Due after One Year
First National	_____ (A)	_____ (B)

(A) Total goes above in current assets
(B) Total goes in outside column as total long term debt

CAPITAL & NET WORTH

Authorized Capital Stock --Refers to the par value of the stock (if corporation)

Retained Earnings --Amount of profit left in business from previous year

or

Retained Loss --Amount of loss carried over from previous year

Profit (or Loss) from Period --Figures carried over from next sheet show income and expenses. This figure is either added or subtracted from retained earnings and retained loss.

ASSETS

Current Assets

Cash on Hand	$ 115.32	
Cash in Bank	3,529.56	
Accounts Receivable	20,909.83	
Inventory	16,000.00	
Total Current Assets		$40,554.71

Fixed Assets

	Cost	Depreciation	Book Value	
Machinery & Equipment	$73,509.00	$3,903.99	69,605.01	
Furniture & Fixtures	11,285.00	255.06	11,029.94	
	84,794.00	4,159.05		
Total Fixed Assets				80,634.95

Other Assets

Prepaid Insurance	500.00	
Other Investments	15,000.00	
Goodwill	10,000.00	
Total Other Assets		25,500.00
TOTAL ASSETS		$146,689.66

LIABILITIES, CAPITAL AND NET WORTH

Accounts Payable	11,885.10	
Notes Payable	1,500.00	
Accrued Interest	2,117.19	
Accrued Payroll Taxes	1,789.45	
Current Portion of Debt (see below)	2,437.00	
Total Current Liabilities		19,728.74

Long Term Liabilities	Due within One Year	Due after One Year	
First National	2,437.00	15,000.00	
Total Long Term Liabilities			15,000.00

CAPITAL

Capital Stock at Par Value (100 shares @ $1,000.00)	$100,000.00
Earnings for Period	11,960.92
TOTAL LIABILITIES, CAPITAL, AND NET WORTH	$146,689.66

214

THE WEEKLY PRESS
Statement of Income and Expenses
for July 1, 1971 – June 30, 1972

Income:

Display Advertising	$62,486.00	
National Advertising	2,231.00	
Legal Advertising	6,357.00	
Classified Advertising	1,636.00	
Job Printing	25,696.00	
Merchandise	2,818.00	
Circulation	12,133.00	
Other Income	1,505.00	
Total Income		$114,862.00

Expenses:

Officers' Salaries	7,000.00	
Regular Salaries	32,860.00	
Payroll Taxes	3,000.00	
Other Taxes	1,567.00	
Rent, Lease	2,400.00	
Newsprint	15,000.00	
Merchandise	1,350.00	
Office Expense	816.00	
Printing Expense	8,450.00	
Newspaper Expense	12,060.00	
Repairs	417.00	
Freight, Postage	2,400.00	
Insurance	1,117.00	
Legal, Accounting	470.00	
Utilities	3,800.00	
Auto Expense	275.00	
Dues, Subscriptions	65.00	
Correspondents	1,291.00	
Donations	55.00	
Interest	1,896.00	
Travel, Entertainment	1,140.00	
Advertising	25.00	
Miscellaneous	286.00	
Depreciation	4,159.05	
Bad Debts	1,003.87	
Total Expenses		102,902.92
Profit for Period		$ 11,960.92

Fig. 10.3. Completed financial statement.

215

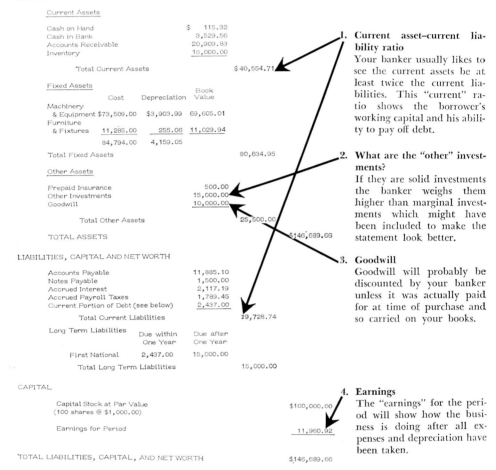

THE WEEKLY PRESS
at the end of business
June 30, 1972

ASSETS

Current Assets

Cash on Hand	$	115.32
Cash in Bank		3,529.56
Accounts Receivable		20,909.83
Inventory		16,000.00
Total Current Assets		$40,554.71

Fixed Assets

	Cost	Depreciation	Book Value
Machinery & Equipment	$73,509.00	$3,903.99	69,605.01
Furniture & Fixtures	11,285.00	255.06	11,029.94
	84,794.00	4,159.05	
Total Fixed Assets			80,634.95

Other Assets

Prepaid Insurance	500.00
Other Investments	15,000.00
Goodwill	10,000.00
Total Other Assets	25,500.00
TOTAL ASSETS	$146,689.66

LIABILITIES, CAPITAL AND NET WORTH

Accounts Payable	11,885.10
Notes Payable	1,500.00
Accrued Interest	2,117.19
Accrued Payroll Taxes	1,789.45
Current Portion of Debt (see below)	2,437.00
Total Current Liabilities	19,728.74

Long Term Liabilities	Due within One Year	Due after One Year
First National	2,437.00	15,000.00
Total Long Term Liabilities		15,000.00

CAPITAL

Capital Stock at Par Value (100 shares @ $1,000.00)	$100,000.00
Earnings for Period	11,960.92
TOTAL LIABILITIES, CAPITAL, AND NET WORTH	$146,689.66

1. Current asset–current liability ratio
Your banker usually likes to see the current assets be at least twice the current liabilities. This "current" ratio shows the borrower's working capital and his ability to pay off debt.

2. What are the "other" investments?
If they are solid investments the banker weighs them higher than marginal investments which might have been included to make the statement look better.

3. Goodwill
Goodwill will probably be discounted by your banker unless it was actually paid for at time of purchase and so carried on your books.

4. Earnings
The "earnings" for the period will show how the business is doing after all expenses and depreciation have been taken.

FIG. 10.4.   What the banker looks at in your financial statement.

show how a financial statement works and how it can look.

The machinery total is notoriously low for newspapers (see Figure 10.4) since we use a comparatively small investment to produce a large cash flow. The cash flow figure is a more accurate barometer of our business than what our investment in machinery is.

This cash flow is one of newspaper's prime assets. It shows how much cash you are generating in your business. To determine cash flow you subtract the gross expenses from the gross income. This is gross profit, or cash flow. Your cash flow can be $40,000 before you pay yourself, before principal payments, before depreciation, although your "earnings for the period" on your financial statement may show only $5,000. When talking with your banker make certain you have your "cash flow" figures.

Income and Expenses from Figure 10.4 (Statement of Income and Expenses) can be separated into departments if you have split expenses that way (i.e., job printing wages separated from newspaper wages).

★ COLLECTING PAST DUE BILLS

There is no excuse why we newspapers put our accounts receivable in such a mess. We should be able to keep our customers current, and I think we would if collecting wasn't such a disagreeable task.

You need to institute an automatic collecting system that immediately picks up the delinquent account, reminds him at fifteen-day intervals of his delinquent status, charges interest at the end of a specified period and grows progressively nastier until the customer pays.

Fortunately for the newspaper business, nearly all of our accounts are with other businessmen whose credit rating is above average. However, enough of the slow-pay kind merits our finding a system of collection.

When you're trying to collect owed money, a system that moves on a beginning delinquency quickly is the most successful. Your delinquent customer has to be convinced each day that you are just getting ready to pick up the phone to call him. It is most important that he knows you know about the bill. Many debtors believe if no one hollers about the account, the "guy doesn't need it yet."

First, we should try to understand this debtor. Although we're all afraid of offending him by asking for our money, he really won't be offended. Some will *expect* you to collect the bill in person. They'll wait for you to come around instead of volunteering payment themselves. Usually he won't trade with you until his account is paid up again. All the while he's owed you money he has probably paid someone else cash. The secret is not to let an account go unpaid too long. The longer it's unpaid, the harder it is to collect, and the more

money you've lost from the debtor who's taking his business elsewhere.
So go after it.

The best time to start collecting is when the account moves past
thirty days. We devised a system of constant reminders as the delinquent account moved through to ninety days. These reminders grew
increasingly tougher and ended with the ninety-day-old account being
turned over for collection. We discovered waiting too long to collect
was only more difficult. An account should never go ninety days. The
constant reminding brought results.

Here is the system we use:

1. We send out the regular bill at the end of the month as usual.
2. We send the second bill at the end of the second month showing the balance due.
3. A reminder is sent on the fifteenth of the third month, giving
   the past due balance, plus the current balance.
4. If still not paid, a letter or call is made on the tenth of the
   fourth month. The letter is a form letter asking if there is
   some reason why the account hasn't been paid and if we may
   expect payment soon.
5. A final, tougher letter is sent on the thirtieth of the fourth
   month informing the customer that the account, if not paid,
   will be turned over for collection within ten days.
6. If still unpaid, the account goes to a collection agency. (If
   we felt it was possible to collect ourselves with a little more
   effort, we moved the account into the card file system outlined
   below and did not turn it over for collection.)

The reason this system works is the constant pressure on the account to pay and the regularity of the reminders.

A bookkeeper, even a part-time one, can handle this system. The
bills, reminders, and letters must be sent out in right sequence at the
right month to keep the system going. Once the number of past due
accounts dwindles, there is time to handle the chronic nonpaying ones.
The bookkeeper doesn't have to make any disagreeable calls herself.
When the past due account moves into that stage, the manager takes
over, either signing the letters, making the phone call, or making
personal contact. His work is also cut down because he is handling
fewer old accounts. The thirty- and sixty-day delinquents are not
allowed to move into ninety days.

If you want to go after the over-ninety-day bunch, or if you've
inherited a large number of bad accounts, you can use an additional,
long-successful card file system.

Past-Ninety-Day Accounts. Place your slow-pay and uncollectable
accounts in a card file system. Arrange the file into four weeks. With

this card file, using a telephone or a personal call, you're going to ask each debtor to start paying on his long past due account.

First, contact the account. Tell him you realize the past due bill is affecting the business relations between you two and you'd like to change this. Don't be belligerent or apologetic and don't threaten. Act very natural, as if it were normal business to be saying, "You owe me money." This initial contact is to acknowledge you know about the past bill and you are concerned about your loss of business. You're opening the door for arrangements to pay the account, partially or in full, to resume business between you two again.

If he says, "I'll pay you next week," slip his card into next week's compartment. Then if he doesn't pay next week, *be sure to contact him again* exactly the same way. Try for a firm commitment again, slip the card ahead, and in another week try again. Don't give up. Persistency is one key to this method, and so is your apparent consideration for his account and his business. You'll find the account is more receptive to paying; he's conscious of the principle of paying the creditor who is hollering the loudest. Yet he isn't offended by undue pressure.

This method has collected thousands of dollars throughout the United States by little businessmen like you and me. You can always turn bad accounts over to a collection agency or take them to court. But the card file system works and you pay yourself the collection charges!

Go Ahead and Charge Interest. Charging interest is the best collector you'll hire. Interest is one charge a customer wants to avoid. Even if it's only fifty cents, there's something about paying money *for* money that galls a customer.

These interest or late charges earn from 12 to 18 percent money for you by themselves. They will also cut down the number of delinquents you have. So interest makes money for you two ways!

★ KEEP THE BUSINESS RUNNING

Based on his experience analyzing newspapers nationwide, Kansas newspaper broker and consultant Marion R. Krehbiel makes these points about newspaper business management:

1. Gross—Any good weekly should gross (including normal job work) $30 minimum to $50 maximum per capita of town population (2,000 population equals $100,000 gross maximum). An acceptable average is $40 per capita. Dailies should gross a maximum of $60 per capita, with $50 as the acceptable average. Another way of measuring your gross in a weekly is

1 percent of *county* retail sales (if you're the dominant weekly in the county and there are no dailies). These retail sales figures should be taken from a source likes *Sales Management* magazine's survey of buying power, not sales tax returns, Krehbiel suggests. For a daily, 1 percent of city retail sales is the acceptable median.

2. Circulation—For weeklies, Krehbiel says, the national average is 85 percent of town population (2,000 town equals 1,700 paid circulation). If you're under that, you need a strong circulation campaign. A daily should have 60 percent of town population.

3. Production—If you're offset, printed at your plant or a central plant, you should be getting about $15,000 gross per employee (including publisher). (Ten employees equals $150,000 gross.) Krehbiel advises to count part-timers on a time-percentage basis to equal one full-time employee. So if you have the equivalent of fifteen full-time employees doing only $100,000 gross, you're 50 percent overstaffed. (If you are letterpress, you should figure $12,000 per employee.)

4. Payroll-Volume Ratio—Your ideal ratio of payroll (including minimal salary for the owner) to gross volume should be 35 percent. If you are semiweekly, the figure is 40 percent, and if you're a daily, 45 percent. No matter what kind of a newspaper you're running, you're going to find out that anything near 50 percent and you're at break-even, at 55 percent you're having trouble, and at 60 percent you're going broke. Payroll is your biggest expense and it *can* be controlled. With normal payroll, the average weekly should net, pre-tax, 20 percent of gross. Make that 15 percent for semiweeklies and 10 percent for dailies.

5. Accounts Receivable—Your receivables in any newspaper should never get above 1½ times your average month's gross volume ($120,000 gross equals $10,000 a month, so keep receivables below $15,000). If they're above this limit you need a collector on the street twice a month.

6. Operating Capital—Never let your operating capital (excess of cash and receivables over payables and other current liabilities) get below 15 percent of annual gross. (If $100,000 gross, have at least $15,000 in cash and good accounts at all times—$20,000 or 20 percent is even better.) If you get above 30 percent you ought to get out of the newspaper business and go into banking.

7. Maximum Debt Load—Never get caught in a debt that can't be amortized, principal and interest included, at 1 percent of annual gross volume per month ($100,000 gross equals $1,000 per month payment of principal and interest. If you want

to build a building, don't go above 50 percent of gross in total indebtedness—and don't forget to count any other debts you still have outstanding in this total. If you want to convert to offset, you can go up to 70 percent of gross, maximum, if you have no other debt obligations to meet. Offset will make you more money; owning your own building is a 7 percent investment at best.

8. Fair Rental—The average rent, daily or weekly, runs about $40 per month per each $25,000 in gross volume ($100,000 gross equals $160 monthly rent). Some are much higher, some much lower, but this strikes a fair median. If it's simpler, figure about 1½ percent of annual gross volume for annual rent. If you're renting from yourself, this doesn't apply.

9. Commercial Printing—In weeklies, 25 percent of gross in job work is the average. Weeklies can still use job work to sop up a little idle time, but if above 25 to 30 percent of your gross is in job work, you're getting into the printing business. You probably will have to hire extra help just for job work, which is always a losing proposition (job work will make you 5 percent at best as against that 20 percent newspaper profit). Don't count offset printing of other newspapers as job work; it's more profitable and should be accounted separately and carefully costed out.

10. Local Ad Rates—Raise ad rates 5 percent per year. Inflation in our business has been as high as 8 percent and as low as 3 percent in recent years, and a 5 percent rate raise per year will just about keep up with inflation. Raise rates in a four-week month following a five-week month. It's also best to raise just ahead of the heavy last quarter when the advertiser needs you more than at any other time of the year. The ideal setup would be a five-week August with a raise September first.

11. Bank Deposits—One good way to measure the strength of your town is by deposits in banks and savings and loan firms in the town. The national average in 1970 was $2,200 per capita (2,400 population town would mean $4,800,000 in deposits).

Post Ahead. Don't wait to post invoices to your customer's accounts. If he orders register forms that arrive October 17, post the charge to his account immediately.

If you wait to post the account until you pay your own invoice on the tenth, the customer won't pay you until the tenth following. You've operated for thirty days longer on your money; you could have operated on the customer's.

Ordering. Order one month's (or several months') supplies at one time. Scattering orders throughout the month costs extra freight and time.

If you won't order during the last week of every month, you will have an extra thirty days to pay. If you order just before the billing date closes or the month ends, you'll be billed immediately.

A good order book is absolutely necessary and should tell you a) what you need, b) when it was ordered, c) who it was ordered from, and d) has it ever come in.

I've found most problems about ordering solved with answers for these four questions in one book. Supplies needed can be marked in the book. It also shows if the stock or chemicals have been ordered, how long the order has been on the way, where it was ordered so you know who to call, and if it has arrived yet. Figure 10.5 shows a good order book form.

What to Do about Theft. Can your employees steal from you? Of course they can. An employee can find it very simple to dip into the

QUAN	SIZE	ITEM DESCRIPTION	ORDERED FROM	DATE ORD	ORD BY	DATE RCVD	RCVD BY	B O

CODY ENTERPRISE 1361

FIG. 10.5.   Page from a good order book.

cash drawer. All he needs is nerve. And he's helped by a loose, sloppy bookkeeping system. A tight set of books is important, because constant checks and continual balancing make the dishonest employee nervous. He is not as likely to take the chance under a good bookkeeping system. But a loose one, coupled with an indifferent boss, is too much temptation.

How can an employee steal from me if we balance every night? If she balances herself, it is very simple. She manipulates the cash and doesn't write a ticket for a transaction. You can't catch her since she handles both the balancing and the cash transaction.

If someone else does the balancing, our employee must be a little more subtle. Let's say a customer, Mrs. Brown, buys a ream of paper for $3.50. Our Dishonest Lil (or, of course, it could be Dishonest Lou, too) doesn't make out a ticket or mark this transaction down. If the sale is run through a cash register, Lil rings up a no sale or just 50 cents. Whatever she has on the register—the 50 cents for instance—she leaves in the till. The rest she takes out whenever she wants to before you balance. All the written transactions show only 50 cents came into the business. Actually, $3.50 did, but Lil got away with $3.00 of it. The theft won't show up until you take inventory. Since you probably will inventory but once a year, Lil has a long time to deplete your cash. She can get away with $20.00 a day very easily.

If Mrs. Brown wants a receipt, old Lil is stuck. She has to make the receipt out right so the ticket shows the entire $3.50. If you're under a numbered ticket system and every ticket must be accounted for, she can't make up a duplicate receipt for Mrs. Brown showing the $3.50 and throw away the business ticket, so Lil has to forget Mrs. Brown who wanted a receipt. She'll have to wait for another customer. This kind of thievery goes on in every kind of business all the time.

Now look at what Lil can do with a newspaper's subscriptions. She can manipulate the cards to show the subscriber paid, but not ring up or write up the transaction. She does it by accepting a $5.00 cash subscription payment from Mrs. Brown. She marks up Mrs. Brown's card "paid" for another year. But she never enters the cash amount in any book or on any ticket or rings it up in the cash register. That $5.00 is Lil's as soon as she takes it back out of the cash drawer. If she has access to the cards, she can eliminate Mrs. Brown's coming back in to say, "I did, too, pay this." Even if she doesn't mess with the card, it's an entire year before Mrs. Brown says she paid.

Taking subscription money shows up in the total amount of circulation money this year as compared to last year. Several months or even a year can go by before you can discover the shortage. One hundred dollars a month in lost subscription money is not much fluctuation, but $1,200 is.

Again, the receipt will bug her on the cash transaction. But she can do the same thing with a check in the mail where no receipt is necessary. If she doesn't write it down or ring it up, she can take the check's equivalent in cash.

She does not have to take Mrs. Brown's money and physically put it in her pocket right then. She can put it in the cash drawer at the time Mrs. Brown is there and then "draw it out" later.

The disturbing part is that you can still balance and not catch her.

If they want to steal, they're going to try to do it.

Fortunately, we have some warning flags. If these show up in your newspaper office, keep your eyes open for something else:

1. The deposit slips show very little cash has been deposited for awhile. (This means the right amount of cash is not staying in your business.)
2. You notice a lack of operating capital and a month that should have been a good one is short.
3. The employee becomes very nervous, has little bits of paper tucked around her desk, and seems to be hiding things when you walk up.
4. The employee starts to dress too well, buy more than she formerly did (or her kids do).
5. The employee doesn't want anyone to substitute for her, becomes very possessive of her job, refuses help, doesn't want a vacation.

Preventing theft requires that you be organized yourself. If you haven't already, adopt a very tight bookkeeping system—ticket numbering, balancing, tying in accounts receivable to cash received.

Don't allow a loose paid-out system. Don't let everyone take money out of the cash drawer, only one or two people. Account for every paid-out on a sales ticket.

Balance at odd times. Spot check your whole system. Continually compare this year's figures with last year's.

Do not let the same person who takes in the money at the cash register make the deposit.

Bond everyone under a blanket bond. ("Always bond those you trust" say the bonding companies. You won't give money-handling jobs to those you don't trust and the "best" employees are sometimes those who let you down.)

Observe an employee more closely if he or she becomes nervous or adopts "my own system."

Lotteries. Watch for lotteries. The post office department says your newspaper can't carry any information about a lottery and still be mailable. The policing burden is yours. Look for these three conditions, says the post office:

1. Is chance involved?
2. Is there a consideration, a prize awarded?
3. Is there restriction? Do you have to buy something, a card or ticket or make a purchase from the store?

According to postal regulations, any contest which has all three conditions constitutes a lottery. But *all three* must be present. Most merchants running such contests eliminate condition 3. "No purchase required" does it neatly. Now anyone can enter, purchaser or non-purchaser. In actual practice the contest is not weakened since people must come to the store to register. If the "no purchase required" is used, the line must appear in the ad.

Going Extra Pages. When does the profit start slipping in going to extra pages? For generations now, we've been told the magic figure was 60 percent advertising per issue. Falling below a 60–40 ad-news ratio was to invite red ink. I'm sure this figure is as good as any. I don't know how you arrive at a figure that is the "right" profit to make except that 60 percent advertising is obviously more of a money-making proposition than 50 percent. I accept this long-standing rule of thumb just because I've never come up with any better one.

As the years went by, I found myself drifting away from that ancient printer's admonishment "never to drop below 60 percent ads" because I found I didn't like tight papers. I like advertising revenue but I think I hate tight papers more. Unless it meant another press run, I found myself filling up two more pages even if we ended up with a 50 percent instead of a 60 percent twelve-pager.

I could justify my decision because I hate overset; I like abundances of white space; I don't like ads buried or stacked; I prefer big pictures, airy, well-displayed pages; and I wanted to plug my own products, my own business.

On my old flatbed, when it was the same press run at ten or twelve, I had two more pages to play with by going to twelve. I had more room for news and pictures. My overset, though not entirely eliminated, was cut down. My newspaper looked better. The ads weren't jammed on top of each other and had more display, the increased white space gave emphasis in many ways (e.g., three columns of type across four columns of space, picture stories, better editorial page make-up).

I could push my own product with more consistent advertising. Tight papers had wiped out my own advertising. Now there was room to push and promote. I was also in a tough competitive situation and felt I needed friends.

I just held that 60 percent not so sacred. The press run dictated

it. If I had to make another run, I stayed at the higher percentage.
If it was a tight ten or a loose twelve, I went with the twelve.

If you find yourself in a similar situation or state of mind, remember that going extra pages is dependent upon your presswork
available and whether you already have the type and pictures in
overset. *You cannot make another press run or set two more pages
of type and come out.* Now we're talking about more stuffing, more
press runs, more plates. Every press has its natural breaking point.
Ten-to-twelve pages is no more presswork on an old flatbed, nor is
fourteen-to-sixteen; but twelve-to-fourteen and eight-to-ten are. In
collated tabloids that run two up on sheet-fed offset, additional pages
aren't much more effort; but it takes another press run, another plate
and negative. You can easily go more pages on a web unless you hit
a unit break. A two-unit web offset has the same eight-to-ten-page
break that the flatbed has. A three-unit has a similar break going from
twelve to fourteen.

Going those two more pages within available presswork doesn't
involve much in newsprint costs. One eight-page broadsheet newspaper has about one cent's worth of newsprint in it.

If the type is up, if you have house ads ready for such times, if
you have pictures already screened, then you are not spending much
in production costs to go from a 60 percent ten to a 50 percent
twelve. But you have two more pages of newspapering. The cost of
those two extra pages is small compared to an impact of a picture
story, more comprehensive news coverage, or a house ad that will
generate its own revenue.

You can't afford to give away too much space, but in the long
run you can't afford to be too stingy with it either. You don't make
friends with overset.

Table 10.1 shows the various advertising percentages for a 168-
inch broadsheet paper.

TABLE 10.1.   Advertising Percentages for a 168-inch Broadsheet

				Inches of Advertising					
	8	10	12	14	16	18	20	22	24
Ad Ratio									
40%	537	672	806	941	1,075	1,210	1,344	1,478	1,613
50%	672	840	1,008	1,176	1,344	1,512	1,680	1,848	2,016
60%	806	1,008	1,210	1,411	1,612	1,814	2,016	2,218	2,420

Going to Color. Running more ROP color has similar barriers to break down. Weeklies hesitate to run color because of the cost and time involved. Web offset is changing this. It's much easier now, and we all should be running more color.

★ HOW MUCH IS A PAPER WORTH?

Marion Krehbiel sets the value of the average offset weekly at 115 percent of a three-year average annual gross volume "stripped."

He uses "stripped" to mean the bare and basic newspaper as a going business, with adequate plant and inventories, with all bills paid and no indebtedness, but without the building and without cash or accounts receivable.

Values for offset dailies are 150 percent of the three-year average gross stripped, and letterpress values are 125 percent of the three-year average gross stripped.

In offset weeklies it doesn't matter whether you print your own paper or have it printed in someone else's plant; the value of the newspaper is the same.

In offset weeklies printed outside in a central plant, the value is 105 percent of gross stripped. With your own press in an A-1 plant, it's 130 percent of gross stripped.

If you're incorporated, to determine the value of your capital stock take the basic 115 percent gross stripped figure, add back in the building if the corporation owns it, the cash and receivables above payables, deduct any indebtedness and the balance would be what 100 percent of the capital stock in your corporation would be worth.

There are some additional factors which affect the stripped value of a paper. Krehbiel notes if there is less than 1,500 population, if more than 40 percent of gross is in job work and/or office supplies, or if any local paper or free sheet carries more than half as much lineage as you do, you should reduce this final value by 30 to 35 percent. If you're not in a county seat or largest and strongest town in the county, deduct 10 percent from final value. If the paper is suburban, paid or part paid, deduct 10 percent.

More pluses and minuses that must also be considered are area-per-capita income; retail sales; larger towns and papers within 10 to 15 miles; quantity of food ads; national dealerships; small county population; banking climate; schools; churches; local college; available transportation, water, power and labor supply; high union scale; predominant racial or religious groups; type of agriculture; local industries; local taxes; rent, term of lease; less than two years of present ownership. Also, are you on an interstate highway or near a commercial airport?

★ WHERE SHOULD YOU NEWSPAPER?

You can newspaper in any town that will economically support a paper. This is a business determination, not a journalistic one and we come down to that principle of a newspaper being first a going business before it can be a good newspaper. This economic restriction—that the paper must be a profitable business—is the only limit there is to newspapering. A 2,000 population town newspaper can be just as much a gem as the 20,000 population one. Whether it's twelve or thirty-two pages a week, your newspaper is what you make it, how you create it. It grows where you put down your roots. With the first issue, you have license to make it your own. But besides the words and the pictures and the heart of this paper, you also control immediately the paper's financial capabilities. No matter what the paper was like before, right now, on this day with this first Wednesday behind you, it is you. Whether you choose one town over another, I doubt that your paper would be much different in either place. Your individual mark will always be on it.

What to Look for in Buying a Newspaper. Judging a newspaper's possibilities will depend a great deal on your personal taste, whether you like the town and the country, and if the paper is within your financial capabilities. The pluses and minuses of Marion Krehbiel's paper value formula (page 227) will refine a town's newspaper possibilities for you.

The smaller the newspaper—up to $65,000 gross—the more mechanical work you will have to do yourself. You can't hire a lot of help unless you are willing to take a cut in the net profit.

The small to medium size newspapers, like one grossing $100,000, will not make so much money in dollar amounts as one twice this size though in proportion to investment it might make a higher return for the owner.

In larger newspapers, from $150,000 on up, the potential will not be as limited as it is in smaller circulation papers. The town itself is probably headed for more growth sooner.

As the newspaper increases in size, the editor or publisher has less of the drudgery and petty details. More employees and more delegating is possible.

Don't involve yourself in a hopeless competitive situation—a small weekly against the bigger, more established one; or a struggling weekly against the successful daily. The joys of newspapering, as great as they are, can't overcome those frustrating economic pressures of a weak business.

For the same reason, don't invest in a newspaper with hopeless machinery problems. If you recognize that the press is old or the machinery will be needing work, don't look at the paper's price as a bargain. Instead, you will be fighting financial and mechanical frustrations rather than being free to newspaper.

Don't pay too much for a letterpress newspaper. You will probably have to convert it to offset eventually and you don't want to pay for a paper twice.

Look more closely at a newspaper if you find it has changed hands frequently. Several successive owners are usually a warning signal.

Starting a paper from scratch is very tough work in face of competition. Even an unexciting, poor newspaper is solidly established in the community ahead of you. Invariably a poor newspaper, threatened by competition, improves immediately to meet the threat. The existing newspaper usually has financial resources to fight a better fight than you have in just starting out. You are the "newcomer," he is "one of us." Even if you do make it to equal footing with the other newspaper, you may still be in a competitive situation for a long time.

Working on a Community Newspaper. If you can't or don't want to buy a newspaper, find one where you can learn the most about community journalism. Look for a progressive editor or publisher because for the same amount of time invested you will learn much more. Many publishers are on the lookout for young journalists who can become assistants or even eventual junior partners. These are ideal situations for experience and total exposure to newspapering. Learn every phase, even if it means on your own time. Don't specialize during this apprenticeship. Sell ads, price jobs, go into the darkroom. Be especially aware of management and the business end of newspapering since these will be vital to you when you move to your own paper. The best time to learn them is under someone else's guidance.

★ MISCELLANEOUS BUSINESS TIPS

When you make arrangements to buy anything on time be sure you reserve the right to pay it off in advance. Don't commit yourself to five years at 8 percent and no advance payment when you might be able to find someone willing to give you 7 percent later.

Interest should be paid on the unpaid balance only. Don't accept flat interest charges. A flat interest payment of $36.00 spread over twelve months on a $600.00 loan looks like 6 percent interest. But it's far more than that. True 6 percent interest would amount to only $19.50 if you paid the $600.00 back in twelve payments and paid interest on the unpaid balance only.

Buy your own building as soon as you can arrange it. Renting is expensive and limits expansion. The real estate is good investment in itself.

Be properly insured. Fire in a print shop does damage enough, but water from fire hoses brings its own clean-up problems afterwards. You don't soak up a shopful of equipment without creating a rusting, gummy mess. Adequate insurance is your protection, particularly if you're just starting out in weekly newspapering. You may have to pass around the insurance premiums so the town's agents can get back some of their advertising money, but have enough insurance among them. If you don't know what "enough" is, your favorite agent can analyze your policies and advise you on proper coverage. If he also suggests business interruption insurance (protecting your income in case fire knocks out your plant) don't shrug it away. Business interruption insurance is high-priced but so is revenue from one week's newspaper. Most newspapers can continue to publish (in a neighboring plant or with makeshift equipment), but often at a loss of normal potential. Business interruption insurance fills this gap. As you become more financially solvent, you may depend less on this coverage. In starting out, it's a welcome partner.

Do everything you can to make your operation smoother. Many shortcuts and efficient methods, once tried, will make you wonder, "Why didn't we do this ages ago?" One publisher once listed eighty-four such labor savers for a national magazine. The next month he probably had another eighty-four. Borrowing those heavy canvas U.S. mail sacks to facilitate taking the papers to the post office is scarcely worth mentioning. Yet its small efficiency contribution grows mightily after twenty years of post office trips.

Don't be too hasty in giving salesmen the bum's rush. They bring in a surprising amount of news from the outside world. For this they're invaluable to the weekly publisher in his isolation. You owe it to your business to keep abreast of the changes and improvements, to be aware of new products. A salesman is often the most articulate, most up-to-date source of what's going on in the profession.

Watch your own credit. The street runs two ways. Pay as promptly as you insist others pay you.

If you don't own your own building, be protected with a proper lease. Ask your lawyer's advice on this and all other business matters where you need protection. You should have him check all your business arrangements.

If you plan to trade in some equipment or sell it to some other printer, clean it up first. The used merchandise market has an axiom that "clean junk sells better than dirty junk."

Promote your own business first. Civic and community projects are every businessman's obligation but never at the expense of his own business. The most effective and worthwhile contribution an editor can make to his community is to publish a superior newspaper.

Check *every* invoice. Your time will be repaid many dollars over in knowing what prices should be, in making sure a wholesaler didn't charge you the wrong price or ship you the wrong material or forget it altogether. Add up their totals. An amazing number of mistakes are made.

Don't bog down in the same old ruts. Look for new ways to newspaper. Visit another newspaper shop every so often. Wander through their backshop and see how some other printer operates. Go to press meetings. Pore over the trade magazines, the cost studies, the new products sections. Listen to the salesman's pitch. Subscribe to other newspapers (particularly prize-winning newspapers which are conscious of good newspapering) for ideas in make-up, typography, column items. I am never too proud to borrow someone else's ideas; and I have seldom taken a paper that didn't give me an idea to better my own.

If you make paydays every two weeks instead of every week, you'll cut your payroll bookkeeping costs in half.

A sales ticket system eliminates errors, keeps track of sales and charges better than any other way. If you use tickets, keep track of the numbers. Insist that every number be accounted for. Use a ticket for every transaction, for every payment out of the cash drawer.

Observe check numbers when writing checks. Keep your stubs up-to-date and a constant running balance. Your check numbers are excellent cross reference guides.

Don't do it all yourself. The best advice to any manager of a business is to delegate the work to others. Even if they don't do it as well as you do, your valuable time should be spent elsewhere.

Don't use outdated letterheads and envelopes. Your statements and business forms should be models of well-arranged, nicely printed jobs. We printers have a tendency to slight our own printing. We do excellent printing for everyone else but ourselves. "Let me have your business card and I'll write," a man said to me once. And I had to say, "I'm sorry, I don't have any business cards right now, but I do know a place where I can get some printed!"

Pay yourself first. You are the most important employee the place has.

Here's Five Dollars for My Perscription

A NUMBER of new subscribers were accepted at the *Standard* office this week. We do this right along when properly approached with two dollars.

The *Greybull Standard*, 1912

F OR all this newspaper work, someone must read it. Who wants to play to an empty house? We need a long line of subscribers waiting to see our Thursday productions, and the longer the lines the more chance of our success as newspapermen.

We know circulation is tied directly to advertising results, which in turn are tied to more advertising and more satisfied businessmen advertisers, which in turn help you produce a superior newspaper. We sell papers to help sell advertising. We want to reach as many potential customers as possible for an advertiser who may advertise again. But we can sell circulation on its own merits, too. In the rush to sell full page ads, those $5 a year subscriptions seem like peanuts, but those peanuts add up. The $20,000 from 4,000 subscriptions can pay a lot of mortgage.

Even if circulation didn't make money, we still would seek it. As newspapermen we have a personal reason for selling as many papers as we can. We want people to read our newspapers. It is not just a money making project. If I take a picture I like, I want others to see it. My editorial thoughts are not put in black type for my pleasure alone. I want them to influence or to entertain, to be read by others. The news story I write is to be shared. I would edit this newspaper of mine for the world if my press run could make it!

To get the revenue and professional satisfaction successful circulation brings, you must work at it. The secret of circulation success is its steady drumming. The reader you're trying to reach is not a static sales objective. He's a newcomer or an old-timer. He moves, dies, gets pinched financially, forgets, he may even get madder than heck! He needs selling from you. If he's new in town, he needs an introduction. Give him your hand to shake. Even the old neighbor, once loyal and faithful, may drop off and need coaxing back. The housewife who picks up a paper on the newsstand should be cajoled into a steady year after year subscription. The irregular reader needs to be encouraged to become a yearly buyer. It's a continual job of selling, a constant pressure to place your newspaper product before the customer and say, look what I have to sell you this week.

All newspapers can increase circulation, or maybe more accurately, can keep up with population changes. No town's population remains entirely static. There are company transfers, employee changes, new owners of businesses, and a large teacher turnover. In fact, statistics show that on the average, one-quarter of the population will have changed every five years in your town. Will these new arrivals be new subscribers?

New circulation isn't all new people. My sales pitch is as much to the people in the neighboring rural communities or the competitive town as the new guy on the south side. A person can live in a community a long time and never get around to being a regular subscriber. Rural area people tend to pick a town to call "our town" and the town's paper becomes theirs. They can be coaxed away with a better paper and a better sales pitch.

The more the circulation potential, the more job it becomes (eventually a full-time position on larger papers). Regardless of a paper's size, circulation takes work. On the smaller newspaper where the circulation manager may be just a corner of an already cluttered desk, it's sometimes more work than an editor wants to spend. But circulation promotion is effective when effort is spent on it.

Any system you devise for circulation will be successful if you keep in mind that to gain new subscribers, you must sell them. Consider them potential customers for awhile instead of readers if that will help you find a sales pitch. It takes actual selling—door to door possibly, certainly person to person—to increase circulation.

I made the early mistake of relying too heavily on my newspaper product to sell itself. It was true, some departments of my paper became natural salesmen themselves—better rural correspondents, a TV schedule, a good columnist, pictures. I understood the value of additional sports coverage, knowing that nothing appeals to a small neighboring rural community so much as having its high school sports covered in the county paper. I was correct as far as I went. Circulation success is tied to the quality of the newspaper. But I neglected the need to sell the newspaper as a product itself.

You must work at circulation selling as hard as you do advertising selling. Normal circulation growth that accompanies town population growth lulls the publisher into thinking his circulation is "keeping up." It's true, subscriptions will come through the door unsolicited, but more arrive when you hustle. The publisher who doesn't have some kind of circulation promotion month by month isn't keeping up. You don't realize true circulation growth without constant promotion.

One benefit of circulation selling is that once the customer is hooked, he's hooked good. The renewal rate is astonishing. Short of moving away (and sometimes even the movers stay on), most of the new subscribers will become old customers. Happily for us, our sales approach may need to work only this once and we've landed a customer who will be steady and of long life. I don't forget my old subscribers, but my interests lean toward the potential new name on the subscription list.

If you can dream up new ways to reach these nonsubscribers, you are beginning to solve your circulation problems. There may be 4,000 ways to do this. Every circulation article I read has a new idea, but all are basically the same. They say to sell newspapers like you'd sell brushes door to door; knock on doors, send out samples, hire every possible salesman, use new gimmicks, advertise. To an editor passionately creating every week's issue, thinking of his newspaper in terms of brushes may be painful. But constant selling improves the circulation of even the best newspapers. And no matter how well edited your product, if you don't sound like a barker sometimes, you're not realizing your circulation potential.

★ SELLING PAPERS

I'll sell a subscription any way the customer wants it. Many of my six month "trials" have turned out to be steady year after year customers. I keep drumming constantly. The subscription sold in August is as good as the gift subscription in December.

I enlist all the help I can in selling subscriptions. The more salesmen selling the paper, the better my average. Correspondents may sell for a cash commission, and newsboys or carriers can be the greatest part-time hustlers in the world. The kids are natural outlets for your subscription sales pitch since they are familiar with the new people, nonsubscribers, and once-in-awhile buyers on their routes. You're concentrating a salesman in a specific area, and you can capitalize on their natural competitiveness and eagerness to win something. Finding an incentive that kids like is easy—prizes, cash, or points toward a grand prize (like an expense paid trip to a bigger city).

Look for the special ways to sell subscriptions like introductory offers to newlyweds or lower rates to college students. A stuffer in newsstand copies can encourage a trial subscription.

Always remember that you never saturate a newspaper market; your customers will be changing constantly.

Sampling. I like the idea of putting the product in the customer's hands and selling him while he's reading it. It seems to be very important in selling subscriptions that the potential subscriber sees the paper and actually feels the merchandise. This is sampling's strong point.

Postal regulations (1967) allow you to "sample," to send 10 percent of your total estimated weight of copies to be mailed to subscribers during the calendar year, at any time during the calendar year, as many times as you wish. (You can sample over the 10 percent limit, but you must pay additional postage.) It's the cheapest, easiest way to reach a large number of potential readers with a copy of what you're selling. You may want to sample one area at a time, working one side of the street today, the other side tomorrow.

The best time to sample is when you have a particularly good issue coming up. Or do it during a town-wide sales promotion when your extra copies to prospective customers will help the promotion go over (and earn you points with advertisers).

Sampling by name is an impressive personal invitation, but you can't send these personally addressed samples without paying full postage. The post office says you may sample by name and street address only if you send to all patrons on a route or to the boxholders, nonsubscribers and subscribers alike. Copies may not be addressed personally and mailed only to nonsubscribers. The full postage price and extra time is worth it many times, though, especially if you follow up with a card or letter.

Always run a house ad about subscriptions in your sampling issue to show price, add incentive, and clinch the sale. Or include a card that can be returned to buy a subscription.

Heavy sampling before a subscription campaign will soften the market.

Sampling should be done regularly and consistently. It costs only the postage, the time to add the required SAMPLE COPY line near the nameplate, the extra newsprint and press time. You can't take a copy to a possible subscriber as cheaply.

Selling to Individuals. The constant flow of new people in the community is easy to overlook, yet each new family is a prospective subscriber. The timing of a sample copy may miss his first weeks or months in town. He may be in a mobile home ignored by the newsboys. He may be a teacher renting a house only for the school year. He needs a welcome from you. If you prefer to work on an individual basis, you can usually find a source that can supply a continual up-to-date list of new arrivals in the community. The light company or gas office or maybe even the city hall may help.

If you want some extra sell, follow up the last introductory issue with a little note: "We've been sending you the paper for the past several weeks . . . we hope you'll decide to let us keep sending it. . . ." You have a foot in the door, a chance to show the product, and you're closer to a sale.

The Campaign. For adding subscribers in a hurry, nothing grabs more arms to twist than the subscription campaign. Here is where we make dramatic gains. Whether an outside service comes in and does all the work or whether you go for the smaller splash of your own, the campaign adds names.

I suspect we editors don't run campaigns often enough. We indulge in the campaign splurge and then shelve its usefulness until years later. Looking back, I see I should have run them more frequently. (Our biggest renewal months in years past, outside of the Christmas gift seasons, are those in which we ran big campaigns.) No matter what campaign gimmick you use (big cash prizes, dozens of small prizes, a combination of one big and several small, premiums, magazine subscriptions sold in conjunction, cash commissions), it will increase a subscription list.

I've run several good campaigns in which a certain number of subscriptions earns the salesboy a new bicycle. I think this kind of campaign is successful because:

• It isn't expensive when compared to its potential returns. The campaign's cost should be matched against the area's subscriber potential. If you're shooting for a big increase, the prize or prizes should be proportionate. If you'd like to pick up the 100 nonsubscribers in the adjoining town, don't do it with a $3,000 automobile prize. If you already cover the area fairly well and are making the annual roundup of strays, consider the cost per subscriber gained.
• It involves the entire family. Kids aren't particularly good salesmen, but there are more of them! And they have parents, brothers, aunts, and uncles. When one member will benefit from a contest, the entire family will help him win it; so will neighborhoods and rural communities.
• The prize or premium is something somebody wants. Johnny

wants the bicycle more than an American flag or a cookbook. Match the premium to your contest salesmen. The more desirable the prize, the more the participation. Don't be chintzy on prizes. Make it worth their time.

• There are enough prizes. Every twenty subscriptions earned a bike in the campaigns we ran. There was no limit. If you have one big prize, plan on premiums for the winners of second, third and so on. It works to give cash commissions to the also-rans after they've sold so many. The more winners, the better help you'll get from your amateur salesmen.

Don't give away renewals in a subscription promotion. The renewals are already revenue-producing repeat business. It's new subscribers you want.

A campaign that is too expensive is unnecessary. You can find good ones that will at least break even; some may even make you money. Let the new subscriptions themselves finance it. It isn't necessary to go in the hole just to add names.

A campaign should never replace the concentrated month by month pressure to sell subscriptions, so don't confine your circulation efforts to one campaign every year or two. The little touches—because they are steady selling—can't be eliminated. In fact, the big campaign is helped immensely if your steady sales pitch has already prepared the market.

Subscription Rates. Your subscription rates should reflect the quality of your paper and its value to the reader. If you question whether your rate is right or wrong, you should check to see how long it has been since your subscription rate was raised; and what the rates of other papers are, comparable in size and circulation to yours. Your rate should always be high enough. Shade the rate in your favor, not the reader's.

Never raise less than a dollar. You can "hide" a raise in an increased newsprint cost announcement or postal increase. It is easier to announce your raises then, too, since the reader will understand your position better.

Give people a chance to renew at the old price before the new prices go into effect. You receive the advantage of an influx of "new" cash; and you make friends by allowing your readers to save money.

Remember one full year will go by before you will realize the full effect of a subscription raise. It takes that long before all your readers come under the new price.

★ DELIVERING PAPERS

Your paper will reach the reader from the dependable hands of the postman or off the newsstand or through a carrier boy system.

The post office will see that your paper is delivered to box or doorstep through rain and snow and school vacations, but they have half a book filled with regulations you must follow. You won't need to wonder if you're following them or not—the post office department will inform you quickly enough.

Newsboys. With newsboys, it is the other way around. You set up all the regulations and try to make the boys follow them! This is not always an easy task. Unlike his counterpart in the daily field, he may not develop the dependable morning-after-morning routine. Since he may not collect or assume the business arrangement the daily newsboy has with his customer ("I'll pay you if you deliver the paper") he's understandably less conscientious. Just the normal problems of growing boys can create continual chaos. They forget, they can be lazy. They'll dump half an armload of store circulars in the ashcan in back of your best advertiser's place. Or the one guy in the block who won't get his paper until the next day is the manager of the town's biggest store. Homework, bedtime, and a cold morning in January can dent the newsboys' resolve.

You have to find ways to encourage the boys to do a conscientious, good job. It helps if the newsboy feels a definite tie with the newspaper. He must answer to someone he is just a little afraid of. He must be impressed with the seriousness of missing a paper or being late. He has to be made to feel part of the newspaper business, part of something important, that his job is indispensable.

You can't skimp on their pay or you'll lose the good boys. You can't be overbearing and inconsiderate or they just won't work for you. You have to understand their problems, yet be firm enough to make them do a good job. Don't overlook hiring girls as well as boys. Girls can be more conscientious about delivering papers than boys are.

If you do get an organization of newsboys (and girls) going, they can be valuable helpers. One real asset is the delivery of newspapers to everyone at nearly the same time. This simultaneous distribution has an important effect on shoppers and advertisers. It gives your paper a greater punch, and it's a welcome ally in a competitive situation.

With newsboy distribution, you will be able to include circulars and sale announcements in the paper more often, because the carriers can do the stuffing themselves. They are also a force for distribution of special announcements, extra editions, and flyers that come up all the time.

The postman is more dependable, but he's not as versatile as an eager youngster.

Newsstands. When your reader decides he would rather buy his paper at the newsstand, you lose some control over his reading habits, but you place the paper in people's hands who might not get it otherwise. Newsstands are good salesmen. They are important distributors to casual readers, to new readers, even to "two-paper" families (the wife at home, the husband at work). Newsstands help sell eventual subscribers, they can increase ad readership because the more papers you have out, the more chance for nonsubscribers to see it. Some readers will prefer to pick up the paper at the newsstand every week, obtaining the same regularity as a subscriber.

Many newsstand buyers are casual, spasmodic, even accidental. It is a disadvantage to have a reader choose his own time to pick up the paper. A newsstand "subscriber" may buy his copy Friday or Saturday, maybe after a specially advertised sale or after the Friday night football game. Then the town-wide sales punch is lost.

I believe you should approach newsstand sales with this philosophy: Encourage as many casual readers as possible to become regular newsstand readers, then encourage those regular newsstand readers to become regular subscribers.

Your handling cost is higher with newsstand sales so newsstand sales must pay. It's not the postman or the newsboy but you or your staff who takes the papers around. You must pay the store owner so much for selling your papers. Unless you raise your per copy rate to compensate for these extra costs, your newsstand revenue is less per copy than it should be. (A higher newsstand rate also tends to force the reader into buying a year's subscription.)

Your newsstand should be carefully selected. You want salesmen in the best places, in those good traffic areas. A newsstand that doesn't sell many papers or is hard to service costs you money. You may be willing for a time to install a nonpaying newsstand in hopes of cracking a new corner in the trade territory. Now your newsstand is a selling tool, an introduction to an untapped area. Here you're agreeing to take the losing newsstand for awhile to build toward future circulation gains.

Generally, whenever you must spend time on a newsstand sale out of proportion to the papers sold or the future prospects, you can't come out with a profit.

Hooking the newsstand reader to a regular subscription not only guarantees money in your pocket but helps you control the reader's exposure to advertising and your newspapering efforts.

★ KEEPING SUBSCRIBERS

Once you gain a subscriber, you have fifty-two Thursday mornings to resell him. It's an advantage that provides a high rate of repeat business. Most readers will come in to pay up or send a check for their "perscription." But that small percentage who waver, or procrastinate, or forget, may need reselling when their renewal notice comes around.

The stronger your renewal policies the better. Send cards out promptly. If a reader's subscription expires in June tell him early, don't dribble notices out in August telling him so. Be just as prompt with second notices, and then again on the kill-off date. Don't wait; don't carry them along. If they don't pay, take them off. Readers understand the no pay, no magazine philosophy for their national magazines; they can understand it on weekly newspapers, too.

In my first years of newspapering this was a hard lesson. To have someone ask to be killed off was trauma enough. But to do it willfully myself! Then there was the period of the bad crops. How can we kill off all the farmers, we reasoned, who have just had a bad year. So we kept our list of unpayables. It wasn't until several years later we realized our mistake. People don't thank you for keeping them on unpaid. They would rather be forced to be prompt than to be carried. They hate to pay any bill three years overdue. A $5 subscription to a product they haven't seen yet is easier to pay than $15 for papers they've already read. They ridicule a bookkeeping system that allows them to ride free. They may not even want the paper at all! Have no qualms about killing the delinquencies; they expect it.

Whether you belong to the Audit Bureau of Circulation or not, you should have ABC standards. Keep cards up. Allow no free rides. Account for every subscription. Your subscription list should be accurate month after month. It's just as easy to keep it up as to let it slide and then work extra time shaping it up again.

Put a little "sell" on the card you send out and more "sell" on the second notice. Plug the paper. Tell your renewing subscriber why he should keep reading it. Send along a postage-paid return envelope in the second notice. People will use them.

If you can't hustle a full year's renewal subscription, don't turn up your nose at six months.

Mailing List. If you mail your paper, run your mailing list periodically and check it against the subscription list. Mailing stencils or slugs have a penchant for wandering. They'll wind up in wrong zones or addresses, they'll stay on when they should be killed, or they'll go to the same address twice in the same week. The mailing list and subscription list in your subscription card file should be the same. They won't be unless you babysit them regularly.

A Fresh Sheet of Newsprint Each Week

I HAVE BEEN able to criticize and praise and interpret . . . to congratulate and console . . . to point out a common ground of understanding . . . to discuss the problems of peace one day and the problems of rearing a harem of daughters the next.

I have been able to write . . . write . . . write. What an opportunity that has been.

WALTER R. HUMPHREY, editor, *Fort Worth Press*

★

WEEKLY newspapers always seem reluctant to enter the world. They're balky creatures who resist the push to be created. One of the miracles of weekly newspapering for me has always been how we ever got our paper out. Some Wednesdays I have despaired of seeing a Thurday dawn. When I consider how little time I have and how much is demanded of that precious bit, when I watch the week speeding from Monday to Wednesday—I'm grateful there is inked newsprint at all by Thursday, with or without mistakes, the poorly counted headlines, the missed pictures.

Yet, once a weekly newspaper gives into Thursday's inevitability, it becomes a happy, interesting, exciting creature to know. By Thursday morning, newspapering is fascinating fun again.

There's been great fun in it for me—I think you can see this—and I believe the same enjoyment awaits everyone in the business. It's been my paper. My individual touch is on it. It's my creation, whatever it is or isn't. We all start with the same pulpy sheet of newsprint. But black type in each of our hands transforms this rough piece of Canadian pulp into gray papers, bold papers, bright or dull ones, lively or sedate ones, your paper and mine; and no two of them ever look alike.

Newspapers can accomplish great feats. Nothing else molds so much opinion, generates so many ideas or gives vehicle for their expression. Ideas and beliefs are never as strong as they are in black type. I will listen to your impassioned plea on the street corner, but everyone has a chance to read it in my newspaper. None of us writes for himself alone although each may be his own first and toughest audience. We seek others with our words. Black type can be a constant driving force in a community. When you believe in its essential good and respect its power, a newspaper becomes an awesome force, a continual influence that regenerates itself each week. My newspaper existed as a community partner for two generations before I came along, and it will be going for a long, long time after my time is past. "I may leave you but this newspaper won't," I told an editorial foe once who expressed a hope that I might be leaving town soon. There are many Thursdays in the future, and though you and I won't see them all, some other newspapermen will.

I have hoped to make my newspaper a community necessity. I have wanted to provide an institution whose demise would leave an irreplaceable hole. I haven't wanted people to take my paper or leave it. This attempt to ride a winner week after week, whatever its hectic pace, brings a gratifying life. All that I like about weekly newspapering is tied to the one premise, that my newspaper should be as good as I can make it.

More awaits the editor of a newspaper of excellent quality than one who "just gets it out each week." Professional success invariably brings more of everything, money included. I think I can show a punk newspaper (which may make good money) how it could produce more satisfaction (and more money) if it practiced successful journalism.

I'm amused when a newspaperman says, "I can make more money if I don't try to put out a prizewinner." (Or, "You can't eat awards." That's a common one among the nonwinners.) He doesn't realize what potential awaits the hustling, energetic newpaper. Once you've seen what more subscriptions and more readers do to advertising punch, what a firm editorial policy does for prestige, or how many friends enthusiasm creates or how much business follows that enthusiasm, you'll never again wish for mediocrity.

This mediocrity comes with not caring. I don't know how much it matters today that I stayed up later than I wanted on that Tuesday night ten years ago to write an editorial, but the accumulation of such Tuesday nights through the years has meant something to my readers. That front page picture I've sweated over week after week has earned my newspaper a reputation for pictures. The column I started years ago has not missed one single issue. No one knows this but me and I could have probably missed half of them without causing local catastrophe. But it was a standard I wanted to set, and meeting it helped me meet others. I've tried very hard to achieve this high quality. I set personal challenges and gave way to them only in the sheer panic of some Wednesdays. It was not enough to say, "The people don't know the difference. They'll read it anyway." I wanted the profession to set the standards, not just any Joe Doakes down the street. I believe you can't make something good unless you recognize such standards.

This is what we've been talking about in this book. Each news page has standards of its own. So does each day. Whether you write or sell, if you take pictures or keep the books, those individual standards you and I set determine our newspapers' quality.

We must care about our newspapers. The not caring creates and condones printer's mistakes—smudges, white streaks, dirty plates, ads with insufficient spacing, border tapes not touching or overlapping, improper leading, inconsistent spacing, standing heads worn out. Or sloppy paste up, correction lines cockeyed, uneven inking, smashed blankets, ad type too close to border, overexposed page negatives, offset border fading out, lack of impression, pictures flat and without contrast.

And we editors make mistakes—not counting headlines, outdated logos or no logos at all, just straight type, listless signatures instead of distinctive cuts, running pictures too small, ads not pyramided, neglected correspondents, atrocious inside page make-up, and headlines that don't match.

You have to ask yourself many questions: Am I playing this story right? Is there a word better than this? Am I describing this situation accurately? What did I leave out? Why did I miss that local? Should I wait for the sun? Should I redo this ad? Am I answering all the questions? Am I being fair? Accurate? Interesting? Is it, finally, good newspapering? And further, is it a first-rate newspaper?

When you watch a newspaper develop friends through the years, you realize acceptance doesn't necessarily come from just good journalism. A good newspaper, like a person, is more than pressed clothes and combed hair and a happy smile. It's a warm handshake, a comfortable feeling, an arm across the shoulders, respect, and interest. Your newspaper can be slick and functional on the outside, but it needs heart and soul, too. To make real friends it must be more than a shell of good journalism that uses smooth words and out-sized pictures to cover its real insides.

How do we put soul in these blank sheets of newsprint? It will be your enthusiasm for one thing. And your warmth and personality and whether you're happy, today, in this town, publishing this newspaper. All this shows through newsprint. One clever headline can brighten the entire front page for the reader. A warm column will touch many hearts. A laugh is infectious. Sincerity is contagious. We must have a liveliness about the paper and about ourselves. We can't plod along missing all that's stirring outside. We can't be coldly proper. If our heart shows, let it show. If our enthusiasm tends to run away sometimes, let it run. Let's never be dull. You can forgive a newspaper for many faults, but not for being dull.

We should be interested in everything. How old is that bridge? Is it marble time? Did the ice on the river go out earlier than usual? Are the post office flowers blooming yet? Are the fish biting? What will make the town grow faster? What were the laughs this week?

We should be especially interested in people. We should make them aware of who lives across the street. Involve them with each other: How is Sam since he got out of the hospital? Is John home yet from overseas? Can we help you with that special project? Have the Heywoods started their garden? Congratulations on being a grand-father!

There's much of this "neighboring" in small-town newspapering. The whole town is the family next door. Our papers help to bring us together even more.

And they help us work together, too. Our papers should become active partners with our communities in their struggles to grow bigger, to improve more. Towns need to be stimulated and inspired. They require the catalytic action of a newspaper that keeps suggesting ways to make the town's life better, one that explains what happens or could happen to an idea or a project. A newspaper is usually the only way people can study the pros and cons. They look to newspapers for guidance, and I'm glad they do. It's one of the moral obligations news-papers have always fulfilled. I haven't won all my battles or filled all my hopes. Some may take years yet to happen or may not happen at all, but I hope I've won enough and tried hard enough that people in my town are saying, "If you want something done, get the *Standard* on your side."

Yet we shouldn't become Chamber of Commerce organs either. If some project isn't right or if it's questionable, we shouldn't let it go just because the Chamber or the City Council endorses it. Supporting everything regardless of merit runs the risk of diluting your effective-ness on the important ones. For the same reason, don't become a chronic "aginner" since endless criticism, in the end, becomes no criticism at all.

You won't need to slant the news or manipulate the front page toward something you favor. The good projects will stand by them-selves. You owe your reader the integrity to provide all possible in-formation about a proposal, and if you wish to praise or condemn editorially, he will understand that. But he won't forgive you for try-ing to slant the *news* your way.

The best contribution to your community is the quality of your newspaper and your integrity as an editor.

Newspapering, I've found, takes generous doses of positive thinking. You can't pass on the paper's problems. No one is happy to hear about my troubles back at the office. Fellow townspeople don't want to see my long face or listen to me wail about the help shortage. I try to practice my pessimism in private and not talk down the profession or complain about the overtime and the extra work. The more work we do the more money we take in, and I'm always surprised at the reactions of my customers when I tell them this instead of how hard we're working. When I say I worked last night because the paper suddenly has much more business, this is just as true as saying we're so far behind we can't take care of it. One implies you're running a successful place and the other that you're inefficient, and there's a difference to the customer!

We must avoid the loser's image. Let success show in as many ways as it can, and more success follows. People just can't resist riding with a winner.

I try to be a good sport, publicly, about competition, though sometimes I must do it through clenched teeth. I wasn't always such a good fellow. But my belligerent attitude once forced a customer to take sides, which he didn't want to do. No businessman wants to contribute to the demise of another. And the Main Street is jumpy about two quasi-public-service media fighting publicly. This goes back to the Chamber of Commerce feeling that if we're going to hang, we should hang together. A radio station and a newspaper embroiled in bitterness becomes a public matter, to the outside as well as to the community. My irritation also showed the competitor was getting to me, which eroded the success image I wanted to build. Such a negative approach didn't sell anything.

I have stayed just as tough as I could and tried hard to be number one. But I did it all without tangling in the gutter.

A newspaper should go to as many different kinds of people as it can—the sports-minded, the intellectual, the oldster who wants to remember, the youngster eager to learn. All kinds of people will read a paper, and everyone will have some part of the paper he likes best. You will concentrate, if you're human, on that part of newspapering you enjoy doing the most; but remember, the writing, the editorials, the pictures, the sports, and the society news all enjoy their privileged places. Each part of the paper has an eager audience somewhere. Let's give them something for their five bucks!

If I've made this sound like a lot of work, I can't be faulted for not being honest enough. The work involved can't be denied. But there are many compensations. The mystique of newspapering has always attracted me. Is it because there is more working with the in-

tellect than the hands? Is it the words and writing or the constant flow
of ideas? Or the even more constant flow of people? Is it knowing
much? Is it the professionalism? Or the power?

A woman we hired for part-time paste up on press day once said
she "couldn't wait for Wednesdays to come around." Finding inspiration in a horrible Wednesday is confession of faith enough! But
she insisted, "I never had so much fun on a job." And she's right!
Many of us do have a lot of fun in it. She discovered, coming down to
our chattering, lively office, busy and important for this one day of the
week, that she was as taken by it as the rest of us are. I long ago suc-
cumbed, and while I admit to many hours of despair and weariness, I
have reveled in many wild peaks of happiness, too. When I look back
on it, I see many words I'm glad I wrote, some pictures I know I'll
never get again, some friends that are still around. I flip through the
bound files and see all those Wednesdays of the past, all that newspapering; and I can feel the old adrenalin flowing again.

And next week there's a fresh sheet of newsprint!

INDEX

249